TheStreet.com

GUIDE TO SMART INVESTING IN THE INTERNET ERA

TheStreet

GUIDE TO SMART INVEST

.com
ING IN THE INTERNET ERA

*Everything You Need to Know to Outsmart
Wall Street and Select Winning Stocks*

DAVE KANSAS
and the Writers of
TheStreet.com

CURRENCY

NEW YORK   LONDON   TORONTO   SYDNEY   AUCKLAND

A CURRENCY BOOK
PUBLISHED BY DOUBLEDAY
a division of Random House, Inc.
1540 Broadway, New York, New York, 10036

CURRENCY and DOUBLEDAY are trademarks of Doubleday,
a division of Random House, Inc.

Currency Books are available at special discounts for bulk purchases for sales
promotions or premiums. Special editions, including personalized covers,
excerpts of existing books, and corporate imprints, can be created in large
quantities for special needs. For more information, write to Special Markets,
Currency Books, 280 Park Avenue, 11th floor, New York, NY 10017, or
e-mail: specialmarkets@randomhouse.com.

The Library of Congress has established a cataloging-in-publication
record for this title.

ISBN 0-385-50094-7
Book design by Erin L. Matherne and Tina Thompson
Printed in the United States of America
First Edition: January 2001
10 9 8 7 6 5 4 3 2

To all the people who have made *TheStreet.com* possible,
especially our readers.

Contents

Acknowledgments

As with everything at *TheStreet.com*, this book was a huge effort joined by many. First, I would like to thank the writers who contributed: James J. Cramer, Tracy Byrnes, Dan Colarusso, Christopher Edmonds, Jim Griffin, Thomas Lepri, George Mannes, Mark Martinez, Helene Meisler, John Rubino, and Elizabeth Roy Stanton.

Four others deserve special recognition. Helaine Tishberg shepherded the numerous graphics and charts so critical to the presentation of the material. Tracy Byrnes, in addition to writing, aided in the conception and overall presentation of the book from its earliest days through to finish. Mark Martinez, in addition to writing, tirelessly fact-checked hundreds of pages. Kevin Burke also did extensive fact checking and other tasks necessary to getting the job done.

Many other people in *TheStreet.com* newsroom generously offered their knowledge and expertise to the project. They include John Edwards, Pat Fitzgibbons, Dave Gaffen, Caroline Humer, Justin Lahart, David Landis, Gretchen Lembach, Brian Louis, Ian McDonald, Scott Moritz, Jane Penner, and many others too numerous to name. Other people at *TheStreet.com* drove important, non-editorial aspects, including Tom Clarke, Jordan Goldstein, Cathy Fetell, Abby Marr, Gail Griffin, Peter Drace, Vivian Shpigler, Ronnie Goldman, Laurie Robbins, Millie Alicea, William Maldonado, and Shoshanah Harvey.

Beyond our own ranks, thanks go to Daisy Alpert, Tina Aridas, Alex Berenson, David Byrnes, Andrew Greta, Robert Hagstrom, Michael C. James, Justin Mamis, Chris Marinac, Jason Marks, John Power, Pamela van Giessen, and Michael Zuckert.

We are also grateful to our new friends in the publishing industry. They include our agents, Owen Laster and Claudia Cross of William Morris, as well as William Morris attorney Philip Liebowitz; our lawyers, Robert Stein and Philippe Adler; and at Doubleday, Rebecca Holland and Stephanie Land. Thanks as well to book packagers Chris Fortunato and Tina Thompson, as well as cover art director Ashwini Jambotkar.

A special thanks to Roger Scholl, our outstanding editor at Doubleday, who was instrumental in helping us bring the essence of our Web site into book form.

And, finally, I would like to thank Jamie Heller. One of the original editors involved in the creation of *TheStreet.com* way back in 1996 and an active voice through its evolution, Jamie conceived this book, edited it, and did all the other work required to bring it to fruition. From the most mind-boggling big issue to every mind-numbing detail, Jamie shepherded this book to successful completion. This book could not have been done without her, and I am grateful for her devotion to the enterprise.

As you can see, many good hands worked on this book. I'm honored to have been part of the effort.

L'Etoile du Nord

Dave Kansas
New York
2001

Foreword

James J. Cramer

You want to beat me at my own game? You want to learn what I know and apply it to make big money? I don't blame you. The stock market can be a great place to make money. But what resources are you going to do it with? Are you going to try to beat me with the books that are out there now, the ones that clog the shelves and teach you what you already know or what you'll never even need to understand? I don't think so.

Ever since we started *TheStreet.com* five years ago, we have pushed to give you everything that the top professionals have to make money. We have attempted to level the playing field wherever it may be tilted in favor of the cloistered group of moneymen that has so long dominated Wall Street.

It's hard to believe that in a day when we see commercials about nail salons that are hotbeds of day trading or English-as-a-second-language classes that discuss low commissions, there was a time when it would have been plain wrong to even suggest that people control their finances themselves.

When I worked at Goldman Sachs in the early 1980s, I felt that the professionals had so many advantages over the individual that it would be financial suicide to do anything but turn your assets over to your betters. We had instant information about stocks. We had vast libraries where you could call up microfiche sheets with the latest financials. We had newspapers and magazines that contained new information about stocks that only true stock junkies would have the time and inclination to sort through. Plus, commissions were prohibitive, so individual trading costs were too expensive to justify.

All of that has changed. The Web has put everything I had at 85 Broad Street (the headquarters of Goldman, just a block from the New York Stock Exchange) at your fingertips. Commissions are rock bottom and at times nonexistent. There are whole Web periodicals devoted solely to making the individual equal to the professional when it comes to running money.

Of course, not everyone has the time or the inclination to manage their finances. But we have also learned in the last decade that farming out your finances and forgetting about them can be plainly irresponsible. Clients who want others to handle their money need to keep the handlers honest. You have to be either a smarter client or a smarter investor. Ignorance is no longer an option. There is too much of your money on the line and too many ways available to all to be sure you are getting the best service.

Can you really learn options to the point of trading them? Do you understand what really moves stocks? Do you have any sense of when to sell? Most of the time, this stuff does fly over people's heads. But we at *TheStreet.com* have, from day one, made it our mission to demystify and democratize the process. This is the first plain-English investment guide I have ever seen. It is fitting that the folks who put investing in plain English on the Web would now do the same with the printed word.

Every day I communicate with hundreds of people, ranging from neophytes to grizzled vets, about the stock market. I can't tell you how often they have asked me for help in trying to understand the relationship between stocks and bonds, or the options and common stock markets, or the choice of growth or value stocks. I am always at a loss to say to them anything other than "read *TheStreet.com* Web site."

Now, in *TheStreet.com Guide to Smart Investing in the Internet Era,* we have an easy-to-use guidebook to the markets, a one-stop summation of everything you need to outsmart me and all of the other pros battling to try to beat the market. You want to learn how to set up the ideal portfolio? It's here. You want to identify the best tech stocks? It's here. You want to understand how to examine balance sheets and sniff out problems or opportunities? It's here. You want to trade options like a pro? It's here, too.

Almost every question I've been asked is answered in these pages, and it won't take you more than a few seconds to find the passages that you need to figure things out. So many books tell you how to "get started." So many offer glib assertions and easy tricks and gimmicks that end up backfiring and costing you money. This book speaks in plain English about strategies that win. It may not teach you what you could learn if you sat in at my hedge fund for a good stretch, but you won't have the bruises and the heartache either!

What are you waiting for? Get in there and get dirty. Understand the concepts that can make you money or allow you to grade others who are supposed to be doing it for you.

Get started learning how to match wits with the pros. With *TheStreet.com Guide to Smart Investing in the Internet Era,* you have the game plan. Read it, put it into action, and let's go make some money together.

TheStreet.com

GUIDE TO SMART INVESTING IN THE INTERNET ERA

1

The Investing
Revolution

If you had fallen asleep in 1995 and awoke on the dawn of the new millennium, you would have missed much more than a worldwide fireworks melody. In that half decade, a revolution swept through the investment firmament, with online brokers, online news outlets, and online data providers paving the way for a new chapter in the do-it-yourself world pioneered by outfits like The Home Depot.

That investing revolution coincided with the emergence of all sorts of strange companies that swiftly became enormously valuable. Yahoo! leapfrogged General Motors, and America Online set out to gobble up venerable media giant Time Warner. Wireless outfit Qualcomm defied the loftiest expectations, and optical networking firm JDS Uniphase made a name for itself in the span of a quarter. It all occurred at lightning speed. And it still does. Funky companies pop up, grab our attention, and soar into the stratosphere. Sometimes they come crashing and burning to earth just as quickly.

The way we invest has been radically transformed as well. Trades can be placed from our desks, at work, for less than the price of lunch. And where it once was a huge leap to get a delayed quote online, now investors insist on real-time portfolio tracker updates, real-time news, and after-hours trading to boot.

Unlike the old-time, smoke-filled country club world of investing, the new arena sparkles with increased access, opportunities, and risks for the small investor. Individuals get rich, 20-something entrepreneurs become famous, and the rest of us search desperately for a game plan that will work in this topsy-turvy world.

If the late 1990s marked the early part of the revolution, we are now in the teeth of the transformation. Each day more people venture online, taking a stab at controlling their financial destinies. Wall Street and the keepers of the institutional flames scramble to maintain an advantage. But the people keep coming. They continue expecting more, and they devour new learning at a ferocious pace.

Despite all the fancy electronic footwork and online stock market research, books that can synthesize and make sense of the cacophony remain an essential tool in gaining confidence in the investing process.

But most investment books offer either not enough or too much. On the dummy end of the spectrum, guides are so basic as to be useless for anyone except, well, dummies. Our book aims to be understandable and usable for newbies without skirting the meatier material that really anyone can grasp if it's explained right. As for the books aimed at more sophisticated readers, you'll find blather so incomprehensible that even the wizened professionals are left scratching their heads. Or at the very least, they're put to sleep.

TheStreet.com Guide to Smart Investing in the Internet Era aims to walk the untrod middle ground. We know from our experience at *TheStreet.com* Web site that millions of investors have picked up some learning and at least a patchwork sense of the market. What they are looking for is some guidance that will give them a firm footing, take them to the next level when they're ready, and help them put it all together. Written in the spunky, shoot-straight style of our online news operation, *TheStreet.com Guide to Smart Investing in the Internet Era* provides just that information and help. We take you on a journey of learning that will help you cast off understandable fear. Wall Street may be jammed with big institutions promising you sage advice. But Wall Street's size—and the conventional thinking that can tend to accompany it—is as much a liability as a strength. We help you figure out how to pick the spots where the giants might stumble, so you can go toe-to-toe into the investing marketplace with confidence.

When you've finished reading this book, you will understand the market in the same manner that a pro understands the market—or better. You will understand how to decipher the wild mood swings that have become a regular feature of the investing world. You will be able to arm yourself with the information that will help you enrich yourself and your family.

It's important to tell you what this book is not. It is not a book that will give you a paint-by-numbers approach to wealth. It is not a book about some statistically perfect formula. We believe many of those kinds of books are inexcusable sucker-plays aimed at taking a little more money from you and putting it in the pocket of the authors.

We've set out to do something different. We want to make you *smarter* and *wiser*. We want to give you the savvy that the pros guard so jealously. We want you to have the ammunition to forge your own successful path in an arena that is not nearly so simple to conquer as some of the pundits would have you believe.

This is also not a book that defends the bull market or declares that the Dow should be at 100,000. But hyperventilating nervous Nellies will not hold sway in this book either. Though the stock market has enjoyed a remarkable run, we still believe that over the long term the market has tremendous strength. We will not tell you how to cash in on the coming crash or instruct you on the merits of gold or other "safety" commodities. We believe the technology revolution has revolutionized American business. And while there will always be bumps and periods of uncertainty, we believe the stock market will reflect that revolution for some time to come.

What's behind our conviction? Much of what's driven the market boom of the last 20 years has been the diminished impact of the business cycle. Expansions have grown longer and deeper, while recessions have become narrower and shorter. The resulting long-run growth has created a New Economy, an economy that's forcing stock market analysts to redefine how they view investments and long-term earnings.

Dismissed as blarney by old Wall Street hands, the New Economy rests on several real changes. Productivity gains have improved profits while keeping inflation largely in check. Corporations, benefiting from improved technology, have become more adept at utilizing global capacity to evade the problems that arise with market tightness. Toss in increasing fiscal discipline among the developed countries (take the U.S. budget surplus, for one), and you have a recipe for a lengthy expansion.

Technology has played the starring role in the New Economy's emergence. The Internet has helped keep inflation at bay by slashing costs and improving the efficiency of individuals and corporations conducting transactions on it. Technology itself has benefited from rising productivity and healthy competition, with the cost of hardware and software falling sharply for consumers and business and keeping inflation in check.

The New Economy paradigm may not spell an endless period of growth, but we've seen the dips in the United States become less pronounced. And low unemployment and low inflation have now coexisted for several years, leaving the economists dumbfounded—much as they were during the impossible days of 1970s stagflation, when high inflation and high unemployment persisted together for a time.

Given the backdrop of benign inflation, a technology-driven productivity revolution, and sound fiscal policy, it becomes easier to see why a number of high-growth companies receive mind-boggling valuations. Of course, there will be corrections. And, as we've seen, not every wunderkind of the Internet will justify its valuation. Most won't. But the Internet and new technology have combined to fuel a remarkable period of growth that looks to continue, even if it is interrupted by moments of nervousness.

It is our intention in this book to help you understand the New Economy and its valuable intersection with the stock market. We'll help you figure out which companies stand to benefit, and which companies may have great stories but weak prospects. Though the New Economy has many beneficiaries, it is not the guarantor of universal success. Optimism must be tempered with realism, and we won't flinch from telling the harder truths too.

Finally, this book won't cover all types of investing. You won't find an analysis of the art market or much about heating oil futures. We'll talk a bit about bonds and whether you need them for diversification. But mostly this book is about stocks. We've got no particular beef with other investments. But this book is for New Economy investors with the inclination to make their own decisions about stock picking, with or without the help of a broker. And it's for investors who share our view that over time, equities are well worth the risk.

I will take you on a tour of the key issues you need to understand in today's investing firmament. With the help of some of *TheStreet.com*'s most experienced writers, we will explore several areas of the market. We'll help you become a more confident, less fearful stock picker. And for those of you ready to test your mettle, we'll even introduce you to options and shorting!

In this middle ground, between the dummies and the self-proclaimed savants, there's much we feel we can offer. This, in a real sense, is how I and many others have learned about the stock market and investing. Back in 1994, I was assigned to cover the stock market for *The Wall Street Journal*. At the time, I knew more about hat tricks (hockey) than Red Hats (Linux software firm). So, I went to work. I read books, I talked with professors and hunkered down with traders and strategists, trying to absorb their knowledge. This kind of self-teaching is an invaluable way to learn about something, and it is how many on Wall Street, and now Main Street, have learned their trade.

Our efforts to help you master the market will, in some respects, mimic my own crash course on the markets. We'll start with the economy and work our way through fundamental analysis, researching stocks, and how to read charts. We'll help you figure out when to buy a stock and when to sell a stock. We'll break down the technology sector. We'll even give you guidance on how an individual investor can best handle the tax consequences of buying and selling stocks. We will cover every important nook and cranny to ensure that you are equipped to become a full-fledged participant in this new world of investing.

To make sure we get the latest and best information available, I've called on a powerful group of writers and contributors from *TheStreet.com* to help reveal the secrets to the world of individual investing. Among the people we'll receive wisdom and guidance from are Tracy Byrnes, Dan Colarusso, Christopher Edmonds, Jim Griffin, Thomas Lepri, George Mannes, Mark Martinez, Helene Meisler, John Rubino, and Elizabeth Roy Stanton.

We believe *TheStreet.com Guide to Smart Investing in the Internet Era* will teach you how to become a smarter investor. And ultimately, a richer one. We're not going to claim it's a simple world with simple answers. But there are ways to get a leg up on your competition—even the lurching monster that is Wall Street—and we'll give you that edge. Along the way, we'll try to make sure that you are entertained as well as enlightened.

Will you be? We want to know. Please e-mail us at smartinvesting@ thestreet.com with your thoughts and questions on this book. And please join us in a series of online chats with the contributors to this book on *TheStreet.com* network. You'll find more information at our Web site, www.thestreet.com.

Today's new investment world isn't docile, but it can be tamed. Without further ado, let's dive in.

2

Economics 201

It used to be that a surefire way to bring a conversation to a grinding halt was to start chatting about the economy. But no longer. The economy is central to investors of all backgrounds, from the pro in lower Manhattan to the individual in Iowa. It is part of our national conversation. Federal Reserve Chairman Alan Greenspan, the nation's economic czar, is a celebrity. People watch the Fed like they watch the Yankees. At the heart of the economy's rise in significance is a debate about the New Economy vs. the "old economy."

As the 1990s marched forward, and economic growth showed few signs of letting up, some progressive economists started to argue against old economy thinking—the standard postwar dogma of boom-and-bust cycles. The economic growth cycles were getting longer, recessions were getting shorter and less intense. By the end of the century, the United States was in the midst of its longest expansion since accurate data regarding the business cycle had been kept. Something had changed. But was this a New Economy?

The New Economy philosophy is fairly simple. It argues that massive gains in technology have improved productivity on not just an individual scale but on a corporate scale. With these productivity gains, the economy can grow faster and longer without the kind of inflationary and financial dislocations that have felled previous expansions.

In the late 1990s, low unemployment, which typically had led to wage pressures and higher inflation, seemed to mosey along without jump-starting inflation. Productivity gains, thanks largely to technology, helped keep prices down even as the workforce thrived.

Companies that helped foster these gains—networking companies like Cisco Systems (CSCO:Nasdaq), telecommunications companies like Qualcomm (QCOM:Nasdaq), or companies that started to take advantage of them, such as e-tailing companies like Amazon.com (AMZN:Nasdaq) or online brokerages like E*Trade (EGRP:Nasdaq), got dubbed New Economy companies.

During the middle 1990s, the New Economy advocates were still being dismissed as glassy-eyed zealots bent on arguing for an economic nirvana that the old economy stalwarts believed was impossible. Yet, as we move into the 2000s, the New Economy crowd has moved from Cold Fusion–style curiosities to center-stage players. Even Greenspan gives a nod or two to the New Economy theories.

Old Economy Thinking v. New Economy Ethos

Old Economy: low unemployment leads to wage pressures
and high inflation

New Economy: low unemployment and low inflation
coexist in an investor's nirvana

Part of what has allowed the remarkable gains in the United States economy stems from one-off developments, most notably the end of the Cold War. The end of the East-West conflict opened up a big chunk of the world to liberal democratic capitalism, giving a huge boost to growth. That one-time change coincided with an American emergence at the forefront of practically every important technology. From arcane 3-D seismology for oil drilling to fancy wireless contraptions that fit in the palm of the hand and access the Internet, the United States has placed itself at the heart of the economic transformation of the world.

This remarkable change to a technology-driven economy—the move to the so-called New Economy—remains an issue of debate. Curmudgeonly grousers still believe that we're just in an expanded version of the Old World. But this kind of sustained growth with low unemployment and minimal inflation has gripped the country not for a couple of quarters, but for several years. More and more it seems that the rules have changed. And that's because they have.

Economic rules—theories—rarely remain static. New technology, new thinking, and politics, combine to create a moving target. The Old World rules relied on a manufacturing-driven postwar world that is now a mere shadow of itself. The country has changed, and with it the economy.

Seeing the Shift

Strategists and investors on Wall Street who recognized this change early on have become stars or rich. Abby Joseph Cohen of Goldman Sachs began arguing back in the mid-1990s that the structural changes being driven by technology and the vast new markets opening up overseas argued for a new paradigm for investors. Even in the doldrums of the 1994 stock market, Cohen argued forcefully that a long boom was upon us. She contended that an extended period of strong corporate profits and a strong stock market lay ahead.

I remember when Cohen first explained this to me in her office in lower Manhattan when I was a reporter for *The Wall Street Journal*. Skeptical as ever, I absorbed her charts, graphs, and diagrams but couldn't quite bring myself to believe my eyes. She was arguing for a 1950s-style explosion of growth and prosperity and United States–led dominance that seemed unreal during the period of the mid-1990s, when interest rates were rising and the stock market was struggling to keep above water. But slowly I started to grasp how all these different factors were falling into place, and it was pretty darned exciting. Cohen's insight into what was happening derived from an understanding of the economy and how that was creating a different world for investors. And that was something to get excited about, especially if your job was writing for an audience of investors.

Getting a good handle on the economy is absolutely vital to the investor. If you can understand where the big trends are headed, you can more easily extract rich veins of opportunity. Trying to dive into the stock market without getting a handle on the economy is like showing up at the ballpark without knowing a thing about baseball. You don't need to be an expert, but a basic understanding will help you better predict what is going to happen to your investment portfolio.

So, let's dig into the basics of the economy. I promise to keep it a little interesting. Honest.

Understanding the economy is about understanding everything from why a hot dog costs a buck on Amsterdam and 72nd in Manhattan, to deciphering how higher interest rates impact a home purchase. It's a lot of moving parts, from the macro to the micro, and the wackiness of it all might explain why economists consider themselves practitioners of the Dismal Science. I'm not flying solo on this complicated issue. I've turned to two people to help us out. The first is one of my favorite Dismal Scientists, Jim Griffin. A contributor to *TheStreet.com,* Griffin has spent much of his career musing about the economy for insurance firm Aetna and its investment unit, Aeltus. The second is Elizabeth Roy Stanton, a senior writer for *TheStreet.com* who covers the bond market.

Understanding the Economy

Why not start at the beginning. Imagine the view of earth as seen by a higher life-form from a distant galaxy. Having observed the decline of the dinosaurs, and having failed to predict the success of our weak, slow, apparently defenseless species, these distant galactic researchers might be amazed at humanity's prosperity. They might be able to count our numbers, assess our state of nutrition and health, evaluate the structures we build, and perhaps make some speculative projections that they will check on future trips. They might acquire rich volumes of data and produce well-founded inferences. But would they *understand* us?

In some respects, the alien scientists are similar to human scientists studying an ant colony. They observe and document, but the how and why gets confusing. We rush around on a daily basis, interacting with some of our fellows, ignoring others. What is it that organizes this frenetic activity and has enabled us to surpass the alien scientists' highest projections?

The answer is the economy. This may strike some of you as bordering on the mystical, but stick with me here. "The economy" is the organization of humanity that produces and distributes the things that people need and/or want. Perhaps the economy might be seen as a carrying out of the sentence handed down in mankind's fall from grace: "By the sweat of thy brow shalt thou earn thy daily bread." We (well, almost all of us) are required to work for a living. The economy is the compelling locus of much, if not most, of our waking thoughts as we work within it, study and prepare to join it, or figure out how to manage within it in retirement.

The study of the economy—economics—is not just about numbers or even money. It's about dynamic systems. There is an ecology to the economy in which all parts are connected. Labor conditions in Malaysia have an influence on profit margins in Manhattan and investment decisions in Madrid. The key issue in economics is the *dynamic stability of the system*—can the system absorb shocks or disturbances and, through self-correcting mechanisms, return over time to smooth functioning? Understanding both interconnectedness and the dynamic stability of the system is fundamental to making investment choices. Understanding economics can give you an edge on your less-studied peers.

The Economy Now: Global Capitalism

Think of the economy as a prizefight. Buyers and sellers slug it out for dominance. In the labor market, workers are the sellers and employers the buyers. It can be, and literally has been, war. In product markets, such as for food or clothing, the farmer or the manufacturer is the seller and households (or "consumers") are the buyer. As in the labor market, sellers desire highest prices, buyers seek lowest. History is replete with one side having taken advantage of the other whenever the opportunity arose.

Think of government as the referee, the third person in the ring. Its role is to keep the fight clean, to enforce the rules, to be fair. When everything works right, the battle is fast-moving, aggressive, and possesses an elemental beauty and efficiency. When the fight is fixed or the referee is corrupt, the process is ugly, brutal, and inefficient.

By the middle of the twentieth century in the United States, a reasonably stable balance among buyers, sellers, and "referees" had evolved in the domestic economy. After World War II, trade with the rest of the world was a relatively insignificant part of the overall economy. The "economy" then seemed to be a bargaining process aimed at achieving a balance that satisfied the domestic constituencies of business, labor, and government.

But as Europe and Japan recovered from the war, and as poorer parts of the world slowly began to develop, the stable balance within the United States was upset. Imports competed with domestic businesses, cheap foreign labor undercut unions and siphoned off jobs, and an increasing share of United States economic activity moved outside the geographic boundaries of the country and the regulatory reach of our government. By the end of the twentieth century, *globalization* had gone from an economist's buzzword to part of the informed citizen's everyday vocabulary. Events like the protests at the meeting of world trade ministers in Seattle in 1999 underscore how much globalization, an essentially economic idea, has become part of the mainstream.

The aforementioned New Economy is the most recent and possibly the most profound development in the global economy. Around the world, and connecting the world, a new form of e-business is emerging, creating a world of new products and services, green fields fresh for plowing. Enterprises, long established or brand new, confront the opportunity to invest in and till these fields. At the same time, these new products and services that are largely made possible by the multiple technologies that comprise the Internet are a potentially deadly competitive challenge to the old way of doing things. More than a few jobs, businesses, and financial fortunes will be destroyed by the innovations of the wired (and wireless) world. But a great many more have been and will be created by the turbulent process of change in the economy. These changes are a substantial part of what we talk about in this book.

Capital Markets and the Economy

What about the markets? How does the economy of markets work? A market is nothing more than the presence in one place of a buyer and seller. Consider a sports arena. While most people have tickets to enter the event, a group of people offers tickets on the outside. This practice is called scalping, and while mostly illegal, it provides an excellent example of markets at work. Buyers and sellers meet and bargaining takes place. The third player—that governmental referee—isn't around. (Unless the police catch you in the act.) It's a purer form of cutthroat capitalism. Barking, bluffing, and intelligence-gathering all play a role.

Markets in which many buyers and sellers—and plenty of information—are present are said to be "thick," or liquid, markets. In liquid markets, transactions are easy to do. In a thin or illiquid market, a buyer or seller may have to wait a long time for a counteroffer to come along, or may have to accept a price substantially below the one asked. If you put your house up for sale, you are selling into an inherently thin market—no other product is just like it, and it may take months for the right buyer to come along. Thick markets, such as for United States Treasury securities or the interbank market for foreign exchange—the currency market—involve many potential transactors together in one place. The "after-hours" stock trading markets are currently thin, but they could become much more liquid as more buyers and sellers look for each other during nontraditional market times.

In our technology-enhanced world, cyberspace is increasingly becoming a popular marketplace. Take the case of online auctions. While admittedly fraught with their own set of pitfalls, they nevertheless open up on a global scale that one place where buyers and sellers can come together. The funky old sofa from Grandma's attic that you inherited may be junk to you, and perhaps not worth much to the few visitors to your yard sale. But to someone on the far side of the country, it may be the long-sought-after piece that completes her parlor suite. She is likely to offer a much better bid than the barely interested passersby in your own neighborhood.

In our highly evolved global market economy, an individual has access to virtually anything anywhere, even though others produce it. The only question is whether they can afford it. In a market economy, each of us is both a seller and a buyer. But all of us find ourselves on the buy side of many more markets than we sell into. For most of us, we're on the sell side only when it comes to our labor.

Then there are the markets for capital. We are likely to find ourselves alternately on the buy and sell sides in capital markets. The stock and bond markets are capital markets, but so are those for mortgages and other forms of loans. With online trading, some people take both the buy and sell sides numerous times each day!

These three sorts of markets—labor, products, and capital—make up the three-legged stool of the capitalist market system. Three-legged stools are famously stable structures. Ours has been tipped and wobbled by periodic crises but has been able to right itself and return to relatively smooth functioning.

With the advent of the Internet and associated technologies, global capitalism enters a new era, one in which it becomes possible to connect six billion people—six billion nodes on the network. All six billion of us can now or soon will be able to come together in one place—in cyberspace. The result will be—in labor, product, and capital markets alike—better bids and better offers. Thicker, more liquid markets will make for more optimal production and distribution of goods and services across people and through time. It's a constantly revolutionary process that might have earned Mao's admiration had he been able to comprehend it.

The Big Picture: Interest Rates

We'll get into some details of the micro developments fueling these macro changes in Chapter 4, when we talk about technology and technology stocks. Here we're going to review some of the basic economic and markets concepts that affect all stocks. We'll start with the economy and the bond market, and then move to the stock market.

The economy and the capital markets—including the stock and bond markets—intersect at a key locus: interest rates. The economy drives the movement of interest rates. And interest rates—along with earnings—drive the movement of stocks. As an investor, if there's one thing you need to know about the big economic picture, it's interest rates—where they are and where they're going.

What is an interest rate? It's basically the price of credit—the cost of borrowing. Borrowing a dollar today, or a hundred million dollars, will cost you something. The price of credit today is the prevailing interest rate at which you or a corporation is able to borrow money. The price is set by the market of millions of lenders and borrowers in the money and bond markets.

Interest rates are key because while much of the New Economy runs on money collected from issuing stock, the cost of borrowing money is literally the cost of doing business in many aspects of our economy. From factory construction to real estate investment to public works, large-scale economic activity is often financed with borrowed money.

Interest rates are to stocks like the weather is to our lifestyle—they affect every company and every stock every day. And as with the weather, many people make a living predicting interest rates. But no one—well, almost no one—has control over interest rates.

Bonds, which pay interest, are debt securities, meaning that bond buyers are lenders and bond issuers are borrowers. When you buy a bond, you are lending money to the issuer of that bond, and the issuer is obliged to pay you interest at a fixed rate until the bond matures. Interest is paid on the bond's face value, or principal, which is returned at maturity, unless you sell the bond first. For example, a 10-year bond with a 7% interest rate and a face value of $1,000 pays the investor $70 a year for 10 years. After 10 years you get your $1,000 back.

The Big Bond Market

- By the Federal Reserve's accounting, there was $26 trillion of credit market debt, or bonds, outstanding at the end of March 2000, compared to $15.8 trillion worth of corporate equities, as measured by the Wilshire 5000 Index at the end of June 2000.

- The magnitude of the bond market is why the October 1998 collapse of Long Term Capital Management, a big bond hedge fund, posed a threat to the entire financial system.

The bond in the example—let's say it was issued by AT&T (T: NYSE)—has a 7% interest rate, or coupon. Why 7%? Because at the time of issuance, market forces determined that a 10-year bond from an issuer of the caliber of AT&T should pay an interest rate of 7%.

What Determines an Interest Rate?

- Creditworthiness of the lender (risky v. safe)

- Term of the loan (long term v. short term)

Two key considerations go into this interest-rate determination: the creditworthiness of AT&T and the term or length of the loan. A less creditworthy borrower would have had to pay an even higher interest rate to compensate for the added risk; a more creditworthy one would be able to pay a lower one. Likewise, AT&T would normally have had to pay a higher interest rate to extend the maturity of its bond from 10 years to 15 years. That's because the issuer needs to pay more to convince the lender to lock up that money for a longer period of time, a time during which forces like higher inflation could take hold. The issuer probably could have lowered its rate by setting the maturity of its bond at 5 years.

There are many interest rates out there—on corporate bonds, bank loans, credit cards, United States Treasury bonds, and all other sorts of debt. Market watchers pay attention chiefly to the interest rates paid by the United States government on Treasury bonds. That's because the United States government, as the most creditworthy of borrowers, can obtain the lowest interest rates on its debt.

What the Market Watches

Benchmark Borrower: U.S. Government

Benchmark Rate: 10-Year Treasury Note

Within the Treasury market, people look at the 10-year Treasury note for a general idea of what's going on with Treasury interest rates. The 10-year note is a long-maturity bond with plenty of trading volume to create a robust and efficient market. This is the instrument you'll see quoted in market reports and flashing alongside the major stock indices in market data summaries.

How does the bond market decide what the interest rate on the 10-year note should be? It decides on the basis of what it expects to happen to the inflation rate. Inflation is the enemy of the bond investor because while inflation can fluctuate, interest payments are fixed. If you own a bond that is going to pay you $70 a year for 10 years and give you $1,000 when it matures, any smidgen of inflation takes a bite out of those sums.

If you expect inflation to accelerate, you would not want to pay as much for bonds. The longer the maturity—the longer the timeline for possible inflation—the higher the interest rate you would demand. Conversely, if you expect that inflation will decelerate, or even turn into deflation, you might be willing to settle for a very low interest rate, even on a very long-maturity bond, since over time the payments from your bond would buy larger quantities of goods and services.

Interest Rates and Inflation

- High interest rates indicate expectations of rising inflation

- Low interest rates indicate expectations of low or no inflation

In this way, the bond market tells you what investors who buy bonds—institutional investors, mainly—expect from the economy. Inflation typically accelerates when growth is accelerating, and decelerates when growth is slowing. So long-term interest rates that are high relative to short-term interest rates reflect the expectation that economic growth will speed up, stoking inflation. And long-term rates that are low relative to short-term rates signify that investors expect slower growth and less inflation down the road.

Interest Rate Rules of Thumb

Long-term rates > Short-term rates =
High growth and inflation expectations

Long-term rates < Short-term rates =
Low growth and inflation expectations

As with most things economic, the general rules are often just that—general. Specific, real-world circumstances can differ. In the United States Treasury bond market, for example, the normal relationships between short- and long-maturity bonds got disrupted by supply and demand in early 2000. Basically, a shortage of long-maturity Treasuries made investors willing to accept lower interest rates on them than on short-maturity issues—with the result that short-term

Cautionary Notes

- Investors' expectations don't always pan out. Where the economy is headed is anybody's guess, and the bond market can get it wrong.

- The bond market is a market, and so it's subject to the forces of supply and demand. Sometimes, the movement of interest rates has less to do with expectations about the economy than with actual supply of and demand for bonds.

rates were higher than long-term, even though signs of inflation were perking up. Under these conditions, the Treasury market no longer gave as clean a read on inflation expectations.

Still, the basic concept is worth remembering as you make investment decisions: Interest rates tend to go up in an inflationary environment. And as we'll describe next, that's not good for stocks.

Crossroads: The Stock Market and Interest Rates

Stock market players are obsessed with interest rates and inflation because they have such a profound effect on the United States economy, corporations, and stocks themselves. First, a refresher on why investors care about inflation. Inflation is the increase in prices for goods and services. As prices rise, you get less for your money. And it's harder for companies to do business when prices are unstable and hard to predict.

It can also be confusing to recall why stock investors care so much about rates. There are basically three reasons, all of which are related. First, interest rates affect lending to corporations. When United States Treasury interest rates rise, interest rates for corporate borrowers generally follow in turn. That means it costs more for companies who borrow to grow. Higher borrowing costs can either slow their growth or hit their profit margins. The higher cost of borrowing is one of the reasons stocks tend to go down when interest rates go up.

Second, interest rates affect the price consumers have to pay for all sorts of loans, from car loans to mortgages. The more consumers have to pay for a particular item, the less likely they are to purchase it. Higher interest rates help to slow the economy by slowing consumer spending. A slower economy can hurt stocks that do better when people and companies feel like they have a free dollar to spend, like retail stocks and technology stocks.

Finally, stocks react strongly to interest rate shifts because of the issue of asset allocation. Bonds—whose prices move with interest rates—offer an alternative investment to stocks. If bonds are paying higher interest rates, then bonds become an increasingly attractive investment relative to stocks. If bonds are paying lower interest rates, then stocks become increasingly worth their greater risk. Thus, the prices of stocks can fluctuate as investors flee to or from bonds.

Why Interest Rates Affect Stocks

- Interest rates affect the costs of borrowing for companies

- Interest rates affect the costs of borrowing for consumers

- High interest rates on bonds can make bonds more attractive than stocks

These are the main reasons that interest rates matter so much to stock investors. It's concern over these things that prompts investors to try to decipher which way interest rates are going. Their main source of signals on rates is the Federal Reserve.

The Federal Reserve

The Federal Reserve is the central bank of the United States, and it can influence the direction of interest rates. The Fed doesn't have total control over rates by any means. It shares the power with the gargantuan bond market. But the Fed controls the "fed funds rate"—the rate at which banks lend excess reserves to one another overnight—and the bond market sets other interest rates relative to the fed funds rate. So a move in the fed funds rate—or anticipation of a move in the fed funds rate—can and usually does affect all other interest rates.

Strictly speaking, the Fed doesn't even control the fed funds rate. Rather, it takes measures to bring the rate in line with the target the Fed sets for it. The fed funds rate will tend to rise above the Fed's target for it when bank reserves become scarce. In that case, the Fed injects additional reserves into the banking system by buying Treasury securities from the banks. The money the banks receive from the sales inflates their reserves—basically creating more money in the system. In turn, the fed funds rate goes down as the additional supply of money makes borrowing it cheaper.

This power to control short-term interest rates is enormous, and it explains why the bond market cares so much about the pronouncements of the Fed. If the Fed thinks the economy is growing too fast— if the economy is "overheating"—the Fed will raise interest rates to stifle growth a bit and stave off the debilitating scourge of inflation. That's what happened in late 1999 and 2000 when unemployment hovered at a 30-year low of 3.9% and signs of inflation crept in. The Fed started raising rates.

If, on the other hand, the Fed sees no signs of inflation but instead thinks the economy needs some extra juice, it will lower rates. That's what happened in the wake of the Asian economic crisis of 1997, when troubled financial conditions threatened a worldwide slowdown in economic demand.

Because the Fed has so much power over interest rates, the bond and stock markets monitor nearly every utterance from the Fed's chairman and its other members. A handful of times over the course of a year, the chairman speaks publicly, almost always reading from prepared remarks. Those comments can move the markets even before the chair starts reading them, since the Fed has taken to publishing them on its Web site (www.federalreserve.gov) at the hour the speech is scheduled for.

Those pronouncements, though, are rarely if ever crystal clear about what the Federal Open Market Committee (FOMC)—the Fed panel that sets the fed funds rate—is going to do at future meetings. The market is basically searching for hints. For example, on June 17, 1999, Chairman Alan Greenspan gave a speech before the Joint Economic Committee of Congress that suggested quite clearly—to those accustomed to parsing his words—that the FOMC was likely to raise the fed funds rate at its next meeting on June 30, which it subsequently did. "When we can be preemptive, we should be, because modest preemptive actions can obviate the need of more drastic actions at a later date that could destabilize the economy," Alan Greenspan said. In Greenspeak, "preemptive" is code for raising interest rates.

Even when he's not dropping hints about the future course of interest rates, the chairman can move the markets just by revealing a glimpse of his frame of mind. Remember Greenspan's December 5, 1996, musing on the question: "But when do we know when irrational exuberance has unduly escalated asset values, which then become subject to unexpected and prolonged contractions as they have in Japan over the past decade?" The mere suggestion by the chairman that the stock market was "irrationally" overvalued sent the market into a brief tailspin.

While no one can predict interest rates with certainty, mere speculation about their direction can have a huge impact on stocks. Since the bond market indicates which way investors think rates are heading, stock investors consider it worth paying attention to.

Tracking the Fed

Most of the economic terms you hear bandied about in the financial press—CPI, PPI, jobs report—are measurements of the economy's growth and the direction of inflation. The Fed studies this data to help it decide whether to raise or lower interest rates. Economists and market strategists also track the data closely, in an attempt to predict the Fed's actions and in turn the path of interest rates. The interest-rate-driven bond market often moves in anticipation of what the Federal Reserve will do based on the available economic data.

Various points of economic data dribble into the market from federal agencies as well as independent data tracking sources nearly every week of the year. The bond market reacts to the data points to different degrees, depending on the weight the economic community gives the data. A bond market that expects growth to accelerate based on the data will set interest rates high, essentially by selling bonds. If it then gets data indicating that growth isn't accelerating, perhaps interest rates are too high and they need to come down. That's achieved by buying bonds. Likewise, a bond market that sets interest rates low because it expects growth to slow will move them higher if it gets information indicating that growth isn't slowing.

In this data dance, the trickiest steps are the ones on the first Friday of the month, when the Bureau of Labor Statistics, a division of the Department of Labor, releases the "employment report" for the previous month.

The employment report is revered because, better than any other economic report, it tells how quickly the economy is growing at the moment. Other economic reports look at only one segment of the economy, or they measure past growth. But the so-called "jobs report" looks at the entire economy, and we get it hot out of the oven.

The jobs report indicates how many new jobs the economy created in the last month. (Specifically, it counts nonagricultural, or nonfarm, jobs.) But the report contains other useful information as well. It tells us how fast wages and salaries are growing, by calculating average hourly earnings. That's important because wage inflation can lead to

Relationship of Bond Prices to Interest Rates

When bond prices go up, market interest rates go down, and vice versa. Here's why: Bonds pay fixed interest rates. But as the buyer of a bond, you may obtain a market interest rate, or yield, that is either higher or lower than the bond's fixed rate. It depends on how much you pay for the bond. For example, suppose you buy a bond with a face value of $1,000 and a 7% interest rate. If you pay 100 cents on the dollar for it, you get a yield of 7%. Yield is the fixed interest rate divided by the bond's market price, approximately $7/100$ in this case. But if you pay more than $1,000 for it, your yield will be lower than 7% because the market price—the denominator—has grown, while the interest rate—the numerator—is fixed.

Why would you pay more than face value? Say interest rates in general have declined, and brand-new bonds of the same type, selling for 100 cents on the dollar, now pay a rate of 6%. You'd be willing to pay more for one that pays 7%.

Thus, the higher the price, the lower the yield, and the lower the price, the higher the yield. This is why bond prices and market interest rates move in opposite directions.

price inflation, as people have more money to spend. The report also calculates the unemployment rate. While the unemployment rate doesn't tell us anything about the future, it has a great deal of resonance with the broader population and with politicians. A rising unemployment rate starts them clamoring for the Federal Reserve to cut the fed funds rate to stimulate the economy, while a falling unemployment rate can give the central bank political cover to raise the rate.

There are dozens of other economic indicators, but there are only about eight, including the jobs report, that the bond and stock markets get really excited about.

Data That Juice the Markets

- Gross Domestic Product (GDP): The economic growth rate, measured quarterly.

- The Consumer Price Index (CPI): The broadest measure of

inflation, this measures consumer prices on a monthly basis. The "core" CPI strips out food and energy prices.

- The Producer Price Index (PPI): A narrower monthly measure of inflation, including only goods sold at the wholesale level.

- The Employment Cost Index (ECI): A quarterly measure of how quickly labor costs are rising, it considers both wages and benefit costs.

- The retail sales report: Measures consumer spending on goods only, monthly. Consumer spending on goods and services is the biggest driver of economic growth.

- The Purchasing Managers' Index: A monthly private-sector indicator of the health of the manufacturing sector that has become less important as the manufacturing sector has shrunk.

- The durable goods orders report: Measures monthly growth in orders for things like appliances, which predicts future business for the manufacturing sector.

Interest Rates and Your Investing

Now that you understand interest rates, how do you act on them as an investor? To a certain extent, you shouldn't. Basically, interest rates are beyond our control or continued accurate prognostication. And investors' time is generally best spent on things they can control, like how well they understand the promise of an individual company or the trend of a stock chart.

Still, some knowledge about interest rates can help an investor make decisions about whether to invest in a particular sector, or when to time a stock purchase or sale. While the value of a stock will depend on its earnings over the long term, interest rates do affect stock prices in the short term. Keep the following guidelines in mind:

First, while interest rates affect the entire market, they tend to have a more pronounced impact on what are called "rate-sensitive" industry sectors, like financial stocks and retail stocks. Bank stocks tend to perform better in falling or lower interest-rate environments, when the cost of borrowing money is getting cheaper. Same goes for retail stocks, which tend to fare worse in a slower economy, signaled by rising inter-

The Economic Indicators: How They Influence the Market

Most Influential

Employment Report
Consumer Price Index
Employment Cost Index
Purchasing Managers' Index

Gross Domestic Product
Producer Price Index
Retail Sales
Durable Goods Orders

Pretty Influential

Chicago Purchasing
    Managers' Index
Philadelphia Fed Index

Industrial Production and
    Capacity

Somewhat Influential

Beige Book
Existing Home Sales
Housing Starts
New Home Sales
Productivity and Unit
    Labor Costs

BTM Weekly U.S. Retail
    Chain Store Sales Index
Initial Jobless Claims
Personal Income and
    Consumption
Redbook Retail Average

Less Influential

APICS Business Outlook Index
Construction Spending
Consumer Confidence Index
Factory Orders
Housing Market Index
International Trade
Purchasing Managers'
    Nonmanufacturing Index

Business Inventories
Consumer Comfort Index
Consumer Sentiment Index
Federal Budget
Import and Export Prices
Mortgage Applications Survey
Wholesale Trade

Least Influential

Atlanta Fed Index
Consumer Credit
Kansas City Fed Index
New York Business Conditions
    Index

Chicago Fed Index
Help-Wanted Index
Leading Economic Indicators
Real Earnings
Richmond Fed Survey

est rates. When the economy slows, consumers are less apt to buy a new suit or a pair of shoes.

This kind of insight can affect your trading decisions. If you were thinking about buying, say, the Gap (GPS:NYSE) in the spring of 2000, you perhaps should have thought about holding off. The stock was getting hammered along with the Fed's rate-hiking activity.

Beyond financials and retail stocks, some contend that technology stocks get a heftier pummeling than the broader market when interest rates rise. The theory is that these stocks have such high growth expectations factored into their prices, any general slowing of economic growth will crush their stocks. And to a certain extent, it's proven true: The technology-heavy Nasdaq stock index stalled out in 2000 as interest rates rose. And in 1994, another year of rising interest rates, the Nasdaq fell more than the Dow and S&P 500.

Still, the evidence on the relationship between tech stocks and rates is mixed. For much of 1999, for example, tech stocks soared even as interest rates rose. Part of the reason is that investors' faith in the promise of these New Economy companies outweighs what they see as short-term interest rate swings. Another reason is that tech companies have been incredibly successful at raising money in the stock market by selling shares to the public. So many of them are not heavily reliant on rate-sensitive borrowing activity.

In general, whatever sector you're considering, interest rates can help you decide on your entry point for a stock purchase. If you sense you're at the end of a rate-tightening cycle and the economy is set to thrive, it could be a good time to buy stocks that are expected to do well in a strong economy—stocks like Caterpillar (CAT:NYSE), manufacturer of construction and mining equipment, or high-end apparel company Gucci Group N.V. (GUC:NYSE). If you think you're at the beginning of a cycle of tightening credit, then you might consider waiting to purchase these stocks until the cycle plays itself out and instead focus on stocks that you'd expect to chug along even in slow-growth periods, like beverage company PepsiCo (PEP:NYSE).

At the same time, know this: Interest rates tend to affect the entire market, throwing out the proverbial "baby with the bathwater." So if there's a stock you like for the long term based on its corporate fundamentals—a concept we discuss in Chapter 6—an interest rate rise may be a good time to pick up some shares on the cheap.

The Stock Market

The stock market is much smaller than the bond market—$15.8 trillion v. $26 trillion. But it's the market that most individual investors can participate in, and it's the market that historically has offered higher returns. (More on that in the next chapter.) The behavior of the stock market can be analyzed in a zillion different ways, from the "advance/decline" line to volume to sector indices.

Big-Three Indices

The big three stock market measurements, or indices, are the Dow Jones Industrial Average, the S&P 500, and the Nasdaq Composite.

None of these captures the entire United States stock market. Another index, the Wilshire 5000, does that. But the fact that relatively few people watch the Wilshire closely is proof that the performance of a slice of the market can be more informative than the performance of the entire market.

NYSE vs. Nasdaq

New York Stock Exchange: trading exchange, mostly for big blue-chip stocks. (Trick: NYSE stocks have one, two, or three-letter symbols.)

Nasdaq: Computerized trading system, mostly for high-tech and smaller-cap stocks. (Trick: Nasdaq stocks have four- or five-letter symbols.)

The Dow Jones Industrial Average is the oldest and still the most familiar of the Big-Three indices. The folks at Dow Jones & Co. gave the index a major overhaul in November 1999 by adding in New Economy leaders Microsoft (MSFT:Nasdaq) and Intel (INTC:Nasdaq), making them the first Nasdaq-listed companies in the index.

Born in 1896 as a 12-stock index, the Dow's ranks swelled to 30 stocks by 1928. There have been dozens of substitutions over the years, but the Dow Industrials remains a 30-stock index.

It's an impressive group. The companies are considered undisputed leaders in their industries, and all the stocks are widely held and actively traded. But at the end of the day, there are still only 30 stocks in the index, representing only about a fifth of the value of the entire market. And basically, it's a stodgy group. Heck, it took the Dow Jones folks until the turn of the century to give Microsoft and Intel their spots. Finally, the Dow Industrials are not market-value weighted, meaning that each stock contributes equally to the performance of the index, regardless of the company's market size.

It's for all of these reasons that the vast majority of money managers who track an index prefer an index that captures a much larger part of the market: the S&P 500.

Maintained by Standard & Poor's (whose main business is actually rating bonds—go figure), the S&P 500 is a market-value-weighted index of 500 stocks representing about 75% of the value of the total market.

It is a large-cap index. Market size is a main criterion for inclusion in the group. So is sector leadership. At the end of June 2000, the group was 76% industrial companies, 14% financial firms, 8% utilities, and 2% transportation concerns. Tech companies are classified as industrials, and they made up about a third of the index at that time. New York Stock Exchange–listed issues make up 87% of the index in terms of the number of stocks included, Nasdaq-listed companies the remainder.

The Dow and the S&P 500 are called indices because they can be tracked. But make no mistake: There's lots of stock picking going on here. The folks at Dow Jones choose the Industrials, and the folks at S&P pick the stocks for the S&P 500. It's art that becomes science once these powers bless a stock for the index.

The main shortcoming with the S&P 500 is that large-cap stocks aren't always where the action is. When optimism about the prospects of small or untried companies heats up, raising their stock prices, that doesn't show up in the Dow Industrials or the S&P 500.

The Big-Three Indices		
DJIA	S&P 500	Nasdaq Composite
30 stocks large cap equal weighting	500 stocks large cap market-cap weighting	5000+ stocks tech and smaller caps market-cap weighting

It shows up in the Nasdaq Composite and the Russell 2000.

The Nasdaq Composite Index, or the Comp, as it is known, is by no means a small-cap index. It includes all stocks listed on the Nasdaq stock market (there are more than 5,000), some of which are quite large. Nasdaq-listed Microsoft for some time had the largest market value of any United States company. And the Comp is market-value weighted.

But the Nasdaq is where most new companies list. Since its inception in 1971, many of those companies have been technology concerns. And so the Comp is a distinctly technology-flavored index with assertive small-cap notes.

If it has a shortcoming, it's inclusiveness. A lot of Nasdaq-listed stocks change hands relatively infrequently, so their contributions to the Comp may be based on old trading data. Still, the Comp is the closest thing the market's got to a broad-based New Economy index. And in recent years, it's become as or more important to many investors than its blue-chip brethren.

Even taken together, the big-three indices don't tell you everything that's going on in the market. For example, to know what small caps are doing, you really need to look at a dedicated small-cap index like the Russell 2000. If you are focused on Internet stocks, there's TheStreet.com's Internet Index, whose quotes are available under the ticker symbol DOT.

The Economy and Investing

Now that we've got some understanding of the economy and the markets, let's look at what counts most: how it all matters to investors.

Let's go back to Abby Joseph Cohen. She foresaw massive gains in the economy, led by technology. This is also a theme that Byron Wien of Morgan Stanley Dean Witter picked up on. He foresaw gains coming from an explosion in capital expenditure—code for corporations pouring a big heap of cash into technology. Both were mining veins of big economic movements.

How can you do the same? Using some of the tenets we've offered in this chapter.

If you believe that interest rate hikes are taking their toll and the economy is tiring, you might want to look at stocks that do well in low- or no-growth periods. For instance, people continue to purchase soda during flat economic times, even if they aren't out buying another car. That analysis would favor Coca-Cola (KO:NYSE) over Ford (F:NYSE). The same can be said for basic products like cosmetics or drugs.

When the economy is picking up steam or coming out of a sluggish time but interest rates are still in check, you might want to focus on big-ticket items that people have deferred. You don't like to buy a car when things are tough, but once things start to get better, you stretch out for a new vehicle. These are very general ideas, ideas that will get more robust treatment throughout this book. But keep the concept of the economy in the back of your head. When you invest in stocks, you're investing in a company's growth and profit prospects. Having a feel for the economy can help you better understand if your biotech stock or your favorite semiconductor maker is in for smooth or rough sailing in the quarters ahead.

Another way to use economic understanding is to take a look at the global marketplace, not just that of the United States. We've already experienced a fair amount of technology revolution here, and a great deal of that revolution is now being exported. Who is likely to benefit? If you believe that Eastern Europe, Latin America, Asia, and Africa need to catch up to the United States and Western Europe, you might explore investment opportunities in those places. A simpler strategy is to invest in United States companies that are finding success in those nascent markets.

Finally, as for the current economy, it is long in the tooth. It is ripe past the age of most economic expansions. New Economy advocates argue that this condition provides nothing to fear, that the economy is not going to return to the old boom-and-bust cycle, but instead embark on a new era of perpetual growth.

While I like the New Economy, I think that it is a mistake to believe recessions are a thing of the past. Periodic recessions still mar the economy from time to time. A quick glance at Japan shows that even a technologically advanced nation can struggle for extended periods. There may yet be periods ahead when the performance of the United States economy falls short of our recent experience—when real growth will not be strong nor inflation and unemployment low.

But the information-based New Economy does seem less predisposed to those sorts of maladies than the agricultural or heavy manufacturing economies of our past. Cyclical shortfalls of food production and periodic overbuilding of inventories were characteristic of old economies past. The New Economy of today seems to be inherently less susceptible to these cyclical volatilities. With its bar-coded check-out counters and its Web-based supply chain management to B2B communities of just-in-time vendors, this economy seems less prone to disharmonies between supply and demand.

What appears to be true is that recessions are increasingly brief and expansions lengthier. This trend, which is really what the New Economy is bringing us, will remain intact. So even if we get a glimmer of difficulty—as we did in 2000—it will not spell the end of the New Economy. It will be one more modest step back before the growth continues. Too much growing needs to happen in too many places around the world for things to turn south for a sustained period. We believe there's simply enough opportunity for ideas, innovation—and profit—to keep this economy humming for a very long time.

3

Diversifying with Stocks

Diversification is, perhaps, the most enduring of all investment strategies. Regardless of who's offering the investment advice—a broker, a portfolio manager, or a financial planner—the old adage "Don't put all your eggs in one basket" is inevitably trotted out. For most of this century, the advice hawkers have generally interpreted that maxim to mean that investors should spread their wealth between the two different baskets of stocks and bonds and thereby spread the risk. But as stocks have soared while bonds served up a paltry meal over the past decade, those old nuggets beg to be reexamined. In fact, a growing number of investment pros argue that diversification should not center on asset class, but should instead center on stocks and which types of stocks to own.

The idea of diversification is that you can reduce the risk you need to take on to achieve a given level of reward if you select investments that behave differently under different economic and market circumstances. Even if a portion of your portfolio goes sour thanks to current conditions, other parts will do better under those same conditions, thereby limiting your downside. We think that for many people, diversifying within the stock market for the long term makes more sense—and, potentially, a lot more money—than a diversification strategy that focuses on stocks and bonds.

I've asked Christopher Edmonds, a contributing writer at *TheStreet.com* and a veteran money manager, to help guide us through the financial thickets. Chris, who covers the venerable Warren Buffett for *TheStreet.com,* manages several portfolios for individual investors. He has spent a good deal of his life researching the subject of diversification.

Stock market diversification is not some New Age theory. It does entail more risk than a bond-heavy portfolio, but not much more, and over the long haul, arguably, not more at all. And as we'll discuss, there are real risks to *not* investing in stocks.

Of course, if investing solely in stocks violates the insomniacs law for you—basically, if you can't sleep at night because you feel your investments are too risky—it's probably not the right strategy for you. But before sheep counting becomes a problem, let me try to calm your fears about the prospect of an all-stock, long-term investment portfolio.

Challenging Conventional Wisdom

Conventional wisdom suggests that a balance between stocks and bonds provides the best defense against investment risk, against the unsettling volatility of an all-equity portfolio. Yet, given the last several years, bond investors may be wondering just what the heck they're doing holding bonds. While bond returns have inched above inflation, stocks have provided solid double-digit returns throughout the 1990s. (As we wrote this book—mid-year 2000—the year was proving to be an aberration, with bonds outperforming stocks. At the end of August, the total return on the 10-year treasury was 7.5% versus a 4.1% return for the S&P 500 stock benchmark, according to Bianco Research.)

Some financial advisers argue that that fact alone suggests exposure to bonds is more important now than ever—that stocks are inflated and overpriced. But performance isn't the sole reason to think about diversifying with an all-stock strategy. The nature of our changing economy makes equity investing the preferred vehicle for building wealth. Debt, once mighty, has been supplanted by an equity-driven culture.

In the first 90 years of the twentieth century, our economic focus was on physical infrastructure and raw materials—land, manufacturing plants, and equipment. All of those economic inputs were acquired through a combination of equity and debt. When Henry Ford built the first assembly line, he did it with the money of a handful of investors and a lot of borrowed money. Think of the industrial revolution, and what comes to mind? The financiers that made it possible through lending. Consider the automobile manufacturers, textile plants, and utilities. Debt played a key role in their capital structure. In those days, companies quickly built physical assets that served as attractive collateral.

Today the inputs to the New Economy—primarily knowledge and intellect—are less tangible. And the transformation of those inputs into outputs is largely funded by equity. Take the backbone of the New Economy—technology and the Internet. Those looking to finance these endeavors have had less interest in lending to emerging companies and more interest in owning a piece of the action (one reason IPOs have been so hot in the last several years).

Why is there less interest in lending with New Economy companies? Lending is typically a lower-risk, lower-reward investing strategy. It's lower risk because the assets of a company act as security for the loan. But younger, New Economy companies often don't have physical assets to serve as security. At the same time, these smaller companies, while certainly very risky, carry the potential of such huge upside rewards that most investors prefer an equity stake. A changing economy has led to a change in the engines of investment success. Today's wealth is created by owning, not by lending. Therein lies the key to an all-equity portfolio.

Stocks vs. Bonds

Since the beginning of investable time, financial planners, accountants, trust officers—fill in the financial professional blank—have hammered home the need to develop a "scientific" balance between stocks and bonds in one's portfolio. After all, too much of a good thing has to be bad for you.

Financial planners obsess on the "inverse age" or "60/40" rule: Subtract your age from 100 and that is the maximum percentage of your portfolio that should be invested in equities. So, for example, if you are 40, you should have no more than 60% of your portfolio in stocks; if you're 60, no more than 40% of your portfolio in stocks.

That formula may have made sense in the days when the Dow Jones Industrial Average reigned as king of the equity markets. However, in today's equity-driven world, following that old saw is a sure way to needlessly limit potential returns and a more comfortable retirement. Moreover, the 60/40 rule doesn't take into account lengthier life expectancy, longer time in the workplace, and other factors that argue for a deeper risk profile at later ages.

When weighing the trade-off between stocks and bonds, you need to think about four main things. First, stocks historically have enjoyed substantially higher returns than bonds. Second, while stocks are more volatile than bonds in the short term, time mitigates the risks of investing in stocks. Third, bonds, often called "safe" investments, in fact carry risks of their own. Finally, given all these factors, there's a risk in *not* owning stocks.

Stocks Boast Higher Returns

Almost any way you slice it, stocks have outperformed bonds over time. Consider the following investment statistics:

- From 1925 to 1999, large-company stocks returned 11.3% a year on average.
- From 1925 to 1999, government bonds returned 5.1% a year on average.

  Source: Ibbotson Associates

It's easy to assume that the last decade has skewed the relative performance of the major assets classes (stocks, bonds, and cash), and that equities will never continue their torrid pace of the 1990s. But according to *Stocks for the Long Run,* by Jeremy Siegel of Wharton, stocks have returned 7% a year on average (after inflation) from 1802 to 1997, compared with 3.5% for bonds. The fact is, you don't need to count on a go-go era for stocks to be seen as the higher-return investment vehicle.

Consider the following data comparing the historical annual returns

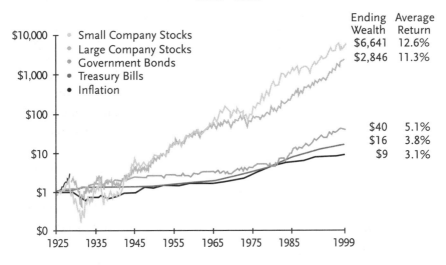

Stocks, Bonds, Bills, and Inflation
1925–1999

	Ending Wealth	Average Return
Small Company Stocks	$6,641	12.6%
Large Company Stocks	$2,846	11.3%
Government Bonds	$40	5.1%
Treasury Bills	$16	3.8%
Inflation	$9	3.1%

between equities and fixed-income investment. As you can see, stocks have doubled the average annual returns from bonds since the Great Depression.

If you can bear the risks in stocks, over time you will likely reap a substantially higher return. Now the question is Can you bear the risk?

The Risks of Investing in Stocks

Investment risk in its most basic form is the level of uncertainty about the returns expected from an investment. The more stable the investment, the less risk. That's why bonds are called "fixed-income" investments—you know what return to expect. There are two main types of risk inherent in investing in stocks: market risk (sometimes called systematic risk) and stock selection risk (sometimes called unsystematic risk).

Market Risk Market risk is the risk inherent when investing in stocks. It's something largely beyond our control. Socioeconomic events and macroeconomic policy that can nudge the market up or down are something very few investors have been consistently successful at either predicting or acting upon to their financial benefit. Even the best investors have said the ability to predict a market's direction is a fallacy. "I don't spend a lot of time thinking about the market," Warren Buffett said at the 2000 Berkshire Hathaway (BRKa:NYSE) annual meeting. "I've never figured out what that does for me." In other words, the nature of the market is that it will go up and it will go down.

That doesn't mean that the market's swings are not a risk. If you need the money you have invested in the stock market just when it's sinking, then market risk is not a risk you can afford. But as we discuss here, historically, down markets have always come back over time. That's why we recommend stocks only for the portion of your portfolio for which you have a long time horizon—a horizon that includes time for that comeback.

How long of a time horizon do you need?

The odds of turning a profit in equities are decent even if you invest for one year. From 1926 to 1999 you would have made money 73% of the time, or 54 out of 74 years, according to Chicago data tracker Ibbotson Associates. But if you had put your money into equities over any five-year period since 1926, you would have made money 90% of the time. Think super long-term, 15 years, and you would have made money 100% of the time.

We think 90% is pretty darn good odds, especially since our econ-

Risk of Stock Market Loss over Time
1926–1999

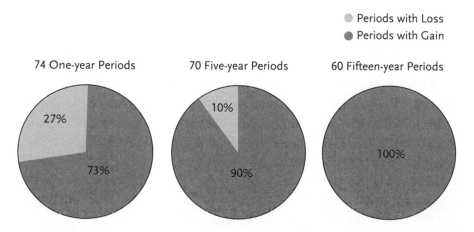

Periods with Loss
Periods with Gain

74 One-year Periods 70 Five-year Periods 60 Fifteen-year Periods

27% 10% 100%
73% 90%

Source: Ibbotson Associates, Inc. All rights reserved. Used with permission.

omy is much more stable than it was back in 1926. Indeed, from 1946 to 1999, of all the downturns of 10% or more, the market has turned the corner and enabled investors to recover their money within four years, according to Ibbotson. That's why we—and most financial advisers— suggest a five-year time horizon for stock investing. That doesn't mean it will normally take five years for you to recover your money—by recent historic indications, the time frame is shorter. Since 1973, only one bear market (10%+ decline)—from the peak in the market before the decline to complete recovery—lasted more than two years, according to Ibbotson. But five years provides the cushion to help ensure the comeback. That's why if you can't afford to wait that long, you want to scale back your equity investments.

Now, those time horizon statistics apply to a large basket of stocks like the S&P 500, a broad market gauge. You'd have been hard-pressed to get the same results if you had put all your money into, say, one stock. That's where the idea of stock selection risk comes in.

Stock Selection Risk This kind of risk is the performance risk of individual stocks you select for your portfolio. Stocks can lose their value, some never to recover it. Many investors who purchased a "dot.com" during the e-euphoria of 1999, for example, may have said good-bye to a substantial chunk of their principal. Loads of these stocks suffered a one-way spiral downward.

The risks of individual stock performance, while not something you can eliminate, is something you can at least mitigate. There are two main ways to reduce your risk of losing your principal. First, good stock picking. This book is all about just that—increasing your odds of selecting winning stocks and identifying your dogs. Even the very best investors pick stocks that disappoint. That's why they diversify—they spread their risk—among a number of stocks. Diversified investors don't expect that every pick will score. Their hope is that their winners will more than make up for the losers.

If you don't diversify your stock portfolio—if, for example, you put all your money into two or three stocks—you face severe stock-selection risk, so much so that you threaten to lose the benefits of a long-term time horizon. If you pick a couple of real no-win companies, no amount of time is going to solve their problems. But if you put your money into, say, a dozen stocks across a number of industries, you can substantially reduce your stock-selection risk.

In sum, if your time horizon is hefty and you pick a healthy bunch of stocks (exactly how many we'll discuss later in this chapter), you can largely mitigate the risk of losing your principal in stocks.

The Risks of Investing in Bonds

Bonds are often called "safe" investments. But in fact that description can be deceiving. Michael Lipper, chairman of Lipper Inc., the mutual fund tracking company, makes this point. "Do you want something where there's very very little chance of loss?" he asks. "If that's the case, I don't think bonds qualify."

Here's why. As we discussed in Chapter 2 on economics, bonds carry two main forms of risk, credit risk and interest rate risk. Credit risk is the risk that the borrower will be unable to pay the lender back. With United States bonds, there basically is no credit risk because, with its taxing power, the United States can make good on its debts. But interest rate risk is a real issue. Interest rate risk is the risk that rates will fluctuate. And that fluctuation affects the value of your bond investment. Here's an example: If you bought a 10-year corporate bond that paid 7% interest for $1,000, for 10 years you'd be guaranteed that 7% payment annually. And you'd get back the $1,000 when ten years was up.

But what if you needed the money, say, three years after you bought the bond? Perhaps now you'd want to sell it. Problem is, you might not be able to get all your money back just when you want it. If interest rates have since gone up, say, to 8% on a 10-year $1,000 bond, then your bond paying only 7% will not command its full face value of $1,000 in the marketplace. Why would someone pay $1,000 for 7% when they can pay $1,000 for 8%?

In that respect, the risk with bonds is not unlike the risk with stocks: short-term fluctuation in value. "My concern always is for people who are going to need to tap their securities because they have been removed from the workplace," Lipper says. "And that might be at a time when the market's not very attractive for bonds."

That doesn't mean Lipper thinks you should put all of your money into stocks. Rather, the average investor who is not sophisticated in the subtleties of the bond market—and that's most of us—should keep money he or she needs short-term access to in cash or in truly risk-free investments like money market funds. The rest can go into stocks.

The Risk of Not Investing in Stocks

If you can now see that stock investing for the long term is less risky than most people suspect, and bond investing is more risky than is usually assumed, the question is What's the risk in *not* investing in stocks?

In a word (or two), a lot! Opportunity cost is the real driver behind the case for a diversified all-equity long-term investment portfolio. The higher returns represent the opportunity cost of not being in stocks. But there's another factor that only makes the case stronger: inflation.

"The risk of not owning stocks comes from inflation which, generally, is a slow, insidious erosion of your wealth," wrote the managers of the Tweedy, Browne mutual funds in a 1998 semiannual report. "The pain is inflicted slowly over time."

Here's why. The value of your bond payment is fixed. No matter what happens with inflation, your bond payment won't rise to compensate for it. Because stocks have more upside potential, they have a better chance to outpace inflation, which has averaged about 3% a year.

To put it all in human terms, the risk of not being in stocks long term is the risk that you'll have substantially fewer funds for yourself and your family. That means the funds for your children, for your retirement, for your quality of life. To the extent you *can* afford to set aside money in stocks over the long term, you *can't* afford not to.

Diversifying Within Equities

Once you accept that stocks are the best vehicle for creating wealth over time, the question is how to diversify *within* equities.

Some folks, particularly sky-high Wall Street strategists, tend to lump all equities together into the same basket. You'll hear news reports like "Lehman Brothers strategist changes his model portfolio to 60% stocks from 50%." But that's just big picture theory. Stocks can behave remarkably differently from one another. Indeed, there's enough variation in the stock market to capture some of the stabilizing benefits that make bonds attractive. That's why it's possible to be diversified among equities.

Two main ways to be diversified among equities are by risk type and by industry. Stocks carry different risk profiles, with some quite risky and some much more predictable. How much risk you take on in your portfolio is a personal decision, depending on a number of factors that we'll review later in this chapter. Here, we'll talk about how to categorize stocks according to their risk profiles.

Another complementary way to diversify is by industry. Stocks in a sector or subsector (e.g., PCs within "tech" or footwear within retail) generally move in the same direction. Without sacrificing reward, you can reduce your risk of any one subsector blowing up by selecting stocks from a number of different sectors. For most investors, whatever their personal risk profile, it's wise to diversify among industries. (In the next chapter, however, we make the case for diversifying within technology—a potentially rewarding strategy for a small subset of investors.)

You see thousands of stocks in those agate-type tables every morning in your local paper. How ever to begin to categorize them? There are nearly as many ways to sort stocks as there are stocks themselves.

For purposes of the diversification strategy we are about to recommend, stocks can basically be broken down into about three different types by risk level: high-octane stocks, core performers, and income engines. We recommend that most equity investors distribute their portfolio among these categories, emphasizing one category or basket of stocks over another, depending on how aggressive or cautious you want to be. The categories are not meant to be—cannot be—rigid. Unpredictable as they are, stocks do tend to defy categorization. "The same stock can go into different phases," notes Michael Lipper. Still, you've got to start somewhere. Note also that the categories apply both for individual stock investors and mutual fund investors. We talk mostly about individual stocks here. But you could as easily apply the same criteria to mutual funds if that's your preference. Look for funds that focus on the category of stocks you are seeking.

High-Octane Stocks

When I think of high-octane stocks, I think about all that is possible in the future. These are the companies that are working on the horizon where tomorrow is taking shape. They are the start-ups, usually without any earnings to demonstrate the profitability of their endeavor.

Yet, that very aura of the unknown is what attracts investors to these stocks—their innovative ideas and daunting future potential. The next great leap in telecommunications or computing, a real genetic breakthrough in the struggle to tame Alzheimer's disease, a better way to purify water or even deliver electricity, all may come from companies in this basket. Many of these companies don't have much more than an idea, a venture capitalist, and a business plan intriguing enough to get an investment bank to bring them public. That's how companies like Apple Computer (AAPL:Nasdaq) got started. Today they feature consistent earnings and mammoth market values. Yet, not long ago they were a huge question mark.

Let's talk about our name for this category of stocks: high octane. We call them high-octane stocks because when these stocks move— in either direction—it's rarely a slow plod. They tend to explode with great energy, to the upside or the down. That's because they don't really have an earnings track record on which investors can judge them. Instead, they're "valued" on investors' beliefs about their earnings *potential,* a highly debatable yardstick. Investors can disagree wildly about a business's future, and they can change their mind instantly with any shift in circumstances.

While these companies offer insatiable investors immense potential return, they carry equally immense risk. Without a steady earnings stream to back their valuation, these stocks can end up trampled as soon as their "concept" becomes stale.

Essentially, if you invest in high-octane stocks, you need to recognize that you risk losing your principal. At the same time, you stand the chance of being rewarded a return multiple times what the broader market will bear. There's just not much of an in-between.

How can you identify high-octane stocks? In general, they have four main characteristics:

1. *Play on the future*
   First, qualitatively, the business model of high-octane stocks is a bet on the future. Of course, all companies of any age need to be remaking themselves and adapting to market changes. But for these companies, they are first *making* themselves. It is not as though they are a fast-food chain trying a new kind of sandwich. The whole premise of their business is something they still need to prove.

2. *Smaller market capitalization*

Next, these are typically smaller-capitalization companies, that is, sizewise they are not behemoths. Given the rapid growth of the overall stock market, market capitalizations are a moving target. Don't be too rigid about categorizing them. But as a general guideline, small- and middle-cap companies can be up to $8.7 billion in market cap, according to Lipper, Inc., in August 2000.

3. *No earnings*

Earnings are a kind of objective metric of the qualitative future concept we discussed in point 1. When a company has earnings, that indicates that its business idea actually makes money—that revenues exceed the costs. It's a key turning point for any company, private or public. Companies like AOL (AOL:NYSE) and Yahoo! (YHOO:Nasdaq) weren't admitted into the S&P 500 until after they first started to report earnings. Until a company has a few quarters of earnings under its belt, its business model is still very much unproven.

4. *Small but often rapidly accelerating revenues that from quarter to quarter may be erratic*

Most public companies will have at least some revenues. But for high-octane stocks, the revenues are not very predictable. That's because business strategies are changing and customer relationships are just getting established. More stable revenue streams tend to be a precursor to earnings.

Remember that the best home-run hitters often carry the highest strikeout percentage. Many high-octane companies are still in the minor leagues. They are looking to make the jump to the majors, but all carry a lot of their own baggage. Many will fail, and a select few will knock the cover off the ball. Hence, stock selection is important. And the ability to balance patience with prudence—knowing when to hold and when to fold—is key to making money with these companies. (More on that in our "When to Sell" discussion in Chapter 10.)

Examples of High-Octane Stocks		
Company/Ticker	Revenue Growth (Year to Year)*	Market Capitalization in $ millions
Virgin Express Holdings (VIRGY:Nasdaq)	1,585.10%	35
SafeScience (SAFS:Nasdaq)	1,300.00%	49
KeraVision (KERA:Nasdaq)	1,212.50%	74
Pennaco Energy (PN:AMEX)	4,500.00%	320
NextCard, Inc. (NXCD:Nasdaq)	2,116.70%	570
Wit Soundview Group (WITC:Nasdaq)	2,457.90%	771
Teligent (TGNT:Nasdaq)	3,030.00%	980
priceline.com (PCLN:Nasdaq)	1,270.50%	4,416
Akamai Technologies (AKAM:Nasdaq)	3,900.00%	6,669
Juniper Networks (JNPR:Nasdaq)	2,600.00%	57,809

*Annual revenue growth comparison based on most recent quarter
Data as of September 12, 2000
Source: MSN MoneyCentral

Core Performers

These are the workhorses of the typical portfolio. The core performers have established businesses with products and services that make money. They are companies on the move with pipelines of new ideas, and the cash, expertise, and management stability to execute.

Core performers generally report consistent earnings and revenues—at least a year's worth, though the longer the track record, the better. Part of the benefit of consistency is that it helps put to rest any questions about the company's viability. But it's also a matter of what Wall Street calls "modeling." If a company has steady earnings, a stock analyst—professional or at-home—can more easily project earnings from the company for the next couple of years. And that makes the company more susceptible to valuation.

Because these companies are modelable, there's less disagreement in the market over their prospects. That generally makes moves in the stock somewhat less extreme and more in line with market fluctuations. And while you can always lose money in any stock, the chance of a real wipeout of principal is less if there are earnings backing a stock's price. (Of course, the more earnings, the less chance of wipeout, which is why stocks with high price-to-earnings ratios are generally more risky.)

As for market capitalization, these companies tend to be the bigger players in the field, with market caps above $8.7 billion.

Can core performers produce outsized returns? Certainly. Cisco Systems (CSCO:Nasdaq) is the archetype here. In 2000, with a market cap of $450 billion—making it one of the biggest stocks—Cisco was still trouncing the S&P 500, up 28% through August compared to about 3% for the S&P. Still, generally, the *size* of outsized moves is somewhat less with core performers than the extremes you'll see with high-octane stocks. The same goes for the downside.

At one point, most core performers were high octane. And even in their more mature state, some can grow at a rapid pace. Yet, they have generally become more predictable and more widely known than the upstarts. These are companies like IBM (IBM:NYSE) and Dell (DELL:Nasdaq) in the technology world and players like Pfizer (PFE: NYSE) and Merck (MRK:NYSE) in the pharmaceutical world.

Here are the main characteristics of core performers:

1. *Proven Business Model*
   These are stocks of companies where the business model is established. That doesn't mean the plan won't get tripped up or sidetracked. But the company has shown that it has more than an unproven concept. Whether it's selling computers, insurance, or oil, the company has an established management team in place that can execute its business model.

2. *Larger Market Capitalization*
   Again, you can't be too rigid about market capitalization. But in general, these companies tend to be the larger cap players, over $8.7 billion, as measured by Lipper, Inc.

3. *Steady Earnings*
   If you've got a proven business concept, it should be generating steady earnings. A year's worth is the minimum you'd like to see, and more is better.

4. *Steady Revenue Growth*
   When revenue growth is relatively stable and in line with earnings growth, that suggests costs are relatively stable as well. All good signs.

Examples of Core Performers		
Company	Market Capitalization in $ billions	5-Year Average Annual Earnings Growth
General Electric (GE:NYSE)	591	14.31%
Intel Corp. (INTC:Nasdaq)	434	19.61%
Microsoft (MSFT:Nasdaq)	362	43.61%
Citigroup (C:NYSE)	340	20.08%
ExxonMobil Corp. (XOM:NYSE)	296	0.23%
Pfizer (PFE:NYSE)	254	18.54%
Wal-Mart (WMT:NYSE)	243	17.46%
SBC Communications (SBC:NYSE)	155	4.59%
Toyota Motors (TM:NYSE)	154	22.32%
Home Depot (HD:NYSE)	126	27.05%

Data as of September 12, 2000
Source: MSN MoneyCentral

Income Engines

The key point to remember when diversifying among stocks is just how many different risk profiles you can find in the equity universe. So far we've talked about very risky stocks, the high-octane brood, and somewhat more stable stocks, the core performers. Neither of these types of stocks is really *defensive*—providing some degree of cushion or counterbalance to market swings.

That's where the income engines come in. The companies in this basket run solid if mundane businesses, and they distribute a significant portion of their profits to shareholders in the form of dividends. The distribution of profits often makes these companies suitable holdings for investors looking for a consistent income stream from their equity investments. Retired investors in particular are strong candidates for these stocks.

At the same time, stocks that pay dividends typically are attractive for more risk-averse investors in general, as dividends serve to stabilize returns and lower the volatility in topsy-turvy markets. Finally, stocks that pay dividends—perceived as safer—tend to attract investors and rise in price in a market downturn, thereby providing a counterbalance for those investors who've held them all along.

Income engines are akin to bonds in that they offer income. But they're better because they also offer the upside potential that you can find only with equities. That's why we we like them. These stocks are the special team—the kicker—of your portfolio. As with any stock, their value can go down. Still, you call on them when you are looking to play conservative and score the almost-certain field goal, the quarterly cash dividend the company pays to you.

This category of stocks is often identified with a certain sector of stocks. The most popular dividend stocks are utilities and real estate companies, especially Real Estate Investment Trusts, or REITs. REITs are companies that invest in a variety of real estate properties.

Income engines often are not on the radar screen for most aggressive investors, but for those who are investing entirely in equities, they probably should be, at least in a portion of one's portfolio. (We talk about this issue in the following pages.)

The number of stocks that pay dividends has dwindled over the past decade, as has the average dividend. As of August 2000, the dividend yield on the S&P 500 was a mere 1.13%, down from about 3.5% 10 years earlier.

What's changed? First, the raging bull market has sent stock prices higher while dividends remained relatively steady. That has the effect of reducing "yield"—the dividend divided by the stock price. The numerator stays steady while the denominator increases. Second, on a more fundamental front, companies have made a conscious decision to reinvest profits in new products, technology advances, and other research and development rather than giving profits back to investors in the form of dividends.

That doesn't mean wanna-be dividend investors should abandon the equities markets. It simply means you have to be more selective in developing your dividend strategy, something we offer assistance with in the accompanying box.

> ### Finding Dividend-Producing Companies
>
> - Look for companies that have a history of paying dividends and increasing them over time. A number of stock-screening tools—try MSN's MoneyCentral (http://moneycentral.msn .com/investor/finder/customstocks.asp), for example—let you screen for companies with high-dividend growth rates. Most allow you to screen based on five-year dividend growth rates.
>
> - Look for companies with manageable payout ratios. The payout ratio is the dividend rate divided by earnings per share (or, in some cases, free cash flow). Be wary of companies that pay out more than 80% of their earnings in dividends. Anything above that may signal difficulty in sustaining current dividends and doesn't bode well for future dividend hikes. (REITs are the exception, as they are required by law to pay out at least 90% of their earnings to avoid corporate taxes. Different screeners handle REITs differently.) Again, most screening tools allow you to look at the current year and five-year average.
>
> - Don't choose a company just because it has the highest dividend yields. There's typically a reason a company yields 20%+, and it's usually not good. When a company's earnings decline to the point they can't cover their dividend, guess what— they'll have to slash it. In anticipation of that, the stock price often slides, pushing the yield higher. Typically, bad news that sends a stock sliding—bad earnings, lost customers—comes before word of a dividend cut. If you see a company with a yield above 10%, keep looking: 5 to 6% is usually reasonable.

Here are the main characteristics of income engines:

1. *Solid, if not stodgy, business model*
   Sure, you can discover some innovative companies among, say, electric utilities. But for the most part, you won't find dividends in the economy's hottest sectors, like high tech or biotech. Dividend-producing companies are more tried and true, which is exactly why you want them.

2. *Mid-level market cap*
   Income engines tend to be mid-cap companies, between $2.3 billion and $8.7 billion, though Real Estate Investment Trusts can often be smaller.

3. *Steady earnings and revenues*
   These companies are mature, with visible earnings and revenues, although you won't tend to see dynamic revenue or earnings growth.

4. *They provide a dividend*
   Ideally, this dividend is above the average yield of the S&P 500, at least in the 5-to-6% range.

Examples of Income Engines			
Company	Market Capitalization in $ billions	Current Yield	5-Year Average Yield
Louisiana Pacific (LPX:NYSE)	1.1	5.5%	3.0%
Cinergy (CIN:NYSE)	5.2	5.5%	5.7%
Dana Corp. (DCN:NYSE)	3.7	5.0%	3.0%
KeyCorp (KEY:NYSE)	10.4	4.6%	3.4%
Standard Register Co. (SR:NYSE)	0.4	7.1%	3.3%
Southern Company (SO:NYSE)	21.5	4.1%	5.2%
American Electric Power (AEP:NYSE)	7.6	6.1%	5.8%
First Industrial Realty Prop. Trust (FR:NYSE)	1.2	7.8%	7.4%
Equity Residential Prop. Trust (EQR:NYSE)	6.5	6.5%	6.5%
Equity Office Properties Trust (EOP:NYSE)	9.3	5.8%	NA

Data as of September 12, 2000
Source: MSN MoneyCentral

The equity universe is actually incredibly diverse, enabling you to do just that, diversify. How you actually diversify among high-octane stocks, core performers, and income engines, however, is a personal decision depending on your risk profile. That's what we talk about next.

Dividing Your Assets

By dividing stocks into these categories, you can start to think about how to invest your assets across the spectrum of high-octane stocks, core performers, and income engines. Diversifying your portfolio involves a personal assessment of your financial goals and responsibilities, your risk tolerance, and your investing experience and energy. You've likely seen theories espousing all sorts of strategies for asset allocation. Every financial Web site seems to boast the ideal asset allocator—that interactive formula that will spit out the perfect portfolio for you.

And, no doubt, under a controlled set of circumstances, every theory works . . . in theory. Reality, however, is quite different. Can an asset allocation worksheet take into account that money you think you might need to pay for unexpected medical bills? Will it take into account the stock options you just got at your new job? Or a recent divorce? Or money you inherited from a relative? Or the downsizing that has temporarily cost you your income?

Life is much more complicated than rote portfolio planning. That's why we suggest a more flexible approach that better reflects the fluidity of human circumstance. We urge you to consider the following questions about yourself. At the end, we will not give you a simple worksheet that will dictate how to distribute your portfolio among our three different baskets. We instead give you some general guidance through examples, which should be more in keeping with real-world circumstances.

Here are some of the factors to consider:

Time Horizon and Age: As we discussed earlier, time is the great equalizer of investment risk. And, as you'll recall, we're not talking about needing 20 years. So while some financial advisers might tell you to scale back your aggressive equity investing at, say, 50, we're not quite so conservative. What's really more important than actual age is your retirement plans—the reduced income you may enjoy if you retire or scale back your work. If your career is thriving at 60 and retirement is still a good 10-plus years off, you can maintain a nice combination of high-octane stocks with core performers and a touch of income engines. But if you're 55 and looking at retirement within three years, then you need to be scaling back on the high octane and beefing up those dividend stocks.

Responsibilities: This is related to time horizon, but it's so important that you need to think about it separately. You could be 28 and well employed, but if you're taking on a big mortgage, now might not be the time for a high-octane heavy portfolio. Same goes for supporting dependents, paying for school, or if you've undertaken a risky career move. Now, if you've got some of these concerns, we're not going to insist that you create a budget—people often don't get very far doing or sticking to that exercise. But if you may need more capital handy in the shorter term than your cash cushion provides, focus your investments accordingly. You don't want to be in the position of holding a lot of Amazon.com (AMZN:Nasdaq) or Red Hat (RHAT:Nasdaq) or Ariba (ARBA:Nasdaq) and suddenly find you have to sell immediately for cash purposes at the very time the market is down 50% from its highs.

Experience: If you're just getting started with stocks, be more conservative, at least at first. There are two reasons. The first is psychological. The market will inevitably hit you with some surprises. In your first foray into stocks, before you've gotten a feel for tolerating the market's vagaries, you might not be able to stomach watching your stocks take a steep dive. With your system shocked, reason may succumb to fear in decision making. Just imagine if you'd bought Qualcomm (QCOM:Nasdaq) in early 2000 at 200, only to see it plunge to 60 that summer. Second, if you're just starting to study companies, you might have an easier time evaluating firms with steady earnings and a proven strategy.

Income and Available Funds: Your income is an issue for obvious reasons—you need to have enough spare money after you pay expenses to invest. You also want enough of an income cushion that you don't have to sell your investments to meet unanticipated expenses.

But there's a more subtle reason you need to consider available funds: If you are going to buy individual stocks, you need a critical mass to build your own portfolio.

Let's say you have $1,000 you are willing to invest in the market. You do your research and come up with five stocks, all with a price of $20, that you want to buy. You're in a bind. You could buy 10 shares of each, but the transactions costs (commissions and exchange fees) would eat you alive. For 10 shares of five stocks, commissions alone would be about $50 at $10 a trade, or 5% of your principal. Or you could choose "the best" stock and buy 50 shares. Then, however, you are gambling your whole pot on the success of one company. That's dangerous for the reasons we have already discussed—it's better to spread your risk among a number of companies than to bet the house on one.

If you're cash scrimped, we suggest you invest in mutual funds until you save enough to buy a meaningful position in a group of at least, say, 10 stocks. What's meaningful? The commission you pay to buy the stock should be no more than 2% of the value of the position. With the plethora of discount brokers, that makes individual stock investing affordable for those with as little as $10,000 or $20,000.

To start to bring together all of these different factors and apply them to our baskets of stocks, we've come up with three examples. Chances are you won't match any of these profiles precisely. But if you can get a sense of how you compare, you can start to build your portfolio accordingly.

Young, single, and new to the game

Average basket ranges:
high octane: 15–40%
core performers: 45–75%
income engines: 5–15%

- Our 30-something single investor is a professional earning more than $75,000 in the early years of wealth building, but he doesn't have much experience with stocks. He's looking for ways to accumulate wealth over long periods of time and, as a relatively new investor, is slightly to the conservative side of the risk spectrum.
- The need for current income is minimal, since his salary is ample for his needs. While a small portion of the equity portfolio may be invested in income-producing securities that provide some protection on the downside, the dividends are typically reinvested to increase the value of the portfolio.
- High-octane stocks occupy a decent portion of the equity portfolio, probably 15 to 30%. Stock selection is key to minimizing the risk of that portion of the portfolio. He should lean toward the larger end of the percentage range only after he becomes more confident in investing.

**Professionally established,
facing big costs of college and mortgage**

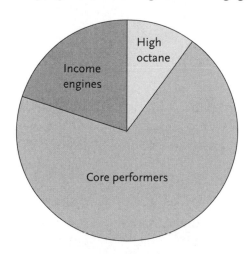

Average basket ranges:
high-octane 10–30%
core performers 50–80%
income engines, 10–25%

- Our middle-aged investor is a 50-year-old who has reached the prime of her career. She is making more than $125,000, but it's time to send her oldest child to college, which will take a bite out of her salary. And there's another college attendee following close behind. Plus, the mortgage payment.
- The bulk of the equity portfolio remains in core performers. A portion of the portfolio is shifted from high-octane stocks to income engines, again with most of the dividends being reinvested.
- The primary objective remains long-term growth, but there's a little less room for downside, on a number of fronts.

Retiree, Loving Life, and Investing

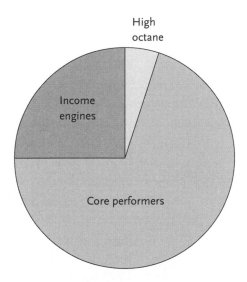

Average basket ranges:
high octane: 5–20%
core performers: 40–80%
income engines: 15–30%

- The sun-and-fun investor is 70-something, firmly planted in retirement. Work and family obligations are largely complete. And this investor has plenty of experience with stock investing.
- With life expectancy continuing to increase, growth remains important, but capital preservation and current income also become primary portfolio cornerstones. All three should be in balance, with an understanding that a combination of current income and portfolio growth serve to fund your retirement living. A small portion of the portfolio might remain in high-octane stocks.

Sector Diversification

Once you have a sense of your investment profile, you'll have a pretty good idea of what baskets of stocks you'll be considering as you build your portfolio. Now you need to select the stocks. Later in the book we discuss how to pick the individual stocks for your portfolio. But before we get to finding and analyzing stock ideas, we need to talk about industry sectors and their role in diversifying your portfolio.

There are hundreds of sectors in the stock market, from auto parts and equipment to publishing, restaurants, and air freight. The universe of publicly traded companies is much broader than the media coverage of semiconductor, telecom, and other hot stocks would suggest. Unless you can withstand—both financially and psychologically—the heftiest risk levels (and some people can—a topic we explore more in the next chapter), you don't want to concentrate exclusively in one sector.

If you load up your portfolio with computer stocks only or drug stocks exclusively, or just heavy equipment stocks, you are taking a risk on the viability of that sector that you don't need to take. While there are standouts on the upside and down in any industry, the stocks in a sector, or especially a subsector (e.g., PCs within "tech" or footwear within retail), generally move in the same direction. Hence, if there is bad news about IBM, it is likely that fellow computer manufacturers Dell, Compaq (CPQ:NYSE), and Gateway (GTW:NYSE) will move lower "in sympathy." Regardless of how strong a sector's revenue growth and earnings may be, there's no need to expose yourself to that kind of concentrated risk—short term or long term. We recommend that you pick the best company or two in your favorite sectors and leave the rest of the stocks in that sector alone. Give yourself some protection by diversifying among different business types.

If you want a good benchmark to check yourself against in terms of diversification, look to the composition of the Standard & Poor's 1500, a combination of the S&P 500, the S&P MidCap 400, and the S&P SmallCap 600. You can check out the sector composition at the Standard & Poor's Web site, www.spglobal.com/sector-scorecard.html. Not only do you get the contribution of each sector to the index, you also get the performance of each sector over various periods of time. That will give you an idea of the "hot" and "cold" sectors.

The index provides a good point of comparison to see how diversified you are compared with the broader market.

Here's how the S&P 1500 index looked at the close of August 4, 2000:

Basic Materials	1.9%
Capital Goods	7.9%
Communications Services	6.5%
Consumer Cyclicals	7.2%
Consumer Staples	10.2%
Energy	5.3%
Financial	14.7%
Health Care	11.2%
Technology	31.8%
Transportation	0.6%
Utilities	2.7%

Source: Standard & Poor's

How Many Stocks Should You Own?

The issue of the number of stocks to own is a thorny one for investors. After all, as we speak of diversification, your intuition probably suggests, "The more the merrier." But diversification does not simply mean owning more stocks. It means owning stocks across the industrial spectrum that work in concert to produce a desired result.

Again, you probably don't want to sink your entire portfolio into one or two stocks. At the same time, as an investor with other responsibilities like a job or a family, your ability to follow more than a dozen or so stocks is likely limited.

The good news: A dozen is probably enough. According to data assembled by Ibbotson, the reduction in stock selection risk beyond the first dozen stocks is minimal.

Stock Diversification

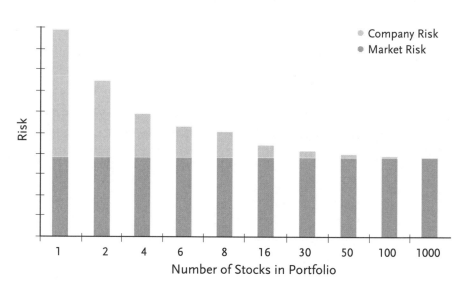

That figure may seem counter to your intuition. However, it is supported not only by data but by some great investors. Warren Buffett is a proponent of "focus investing," owning a handful of great companies that you understand. As he says:

> If you are a know-something investor, able to understand business economics and to find five to ten sensibly priced companies that possess important long-term competitive advantages, conventional diversification makes no sense for you.

By conventional diversification, Buffett is referring to broad-based portfolios of hundreds of stocks. A longtime Buffett scholar, Robert Hagstrom, portfolio manager of the Legg Mason Focus Trust fund, writes in *The Warren Buffett Portfolio*: "Choose a few stocks that are likely to produce above-average returns over the long haul, concentrate the bulk of your investments in those stocks, and have the fortitude to hold steady during any short-term market gyrations." Hagstrom writes that for the individual investor "a few" means "no more than fifteen" stocks. Still not convinced? Maybe Hagstrom's description of the impact of overdiversification will sway you:

> We have all heard this mantra of diversification for so long, we have become intellectually numb to its inevitable consequences: mediocre results. Although it is true that active and index funds offer diversification, in general neither strategy will offer exceptional returns. These are questions intelligent investors must ask themselves: Am I satisfied with average returns? Can I do better?

While there are no guarantees, if you follow the strategies given throughout this book, embrace continuous learning about the market, and remain disciplined, a portfolio of a dozen or so stocks should provide you with both the protection of diversification and the focus to build wealth in the market.

Summing Up

In thinking about diversification and asset allocation, take into account your investment time horizon, age, responsibilities, experience, income, and available funds. Consider how much risk you feel comfortable accepting in your portfolio, given your long-range goals.

You can tailor your long-term portfolio to your goals by diversifying among industry sectors and by spreading your assets among a mixture of high-octane stocks, core performers, and income engines.

If you are selecting individual stocks rather than using mutual funds, we recommend that you limit your portfolio to around 12 stocks.

Now that you have a better picture of the ways you can diversify your portfolio, you're ready to start finding some good stock ideas. That's the subject of Chapter 5. But first we'll focus on a sector that's becoming increasingly important to all investors: technology.

4

So, You Want to Be in Technology?

If you've wondered about the wisdom of investing in technology stocks—let's say the riskiest tech investment you've made so far was in AT&T (T:NYSE)—it may be worth considering the costs of not investing in technology stocks. In this chapter, I lay out the case for committing a hefty portion of your portfolio to technology stocks, for those who want to supercharge their portfolio and can tolerate the risk.

Now, this might sound a little crazy to you. In August 2000 the average P/E ratio for technology stocks was a whopping 49.4 compared with 37.1 for the S&P 500, according to Morningstar. The average beta, a measure of volatility, for technology stocks was 1.28 versus a beta of 1 for the S&P 500 (meaning for a 10% move in the broader market, you would see a 13% move in tech stocks). The risk in tech stocks is significantly higher (as 2000 showed). And you know how many hyped technologies never fulfill their promise.

Despite this, there are tremendous rewards to technology investing. If, like many investors, you've played it safe these last several years and sat on the high-tech sidelines, you've missed the chance to get in on some of the biggest run-ups in stocks imaginable. I'm not talking about one-year wonders, but stocks that have steadily built revenues, profits, and share prices year after year.

From early 1992, when America Online (AOL:NYSE) first became a publicly traded company, to mid-2000, the S&P 500 index grew about 270%—that is, it ended about 3½ times higher than it started. AOL? It grew about 51,000%.

No, that's not a misprint—51,000%. Now look at the growth rates of some other tech stocks:

Ten-Year Performance of Selected Tech Leaders, May 1990–May 2000	
Stock	Percentage Gain
Microsoft (MSFT:Nasdaq)	3,017
Dell (DELL:Nasdaq)	37,000
Cisco Systems (CSCO:Nasdaq)	71,150
Intel (INTC:Nasdaq)	4,013
Oracle (ORCL:Nasdaq)	7,310
Sun Microsystems (SUNW:Nasdaq)	3,933
EMC (EMC:NYSE)	45,456
S&P 500	299

Source: Yahoo! Finance
Data Source: Commodity Systems, Inc. (CSI), www.csidata.com

Those are pretty mind-boggling numbers, something to be reckoned with, and certainly nothing for an investor to dismiss. And keep this in mind when you're thinking about beefing up on tech: Tech stocks already make up about a third of the S&P 500, as measured by their size, or market capitalization. Even more telling, at mid-year 2000 the average diversified growth mutual fund had over 40% of its assets in technology, according to Morningstar. So increasing the tech stocks in your own portfolio to 50% or more isn't as big a leap as it first might seem.

Finally, the number and types of public technology companies are proliferating at a rapid-fire pace. Once there were just Internet stocks. Now that sector has been broken up into content, e-tailing, business-to-business, broadband, infrastructure, and umpteen other types of

Net firms. This kind of fission has affected many sectors of technology, creating a wide range of choice from which an investor can build an increasingly diversified portfolio.

In this chapter, I've tapped George Mannes, a senior writer at *TheStreet.com* and veteran of the technology beat, to help me make a case for the virtues of the tech sector, while laying out its many downsides. In the next several pages, I'll give you the background and insight you need to become a more informed and better tech investor, and to weigh just how much tech you want in your portfolio.

Technology investing is not for everyone. You need to be able to withstand tremendous volatility. Stocks can swing wildly from month to month, week to week—even minute to minute. And to be good at tech investing, you need to know something about technology even if your only decision is which technology mutual fund to purchase. Not many people can boast genuine familiarity with the subject. For your average investor, technology is not as accessible as, say, restaurant or retail stocks. Even above-average investors—professional managers like Warren Buffett—have steered clear of tech stocks simply because, as they have acknowledged, they don't understand them.

At *TheStreet.com* we see all too many investors jump into the latest hot tech trend—"push," "broadband," "B2B," Internet wireless—without really knowing what they're getting into. Otherwise reasonable and prudent investors become so taken with the incredible rise of a few headline-drawing stocks that they toss money at names they know nothing about in the hope of achieving similar gains.

That kind of bandwagon investing is not what *TheStreet.com* is about. In this chapter, I'll discuss how to increase your odds of making wise investing decisions in a sector where such choices are generously rewarded. If you have the kind of long time horizon and psychological constitution that can withstand the increased risk, you may well decide technology investing is right for you. Later in this chapter, I introduce you to some mutual fund managers expert in the field for advice on building your own tech portfolio.

The Explosion of Technology

As anyone who has read about Bill Gates's mansion can tell you, tech stocks can make you very wealthy.

That doesn't mean they will. There's no guarantee of success in the stock market. If you invested in Iomega (IOM:NYSE), the maker of removable computer disks, in May 1996, you may have thought the stock was only beginning its upward run. But shares bought then have lost more than 51% of their value. Shares in Iridium World Communications, the publicly traded stock of a firm developing what looked like a revolutionary satellite phone-based system designed to work anywhere on the planet, traded as high as 49. But after Iridium declared bankruptcy in August 1999, those shares were worth closer to 3, if they were worth anything at all. It turns out nifty phones used mainly by sailors is not a big business opportunity.

But despite individual failures, technology companies and technology stocks have done phenomenally well as a group over the past several years. For example, in 1999, each of the top-ten performing stocks in the S&P 500 was a tech stock.

And that's not a huge surprise. Technology is at the heart of the growing global economy. Companies spend furiously on technology in order to improve productivity and profitability. Between 1995 and 1998, according to the United States Department of Commerce, producers of communications hardware, software, and services accounted for only 8% of the United States gross domestic product. But they accounted for nearly 35% of the nation's real economic growth. By 2006, the department estimates, almost half of the United States workforce will be employed by industries that are either major producers or intensive users of information technology products and services.

Whether you look at big-picture statistics or tiny anecdotes, it's clear something big has been—and is—happening here. Huge amounts of wealth have been created thanks to the Internet, computers, and other technology. It's not driven by a fad; it's driven by the simple truth that technology is changing the face of nearly every other industry in the United States and in the world.

To get an idea of the growth of the tech market, consider that back in 1983, personal computers were already pretty hot stuff. So hot, in fact, that the January 3 issue of *Time* magazine abandoned its usual practice of naming a Man of the Year and selected the computer as its Machine of the Year. But a look at the statistics indicates how much tech spending has changed *since* then. In 1982, *Time* reported, it was estimated that companies sold 2.8 million computers for a total of $4.9 billion. In 1999, according to a preliminary estimate from International Data Corp., manufacturers shipped 45.2 million PCs in the

United States. In 1983 *Time* noted that word processors had displaced about 10% of the typewriters in the 500 largest industrial corporations. Nowadays, PCs, printers, and office networks have left typewriters nearly extinct.

And not all the action has been in PCs, either. The massive growth in technology and the revolutionary improvements have made PCs part of what some wags call "old tech"—the pre-Internet technology of hardware and heavy-duty software unconnected to computer networks. New Tech encompasses everything from Internet-based software to wireless gear to the networking companies that provide the backbone to the Internet. Over the course of a single decade, the Internet has gone from a curiosity to a medium with 65 million users in the United States, according to IDC. In 1980 the cellular telephone industry didn't exist; by 1999, Americans were spending $37.2 billion a year on wireless telephone service. Business spending on software in the United States zoomed from $25 billion annually in 1987 to about $150 billion a year in 2000, according to the Conference Board, a nonprofit research group. They report that information technology business, amounting to between $500 billion and $600 billion a year, accounts for more than 40% of all business investment in plant and equipment.

Technology affects not only what people spend money on but how they spend it. In March 1997 Dell (DELL:Nasdaq) announced that the Web store it had launched the summer before was selling $1 million in computer gear per day. Less than three years later, the company said it was racking up Internet sales of $40 million per day, nearly half of the company's revenues.

Tech has obviously been onto something big. Huge amounts of wealth have been built on the computer and other innovations; companies have gone from zero to billions of sales in record time. It is not hyperbolic to suggest we're in the middle of a societywide change as important and transforming as the Industrial Revolution.

The question is, Does tech have the staying power to hold the leading edge among investment sectors? If it does, what's the best way to approach it as an individual investor?

Will Tech Remain a Stock Market Leader?

Not too long ago, tech stocks were strictly the province of aggressive investors. Tech was a risky niche sector bet, fraught with complicated companies subject to unpredictable successes and cycles. Companies would emerge, flourish, and disappear with alarming speed. But as the technology industry has grown, tech has begun to establish itself as a consistent and strong leader of the stock market. The question is, Is tech a sector with staying power?

By all accounts, it is.

It's not the size of the tech industry. Again, information-technology-producing industries accounted for only about 8% of the economy in 1999. Manufacturing (minus electronic and electric equipment manufacturing) amounted to about 15% of the GDP in 1997, according to the Department of Commerce; finance, insurance, and real estate added up to 18.8%, and government, while sinking, was at 12.6%.

What's more important is technology's effect on many other industries. Think about how many times you've read about automation displacing an employee—a machine doing the job of a person or animal. In shipping, cranes unloading truck-sized containers replaced armies of longshoremen. In law offices, attorneys with computers replace secretaries typing legal briefs. At banks, ATMs have replaced most tellers.

But that omnipresence is not enough to make technology unique. After all, the automotive industry is integral to many other industries. Employees need cars to go from home to work and from their office to a client's office for a sales call. Health care, too, affects other industries. A large corporation has to cover part of the health costs of its employees.

And while technology is certainly a growth industry, it's not the only growth industry—brokerages and insurance carriers grew between 1992 and 1997 too.

What makes technology unique—for the past two decades and for the foreseeable future—is that its growth and change profoundly affect the way other industries operate. New technology can, and does, radically alter the rest of the economy in a way that no other industry could. It's that power that makes technology stocks so compelling.

Let's go back and look at the automotive sector. Perhaps the features of cars are changing, and perhaps the way cars are being manufactured is changing too. But these changes aren't big enough to change the way other industries operate. This year's models may have air bags, and next year's might include a redesigned Ford Taurus, but those are incremental changes.

Meanwhile, every day, technology is making big changes in how business is conducted. Returning to that 1983 *Time* article about the year of the computer, let's consider one of the many examples that were trotted out about how computers were beginning to change people's jobs. A group vice president at an insurance company used an Apple computer over the weekend in his home to—get ready for this—look over a bunch of numbers related to his company's takeover of another insurance company. He could consider different options for structuring the deal, and there were no leaks of information.

Okay. An obscure executive uses a computer at his home to crunch some numbers. This is the lead story in the nation's premier weekly newsmagazine? Obviously, we've come a long way since then. But changes like these are constantly revolutionizing the way we live our work and home lives. Computing power, networks of voice, video, and data—they're everywhere.

At its most basic level, what technology does is replace labor with capital. When we talk about innovative technology, we're talking about something that replaces people with an object. It may replace a person performing a task, like a fax machine that makes it unnecessary to send a bicycle messenger to transport a document from one side of town to another, or a FedEx package to be sent to another city or state. It may cut down on the time it takes to perform a specific task; a person seated at a computer, searching through a database, for example, can find information in a fraction of the time it takes that person to go to the library to find the same article.

Or, technology can substitute for a workforce that would be too expensive for a person or a business to obtain. Placing a computer-generated crowd in the background of a scene in a feature film, for example, is far less expensive than hiring extras.

Wall Street recognizes these efficiencies that technology creates and usually rewards both companies that create technology and those that use it. Let's say a retailer implements a new inventory-management system—one that lets company executives and suppliers see, in real time, how different products are selling in stores around the country. That enables the company to save money—by not shipping additional widgets to stores where they're not in demand—and make more money by quickly responding to larger-than-expected demand in other stores.

When investors reward innovators in different industries who have adopted new technology to their benefit, competing businesses are encouraged to find new or better alternatives. That leads to more demand for technology, which leads to greater appreciation on Wall Street for the companies who create it.

One last thing that makes technology attractive: It moves in one direction in relation to labor—up. Machines always replace people. People usually don't replace machines, unless there's been a disastrously unsuccessful application of technology. Think of all the stories you've read about machines that have displaced people in the workplace. Have you ever read a story about people who have replaced long-entrenched machinery?

One risk to technology investing is recession and a bad economy. In hard times, companies may be reluctant to invest in new equipment. They may feel able to meet demand with what's at hand. But over time the push to progress eventually reemerges.

What Is a Technology Company?

For some companies, the label is obvious. These are the companies whose core function is to create hardware or software, the basic building blocks of computing. But for other companies, the question above is not as straightforward as it sounds. In its broadest meaning, technology is a machine that replaces human labor.

A moment's reflection will tell you that that's not how tech is sized up in the investing world. On lawns across America, Toro mowers have replaced scythes and mechanical push mowers. But you wouldn't call Toro (TTC:NYSE) a tech stock. Electric light is technology, a human invention. But lamp maker Juno Lighting (JUNO:Nasdaq) isn't a tech stock either. Both Toro and Juno Lighting are manufacturers.

So what's the difference between tech companies and manufacturers? Primarily, the stage of their development, and the stage at which their underlying technology has been accepted by the marketplace and human society. A tech stock isn't just about technology, it's about the introduction of *new* technology. Back when people rode horses to get themselves from one end of town to another, an auto company was a tech stock. Now that cars are ubiquitous, it's a manufacturer.

What changes? When a technology is wildly successful and is embraced by society, the companies that make it are no longer tech stocks. A company that makes TV sets isn't a tech stock. A company trying to build an affordable flat-panel, hang-on-the-wall TV set for the home market is—until the day, somewhere off in the future, when all households have these screens in their homes.

In other words, a tech stock is a company caught at a moment in time. Once its underlying technology becomes widespread, it's a manufacturer. The more accepted a technology is, the less it is a tech stock.

What's So Special About Tech Stocks?

So why is this distinction important? For starters, it helps you understand risk. All businesses face risk. They have to compete for market share; they must maintain an acceptable level of quality in the goods and services they provide; they have to ensure that what they sell remains relevant to their customers.

But for tech companies, there's another level of risk. Because tech companies are making new things or making them in a new way, they may not work. Ideas that look good in the lab may fail in the home or office. Or they may not work well enough for buyers to find them a compelling value. For example, 3-D television is something that for years has looked great in a demo but has turned out to be nothing special in real life.

Even when a new type of technology works, the marketplace may just not care. Digital tape recorders that debuted in the early 1990s certainly worked. But the Digital Compact Cassette–format tape recorder failed to become the next-generation audiocassette. And the Digital Audio Tape format failed in the consumer market too, though it has been accepted among professionals. Remember Betamax?

Furthermore, not every version of every successful technology gains market acceptance. Before the Palm's (PALM:Nasdaq) Palm Pilot took off, handheld computers based on Apple's (AAPL:Nasdaq) Newton operating system fizzled.

There's additional risk in any business plan based on new technology because new tech implies change, and things change slowly, if at all. Sometimes people don't want new technology; sometimes it's marketed poorly; and sometimes the people who invent or commercialize it guess wrong about what people will use it for.

Dependence on innovation creates another burden for tech companies: more innovation. Each new technology, each new improvement on a way of doing things, implies a still newer technology that could overtake it if the old tech stands still. Intel (INTC:Nasdaq) is an example of a company that understands this concept well. Rather than wait for other companies to try to improve on each new processing chip it makes, it has fought to make that chip obsolete on its own.

What's Not a Tech Stock?

Sometimes the term "tech stock" is used too liberally. If you think it through, it's the makers of new technology, not the firms that use technology, that properly qualify as tech stocks. But in the market's mind, at least occasionally, the distinction is blurred. The first customers of a new technology may enjoy the tech label too.

Think about the label "Internet stock," for example, and how it applies to one company, Amazon.com (AMZN:Nasdaq). It would be hard not to think of Amazon.com as an Internet stock. It's the most famous Internet retailer. And it's the biggest.

Yet by all accounts, we shouldn't be thinking of it as an Internet stock or, by extension, a technology stock. It's a retailing company— one that just happens to use the Internet. Domino's sells much of its pizza to people who call its stores up on the phone, but that doesn't make Domino's a telephone stock. FedEx (FDX:NYSE) uses a lot of trucks, but we don't call it a truck stock.

So while portal site Yahoo! (YHOO:Nasdaq) obviously is an Internet company, it really isn't. It's a media company. Amazon.com is a retailer, and eBay (EBAY:Nasdaq) is an auctioneer.

The lesson here is to pick your tech stocks carefully. When you invest in a company, ask yourself, Is it a technology creator or a technology user? Is it helping other companies do stuff more efficiently? Or is it just one of the first companies to use a particular technology? What is the core asset of the company?

For a while it may seem as if these distinctions don't matter. During the Internet IPO frenzy of 1999, any stock labeled an Internet stock seemed like a moon shot. But when the market came back down to earth, people started looking more carefully at what each firm did. Does it build out and benefit the Internet infrastructure, such as Exodus Communications (EXDS:Nasdaq)? Or does it use the Internet infrastructure, such as eToys (ETYS:Nasdaq)? The point is, if it's not a tech stock, you're better off judging it by other industries' criteria.

How to ID a Good Tech Company

Certain things are important to any company. Good management. Profits or a credible plan to obtain them. Money in the bank, or at least access to relatively cheap capital. The ability to make acquisitions without wasting money. Not to mention a product or service that people want to buy.

Hard to argue with any of that. But among technology companies, additional investing themes have emerged over the past several years. For example, as illustrated by the rise of Microsoft (MSFT:Nasdaq) and its Windows operating system, technologies coalesce around certain standards. Companies that set those standards are valued accordingly. Another theme: Companies focused on taking advantage of data networks such as the Internet have generally greater promise than those that don't exploit the possibilities of connectivity.

Nothing guarantees success, of course. A company's fate rests upon a near-infinite number of variables. But a survey of key operating tenets unique to tech companies reveals a number of important themes for tech investors. If a tech company's profile or strategy addresses these themes, as an investor you'll know you're on the right track.

Standards

Standards are important to every industry. When Americans buy paper for their computer or their photocopier, they expect it to be 8½ inches by 11 inches—they don't want to stick it in and find out it's 9 by 12. When they buy a car, they expect that it will fit in standard parking spaces, and that the gas pump nozzle at the Exxon station will fit into the tank. When music retailers unpack a box of audio CDs from their distributor, they expect the discs will fit into the racks they have on display.

Customers of technology companies are no different. When they buy a piece of software, they expect it to run on their computer. There are modem standards. Internet standards. Digital TV standards. Sometimes they are worked out in a ritual of cooperation. Other times, they are imposed with the blunt force of market power.

What is different about technology companies is that new standards are always being set, and the rewards can be huge to companies that control standards. Let's say an American paper company devised a new standard office paper size of 9 by 12. What would it gain? Not much—you can't collect royalties from paper sizes. But in technology it's a whole different story. When Windows became the standard operating system on more than 90% of personal computers sold in the world, Microsoft made money on each PC. And because it controlled the standard, it had the chance to influence the future of computing (an opportunity that led to the 1998 antitrust case against Microsoft, in which it was accused of illegally using its dominance of the desktop computer business to influence the direction of Internet software).

When wireless telephone company Qualcomm (QCOM:Nasdaq) settled a dispute with Sweden's Ericsson (ERICY:Nasdaq ADR) over the CDMA wireless standard in early 1999, the agreement was seen as confirming Qualcomm's control of CDMA—and opening up Europe and other major markets to a huge licensing business for Qualcomm. Over the 12 months leading up to the settlement, Qualcomm's stock roughly doubled; over the 12 months after Ericsson's acknowledgment of Qualcomm's patent rights, Qualcomm's stock shot up more than 14-fold. Qualcomm has retreated since then, but attentive investors had a chance to score a big gain.

Standards can be formal ones, enforced by intellectual property laws or standard-setting bodies, or they can be informal standards— standards that are essentially popularity votes. For example, there is no formal standard for the properties of personal finance software. But if a company were going to launch a new piece of software, it would face an uphill battle all the way, because Intuit's (INTU:Nasdaq) Quicken and Microsoft's Money have, as more and more people have adopted them, become effective standards for this type of software.

The rise of Linux—the operating system first written by computer folk hero Linus Torvalds, then developed by a collective of programmers—owes a lot to standards, though in a nonstandard way. Investors are hopeful that Linux software—freely downloadable on the Web or purchasable as a CD-ROM—will grow to become a standard that rivals Microsoft Windows. They also hope that companies identified with Linux will be able to make money from the software, perhaps through Linux-related services they offer, even if you can get the software from the Net free. That's why, after Linux firm Red Hat (RHAT:

Nasdaq) went public in August 1999 at the split-adjusted price of $20, Internet investors bid it up higher than $150 by December, even though its immediate prospects for profitability were thin. (The stock subsequently plummeted.)

The benefit that standard setters enjoy isn't just the sale of hard goods. Often, what technology successes are selling is intellectual property. Microsoft, for example, doesn't have to sell a box with a CD-ROM inside it to make money from Windows; rather, it collects money from computer manufacturers who, working with software supplied by Microsoft, copy it themselves onto the computers they manufacture and pay Microsoft for the privilege. Gemstar TV Guide International (GMST:Nasdaq) has set the standard for a system of easy VCR recording of television broadcasts. For the most part, it, too, doesn't sell widgets—it licenses technology.

That's why patents, when they're enforceable and when they're enforced, can be a crucial asset of a technology company.

Standards don't have to be as ubiquitous as Windows to be useful. For example, the fact that the Palm operating system is gaining popularity among handheld computers, a small subset of computing devices representing a fraction of the size of the desktop market, is enough for people to jump in and build businesses predicated on the continuing success of that operating system.

Starting with the free distribution of Internet browsers from Netscape Communications and Microsoft, the desire to set standards has led to business practices unknown before the days of the Internet. For example, in an effort to build demand for its software that lets Internet publishers stream audio (and later video) over the Web, the company known as Progressive Networks, later RealNetworks (RNWK: Nasdaq), started giving away the player software for listening to that streaming audio. The company appears to be doing well, but acceptance of its player hasn't stopped Microsoft from aggressively trying to promote its own music format, nor has it prevented the rise of the alternative MP3 music format. Indeed, RealNetworks has modified its software to accommodate this new format.

Investing around these standards is tricky. Creating a successful standard isn't a guarantee of success. For years, Hayes, the company that developed computer modems in the 1970s, was synonymous with the standard for computer modems; other manufacturers regularly labeled their own modems "Hayes compatible." Well, that measure of fame didn't prevent Hayes from going into bankruptcy. In the early 1980s, a company called TV Answer (later known as EON) developed an interactive television system known as IVDS and even persuaded the FCC to set aside part of the airwaves so that licensees could implement its system. Companies ended up bidding a total of more than $200 million to offer IVDS. But the service ended up being a commercial disaster for nearly everyone involved.

Still, the fundamental appeal of technological standards is something investors can't ignore. That's because in technology industries, standards are increasingly reinforced by a winner-take-all (or at least a winner-take-most) effect. In a nontech business—advertising, for example—there is room for many winners: large firms, small firms, international agencies, and regional ones. But in the world of, say, Internet browsers, there's room for only one or two.

Standard Setters		
Company	Sets the Standard in	Market Capitalization August 2000
Microsoft (MSFT:Nasdaq)	Windows operating system, office production software	$371 billion
Qualcomm (QCOM:Nasdaq)	CDMA wireless standard	$44 billion
Gemstar (GMST:Nasdaq)	VCR programming, interactive program guides	$30 billion

The Mover's Advantage

Imagine you're in the midst of running a one-mile race at a track meet—four laps around a 440-yard track. It's great to be leading after the first lap, and it's a good sign you'll be a contender at the finish line. But it doesn't guarantee you'll win.

That, essentially, is the situation faced by technology companies. They gain an advantage by being first to innovate. But to hold on to that advantage, they've got to race to stay ahead of their competitors.

In recent years, technology analysts and reporters have popularized a concept called "first-mover advantage." The idea behind first-mover advantage, usually accepted without question, is that there is benefit to developing a product or service before anyone else does. Sometimes this is true, if, for example, it means a company has a patent it can license to other companies. Or it can be a boon if its customers find it too costly or complicated to switch to a rival's product.

The history of technology, however, is filled with companies for which moving first proved to be an insufficient advantage. A half century ago, CBS had the first (and, it thought, the only) FCC-approved system for transmitting color TV in the United States. But RCA's system became the standard. Betamax videocassettes came before VHS. Netscape's Navigator preceded Microsoft's Internet Explorer. CompuServe existed long before America Online. But in each case, the first was vanquished in some way by the second.

And yet, speed matters. Innovation is at the heart of technology; one of the ways successful companies distinguish themselves is by constant innovation. Rather than waiting for other companies to make their successes obsolete, companies do it themselves—constantly creating new products that are likely to turn their current ones into close-out specials, or constantly reinventing what their company is.

Perhaps a better expression for this than first-mover advantage is just "mover's advantage." One company that has it is Yahoo! The company got its start as one of the first and best directories of sites on the Web. But had it remained only that, Yahoo! would be nowhere near the success it has become. It added more and more features to take advantage of the traffic on the site—including free e-mail, financial information, Web site building tools, streamed video, auctions, and shopping. Thus, while first-mover advantage is something to look for, continued agility and innovation are more compelling traits.

Movers and Shakers		
Company	Field	Market Capitalization August 2000
Yahoo! (YHOO:Nasdaq)	Internet news, information, entertainment, utilities	$72 billion
Intel (INTC:Nasdaq)	Semiconductors	$484 billion
DoubleClick (DCLK:Nasdaq)	Online advertising	$3.7 billion

The Network

The network is the context that makes technology really useful. Consider the steam locomotive. It was a wondrous invention that changed the course of history. But the tracks that covered the country from one end to the other were what made it really useful. The car's a fine invention too. But what made it really great is the federal highway system. The telephone? A bunch of telephones is even better.

In the world of networks, this phenomenon is known as Metcalfe's Law. Named for Bob Metcalfe, the founder of computer network pioneer 3Com (COMS:Nasdaq), Metcalfe's law states in essence that a network leaps in value with each new person who joins it. If I'm part of a phone system with a total of four people on it, there's a total of six possible conversations. But if you double the number of people on the system to eight, the number of possible conversations more than quadruples.

Metcalfe's Law: A Graphical Representation

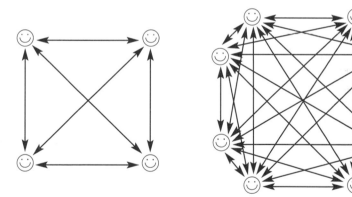

The Internet is the latest example of this basic network concept: The more people and companies attached to the Internet, the more valuable the Internet is.

So, how does this insight translate into investment? For one, it means investors should look at companies that are helping to create this network: Cisco Systems (CSCO:Nasdaq), JDS Uniphase (JDSU: Nasdaq), Corning (GLW:NYSE)—any company that speeds up the network, makes it more efficient, or increases capacity. Because the potential of so many other companies depends on the viability and strength of the network, companies actually building the network or its parts enjoy quite a premium.

Also consider companies that benefit specifically from the network effect that Metcalfe saw. Companies that are built on a foundation of interactions among many people—not just from one store to many people—stand to benefit. As more people join AOL's ICQ instant-messaging service, for example, the value of the service to the users grows at an even faster rate—and these users become more likely to tell their friends how useful ICQ is, leading to more customers. The more people who join eBay to buy or sell merchandise, the greater the likelihood that a seller will find a buyer for his merchandise, or a buyer will find what he or she seeks. That makes eBay more valuable to users. If a company shows an ability to build a network—technical or human—that's a good sign.

Networked		
Company	Field	Market Capitalization August 2000
Cisco Systems (CSCO:Nasdaq)	Networking equipment	$460 billion
eBay (EBAY:Nasdaq)	Auctions	$15 billion
Exodus Communications (EXDS:Nasdaq)	Internet servers	$26 billion

Mobility

A long time ago, we used to sacrifice mobility for technology. Not anymore.

It seems almost quaint now, but at one point, phones were something that were hardwired to walls. Handsets were connected by cord to the phone's base. Computers stayed in rooms and didn't leave. To listen to high-fidelity music, you sat in your living room.

Now 31% of Americans have cellular phones, meaning they can send and receive from anywhere. In June 1989 the industry had annualized revenues of roughly $4 billion; ten years later that figure was about $41 billion.

Computing devices, once immobile, are getting portable too. Along with cell phones, the use of handheld organizers has risen; handheld manufacturer Palm has sold 6 million of its organizers since 1996. With the rise of Palm and other handheld devices, people can e-mail one another even if they're not at their desk. It's unclear where this will go: how many people will have cellular phones; how many people will feel the need to carry around portable computers to manage address books, calendars, e-mail, and other memos.

But it seems likely that people will want the information, communication, and aural entertainment they get on their computer when they're on the move as well. If they download music to their computer, they'll want to take it with them on their portable stereo.

If you think the mobility thing is overdone, well, just look at some of the valuations the market gives to companies that enhance mobility:

Going Mobile		
Company	Field	Market Capitalization August 2000
Palm (PALM:Nasdaq)	Handheld organizers	$22 billion
Nextel Communications (NXTL:Nasdaq)	Wireless communication	$34 billion
Nokia (NOK:NYSE)	Cellular communications	$194 billion

Scalability

Scalability is a term that gets kicked around a lot when people are talking about Internet businesses and technology models. Basically, it's a fancy way of saying that a business doesn't break as it grows bigger—it works on a large scale as well as a small one. At the same time, it's a business concept that is open-ended enough to give a small company the potential to grow, cost effectively, in many directions.

An easy way to think about scalable businesses is to think of one that isn't scalable. Imagine Antonio Stradivari, master violin maker. He makes the world's finest violins—but only one at a time. If he wants to make more violins, he would have to hire people. That's doable if you can find a few trusted apprentices, but after a while the master Stradivari would have so many people working for him, he would no longer have time to inspect each of the violins his workshop makes, at each necessary point in the production process. Eventually, the violins that would come out of his workshop would no longer be Stradivari quality. The business of making such fine violins is not scalable.

In a scalable business, the efficiencies and economics improve as a business grows in size—often because automated processes lessen the need for hiring. One example of a business that appears to be scalable but isn't yet profitable (and whose stock suffered in the first half of 2000) is Internet search engine GoTo.com (GOTO:Nasdaq). The company makes money by selling search terms to different online advertisers; for example, if someone types in "baseball cards," the listings that the search returns are from companies who have bid for the privilege of their listing, with the high bidder listed at the top of the search results page. What's scalable about this setup is that the auction covering each term is automated; in other words, the company doesn't necessarily need salespeople to complete a sale, just an operational Web site.

Scalers		
Company	Field	Market Capitalization August 2000
CNET (CNET:Nasdaq)	Tech news and info	$3 billion
Inktomi (INKT:Nasdaq)	Internet infrastructure software	$13 billion
GoTo.com (GOTO:Nasdaq)	Online search	$800 million

Concepts like standards, networks, mobility, and scalability can help you evaluate the odds that a New Economy company has a promising future.

Tech Sectors: How to Categorize the Beast

As we enter the twenty-first century, technology stocks are like clothes: A new wave of fashion shows up as soon as you've gotten used to the last style.

Look at the Internet. At the dawn of the age of the commercialized Internet, the first companies to capture investors' imaginations were Internet service providers—the companies that supplied dial-up connections to the Net. The hot IPO of December 1994 was the ISP Netcom On-Line Communications Services. Soon after came another well-received ISP, Performance Systems International, later renamed PSINet (PSIX:Nasdaq).

By the summer of 1995, Internet software was the Next Hot Thing—first with browser company Spyglass, developer of the browser upon which Microsoft's Internet Explorer was built, and then with Netscape Communications, the Internet software company whose phenomenal early success in the stock market rewrote the rules of how profitable a company had to be—or, rather, didn't have to be, since Netscape was losing money—to attract investors in the public market.

By the following spring came the next wave of hot companies. Yahoo! and Excite, now Excite@Home (ATHM:Nasdaq), went public in April 1996, turning Wall Street's attention to search and directory sites for the World Wide Web. And so it went. Search engines begat online retailers. Retailers begat Internet infrastructure companies.

To invest in the technology sector, you need a basic overview of the various subsectors in technology.

It's not simple stuff. Billions of dollars have been invested in technology over the past decade, and the stock market has added billions of dollars' worth of value to technology stocks. To get an idea of how things have changed, take a look at the Wilshire 5000 index, which represents most United States–based companies traded on the major exchanges. Over the past decade, the percentage of companies in the index that are made up of tech firms has stayed the same, but their share of the Wilshire 5000's market cap has tripled.

The IPO market shows the same proliferation. The number of tech stocks going public exploded in the 1990s. In 1999, a blowout year for technology IPOs, 73% of public stock offerings were for tech stocks. About half the tech IPOs were for Internet firms.

Date	Percentage of companies in the Wilshire 5000 in the technology sector	Percentage of market capitalization of the Wilshire 5000 attributable to the technology sector
12/31/1990	17.2	10.6
12/29/1995	16.4	15.0
3/31/2000	17.1	32.8

Source: Wilshire Associates

Technology IPOs in the 1990s		
Year	Technology IPOs	Money Raised by Tech IPOs (in billions)
1990	29	$0.63
1991	73	2.6
1992	98	4.4
1993	140	4.8
1994	138	5.2
1995	212	8.8
1996	270	18.0
1997	189	10.0
1998	126	8.3
1999	398	39.2

Source: Thomson Financial Securities Data

It's impossible to categorize all technology companies neatly because they cross so many business lines. Is AT&T a telephone company, a cable company, or an Internet service company? The answer is yes, yes, and yes.

The classification of technology companies is arbitrary in other ways. Much of it's driven by what interests stock analysts. Back in the early 1980s you could easily find analysts covering the word-processing sector. Not anymore. In the late 1990s a significant number of Internet analysts specialized in online retailing. But as more traditional retailers like Wal-Mart (WMT:NYSE) and Staples (SPLS:Nasdaq) go online, trying to separate Internet storefronts from shopping-mall retailers can be arbitrary and pointless. Over time, classifications that people talk about today might seem as strange as an investment analyst covering only dishwashers.

But the process isn't completely arbitrary. Morgan Stanley Capital International and Standard & Poor's, for example, have developed a rigorous taxonomy of publicly traded companies, sorting them into categories such as sector, industry group, industry, and subindustry. Their work can be extremely helpful to people trying to get a broad view of technology and other markets.

These industry categorizations, like almost any classification system, aren't perfect; as new industries are born, sometimes it can be hard to fit them into the established order. But at the turn of the twenty-first century, it's possible to take a snapshot of the different sectors within technology. Let's give it a try, using work from the S&P and MSCI.

Semiconductors

The semiconductor sector comprises the chip makers—manufacturers of silicon-wafer-based electronic circuits at the heart of computers, cell phones, and countless other devices. The semi market is big and getting bigger, amounting to $169 billion in 1999 and likely to grow to $253 billion in 2001, according to market research firm Dataquest. Top dogs include Intel, the company behind the Pentium and most of the other microprocessors used in the PC revolution; Intel challenger Advanced Micro Devices (AMD:Nasdaq); and communications network chipmakers Vitesse Semiconductor (VTSS:Nasdaq) and Conexant Systems (CNXT:Nasdaq).

Semiconductor Capital Equipment

If semiconductors are big business, so are the companies that manufacture the gear used to make them. The semiconductor wafer fabrication equipment industry is doubling from $17.4 billion in 1999 to $34 billion in 2001, estimates Dataquest. The sector includes giants like Lam Research (LRCX:Nasdaq), Novellus Systems (NVLS:Nasdaq), Applied Materials (AMAT:Nasdaq), and Teradyne (TER:NYSE).

Computer Hardware

The computer business is made up in part by desktop computers and laptops found in people's homes and offices—equipment built by companies such as Dell, Apple, and Compaq (CPQ:NYSE). Those companies and other manufacturers, such as Sun Microsystems (SUNW: Nasdaq), also sell servers—behind-the-scenes computers that feed information to other computers over a network, like the computers that house *TheStreet.com* Web site and deliver it to your home. Companies in the sector also include manufacturers of costly workstations, where computer graphics are concocted; mainframe computers that might store data crucial to a large company's operations; and even automatic teller machines. To get a sense of the size of the market, let's look at PCs alone: Worldwide PC sales will amount to about $250 billion in 2004, according to International Data Corporation.

Computer Storage and Peripherals

The storage and peripherals market ranges from disk drives and tape drives for PCs to the growing field of devices used to store huge quantities of information on business networks. Two of the major companies in the storage sector—which, by one estimate, will reach $100 billion in sales by 2002—are Seagate Technology (SEG:NYSE) and EMC (EMC:NYSE).

One major peripheral manufacturer is IBM (IBM:NYSE) printer spinoff Lexmark International (LXK:NYSE).

Systems Software

These are the companies that make software used to run the largest computer systems and networks, including database management software. The biggest fish in this pond is Microsoft, which lately had sales of $22.9 billion over 12 months from its systems software as well as applications such as Microsoft Office. Other big systems companies include CompuWare (CPWR:Nasdaq), BMC Software (BMCS: Nasdaq), and Computer Associates (CA:NYSE). The database market, led by Oracle (ORCL:Nasdaq) and Microsoft, amounted to $8 billion in 1999, says Dataquest.

Applications Software

Applications software are programs not for operating a complete computer system but for running specific tasks. (Note that one of the most famous applications is the Office suite from Microsoft, usually classified as a systems software company—it's just another example of how firms don't fit into neat cubbyholes.)

This software sector ranges far and wide, including graphics software firm Autodesk (ADSK:Nasdaq), video game maker Electronic Arts (ERTS:Nasdaq), and encryption firm RSA Security (RSAS: Nasdaq).

But the applications sector with the biggest hoped-for growth among investors is the B2B e-commerce sector—the companies that will help the nation's and the world's industries take real-world business transactions and put them online. Before 2010, the number of B2B transactions is expected to be in the trillions—a staggering amount. Plenty of companies want to help that process along, including Ariba (ARBA:Nasdaq), Commerce One (CMRC:Nasdaq), and i2 Technologies (ITWO:Nasdaq).

Information Technology Consulting and Services

Overlapping with other software areas, these firms provide information technology consulting and IT services. Some of the biggies include Computer Sciences (CSC:NYSE), Electronic Data Systems (EDS: NYSE), and Unisys (UIS:NYSE).

Internet Software and Services

One group of companies—America Online, Yahoo!, and Internet ad firm DoubleClick (DCLK:Nasdaq), for example—make money by helping marketers target consumers for advertising and commerce. Internet advertising amounted to more than $4 billion in 1999.

Other companies, such as auctioneer eBay, general-purpose retailer Amazon.com, and name-your-price discounter priceline.com (PCLN: Nasdaq), focus on consumer commerce. Dataquest estimates that business-to-consumer sales worldwide will leap from $31.2 billion in 1999 to $380 billion in 2003.

Networking Equipment

These are the companies that make the innards of the Internet—the devices that are used to build the worldwide computer network. The sector is home to one of the most famous tech stocks of the 1990s—Cisco Systems. The king of the networkers had revenues of roughly $16.8 billion for 1999. Other networkers include 3Com and Cabletron Systems (CS:NYSE).

In 2000, the hottest part of this sector was optical networking, or the networks based on sending information via light pulses rather than through electronic pulses down metal wires. One of the up-and-comers among this up-and-coming category was JDS Uniphase.

Telecommunications Equipment

With more and more telecommunications traffic flowing over computer networks, it can be hard to figure out where networking equipment and telecommunications equipment begin and end. The big dogs here supply end-to-end equipment for wired and wireless networks of phones and other communications devices—Nortel (NT:NYSE), Qualcomm, and Motorola (MOT:NYSE), which acquired cable industry supplier General Instrument in 1999. The communications equipment market—comprising both networking and telecom—amounts to $377 billion in 2000, according to Merrill Lynch. About a third of that figure represents wireless spending.

Electronic Equipment and Instruments

This group of companies includes high-tech measurement companies like Tektronix (TEK:NYSE), manufacturer of various sophisticated test and monitoring devices. But Wall Street's real excitement with this category is with the electronic manufacturing services industry—the companies that assemble gadgetry at the behest of high-tech clients who'd rather outsource nitty-gritty work than do it themselves. Donaldson, Lufkin & Jenrette estimates that the sector amounted to $73 billion in worldwide revenues in 1999, tripling to $212 billion in 2004. Some of the prominent names in this category are Solectron (SLR:NYSE), SCI Systems (SCI:NYSE), Sanmina (SANM:Nasdaq), and Jabil Circuit (JBL:NYSE).

Tech Stocks in Your Portfolio

How much of a role should tech stocks from various subgroups play in your portfolio? It depends on your appetite for risk and your facility with the topic.

Tech stocks can—and have—risen phenomenal amounts, both in a single day and over time. But they can also swing violently in the other direction. Shares in e-commerce software company Siebel Systems (SEBL:Nasdaq), for example, grew almost sixfold in value over the year ending March 2000. But that was little consolation to the people who bought the stock near its peak of 175⅛ in early March; amid wild swings in the stock, Siebel closed at 86⁹⁄₁₆ on April 14—about half its price a month earlier (it had regained most of that ground by

August). Henry Blodget, who as chief Internet analyst at Merrill Lynch in 1999 was presiding over a hot sector at a hot moment, suggested in June 1999 that investors put no more than a small percentage—perhaps 5% of their portfolio—into Internet stocks.

Another complication of tech investing is what Bob Turner, chief investment officer of Turner Investment Partners, calls the "ninety-ten" rule: 90% of the value in the tech sector is created by 10% of the stocks. A stock such as Cisco Systems "creates this massive valuation, and the other companies just kind of flounder around," says the long-time tech investor. "That's really always been the case: For every one spectacular success, there are nine failures."

While acknowledging that the point might be self-serving, Turner makes a convincing case for leaving tech investing to professionals like himself. The tech business isn't like other sectors—for example, the drug sector, where investors in a company with top-selling drugs "can ride that for a long, long time." Tech is different: "The volatility is huge, innovation is rapid, competition is aggressive," he says. He's got four full-time tech analysts studying 2,000 different companies, and he thinks the business is best left to the experts. "If you have a bomb to be disarmed, you don't call out the local police force. You call out the bomb squad," says Turner.

If you tend to agree with Turner, and yet still want to be in tech, the solution might be in a tech mutual fund, and there are many out there.

But let's say you can't get tech stocks out of your head. You want to invest for yourself. How to do it?

The best way to start is with a sense of humility. Remember that being aware of a general trend, such as the growth of fiber-optic communications, doesn't necessarily guarantee one's ability to pick specific stocks. The birth of the automobile industry gave rise to hundreds of car companies, but only a handful have survived. The Internet, among other technologies, may live a long and useful life, but most of the companies that investors have obsessed over in the Net's infancy may not. That's why people entrust billions of dollars to mutual fund managers like Turner, who have research staffs that can pick through the minutiae of scores of tech companies.

But if, based on your personal or professional experience and perhaps some of what you picked up in this chapter, you feel confident in selecting your own tech stocks, the next thing to do is consider how much risk you're willing to take. These risks are real. To take an exam-

Top-Performing Technology Funds Five Years Through August 8, 2000	
Fund	Avg. Annual Return %
Firsthand Technology (TVFQX)	53.09
PIMCO Innovation (PIVAX)	45.98
Fidelity Select Electronics (FSELX)	43.15
Fidelity Select Technology (FSPTX)	41.68
Invesco Technology (FTCHX)	39.73
First American Technology (FITBX)	39.20
Kemper Technology (KTCAX)	35.80
Fidelity Select Software (FSCSX)	33.38
Waddell and Reed Adv Science and Tech (UNSCX)	32.51
Hancock Technology (NTTFX)	31.23

Source: Morningstar

ple from 2000, at mid-year many consumer-focused Internet stocks were down more than 80% from their all-time highs. And it didn't look like they were coming back. The tech-heavy Nasdaq Composite index also suffered for most of 2000. Tech investing, like buying stocks on margin, is not only a powerful vehicle for growth; it can also be an extremely efficient way to lose money.

So do you make tech a small part of your portfolio, as Henry Blodget suggests for Net stocks? Or are you willing to put 50% or more of your portfolio into tech?

Diversifying in Tech

Let's go back to Chapter 3 on diversification for a moment. Consider the factors we set out there: age, income, responsibilities, time horizon, investing experience, and available funds. If you land on the more aggressive end of this multifactor analysis, and you have a hankering for tech, then you may be a good candidate for a tech-heavy portfolio. To stay diversified, you'll want to purchase both high-octane stocks and some core tech performers—the Microsofts, IBMs, and Intels. (Dividend payers, such as IBM and some telco companies, are scarce among tech stocks.)

If you're somewhere in the middle of the risk spectrum but still eager to invest in the sector, limit your tech investing to more like 30%.

Make sure you have some high-octane stocks and core performers, but apportion those with an eye more toward the core performers.

If you've got a lower risk tolerance based on these factors, perhaps you should dedicate only a small portion of your portfolio to technology—5 to 15%. If so, don't be afraid to make this the high-octane section of your portfolio.

Whatever portion of your portfolio is invested in technology, the key to mitigating your risk is through diversification—spreading out your risk by investing in an appropriate number of different companies, in an appropriate number of business categories.

The concept of diversification is somewhat tricky when applied to tech stocks. Putting money into a number of different companies can't completely eliminate risk. For example, at times the whole tech sector gets hit. Investors rotate into other sectors perceived at the time to be safer, such as financial stocks or utilities. At other times, whole categories of technology that looked like promising areas for growth don't pan out—not one company at all. In the 1990s, several well-known, well-financed companies placed billions of dollars into developing wireless telephone networks that operated via low-flying satellites. By 2000 none of the publicly traded companies in this area looked in particularly good shape. There is not necessarily guaranteed safety in numbers. But there is more safety in diversification than in choosing one or two tech stocks and seeing them both crumble.

Selecting Stocks

The simplest form of diversification, perhaps, is along the lines of the labels that many investors use to divide companies: "old tech" and "new tech." This terminology, which sprang up sometime after Yahoo!'s IPO, makes a distinction between older tech companies, ones that have been on people's radar screen for several years and newer ones, which seem to have appeared in the last week.

But the distinction is also between a track record of solid performance and the prospect of moon-shot growth. It's between tangible technology, semiconductors and fabrication equipment, for example, and electrons, nimble companies whose only possessions may be a few patents and some electrons on the hard drive. When the market is feeling optimistic and ready for growth, new tech usually does well. When investors want a sense of safety, they retreat to old tech.

For most people, the distinction between old tech and new tech is too vague to be useful. A better idea is to find a more detailed classification scheme and work from there.

To get an idea of what a model tech portfolio might look like, let's look at the holdings of four different tech-focused mutual funds at a moment in time—roughly, mid-year 2000. These aren't recommendations for you to go out and buy the specific stocks listed here, because times change and companies change. Smart choices might be foolish six months later, especially in tech. But by looking at each fund and hearing what fund managers have to say about stock picking and diversifying risk, you can get a sense of how you might assemble your own tech portfolio.

These funds can have dozens of stocks among their holdings. But to make the exercise simpler, we'll look at just the top 10 holdings of each fund, with the largest holdings first. Because these 10 are the top choices, they're a good indication of where managers see performance; for example, the top 10 stocks owned by the Munder Future Technology fund represent 43% of its holdings. (Not all the stocks listed here, such as the MedImmune biotech firm held by Turner Technology Fund, are tech stocks.)

What you can see from these portfolios is that there is a mix in two respects. First, no one is too heavily invested in just one subsector. They

Munder Future Technology Fund MTFAX	
Company	Line of business
Corning (GLW:NYSE)	Optical fiber and other manufacturing
Comverse Technology (CMVT:Nasdaq)	Telecom equipment
Microsoft (MSFT:Nasdaq)	Computer software
Intel (INTC:Nasdaq)	Semiconductors
E-TEK Dynamics (since acquired)	Fiber-optic components
Micron Technology (MU:NYSE)	PCs, semiconductors
Oracle (ORCL:Nasdaq)	Computer software
Veritas Software (VRTS:Nasdaq)	Storage management software
ADC Telecommunications (ADCT:Nasdaq)	Telecom equipment
Cisco Systems (CSCO:Nasdaq)	Networking equipment

Turner Technology Fund TTECX	
Company	Line of business
Cisco Systems (CSCO:Nasdaq)	Networking equipment
Intel (INTC:Nasdaq)	Semiconductors
Microsoft (MSFT:Nasdaq)	Computer software
Oracle (ORCL:Nasdaq)	Computer software
Gateway (GTW:NYSE)	PCs
Dell Computer (DELL:Nasdaq)	PCs
Siebel Systems (SEBL:Nasdaq)	Business software
Ciena (CIEN:Nasdaq)	Optical networking
MedImmune (MEDI:Nasdaq)	Biotech
Ariba (ARBA:Nasdaq)	Business-to-business software

John Hancock Technology Fund NTTFX	
Company	Line of business
Micron Technology (MO:NYSE)	PCs, semiconductors
EMC (EMC:NYSE)	Computer storage
Ciena (CIEN:Nasdaq)	Optical networking
Mercury Interactive (MERQ:Nasdaq)	Internet software testing
Integrated Device Technology (IDTI:Nasdaq)	Semiconductors
Oracle (ORCL:Nasdaq)	Computer software
Cisco Systems (CSCO:Nasdaq)	Networking equipment
Solectron(SLR:NYSE)	Electronics manufacturing services
America Online (AOL:NYSE)	Consumer Internet service
Dell Computer (DELL:Nasdaq)	PCs

T. Rowe Price Science & Technology Fund PRSCX	
Company	Line of business
Oracle (ORCL:Nasdaq)	Computer software
Cisco Systems (CSCO:Nasdaq)	Networking equipment
Analog Devices (ADI:NYSE)	Semiconductors
Maxim Integrated Products (MXIM:Nasdaq)	Semiconductors
Xilinx (XLNX:Nasdaq)	Semiconductors
Vodafone (VOD:NYSE)	Wireless services
Ariba (ARBA:Nasdaq)	Business-to-business software
Altera (ALTR:Nasdaq)	Semiconductors
Ciena (CIEN:Nasdaq)	Optical networking
Nokia (NOK:NYSE)	Wireless equipment

Source: Fund company Web sites, mid-year 2000

diversify within technology. Second, you have a few high-octane stocks juggled in with core performers. High-octaners like E-TEK Dynamics (since bought by JDS Uniphase) and Ariba (ARBA:Nasdaq) are side by side with established brethren Cisco, Microsoft, Intel, and Dell.

Let's take the portfolios in turn. Bob Turner of the Turner Technology Fund goes for focused diversity: First, he identifies the fastest-growing segments in the marketplace—for example, optical communications, storage and servers, and B2B e-commerce. Then he tries to pick the leaders in each of these promising segments.

Alan Harris, senior portfolio manager with the Munder Future Technology Fund, goes instead from specific companies to general trends. The fund starts out picking stocks it thinks look attractive. Then the managers step back and look at what industries their stock selections fall into, such as semiconductors, communications equipment, computer hardware, software, or networking; the next question is whether the various industry concentrations and omissions make sense given broad industry trends.

It so happens, for example, that at mid-year 2000 the fund had found a lot of semiconductor stocks it felt were good opportunities. "We let the industries fall out of that individual stock selection," says Harris, "and we look at it and say, 'Does this make sense for what's going on in the world? Do we want to be overweighted communications equipment and semiconductors, and underweight hardware?'" As described by Harris, diversification isn't a starting point but a reality check.

But whether you start or finish by trying to diversify across tech sectors, it's a safe practice. At the John Hancock Technology Fund, according to co–portfolio manager Alan Loewenstein, the fund's management divides its investments into five different industry areas. Those investment segments include telecom, Internet, semiconductors, software, and, finally, hardware and data storage.

In practice, explains Loewenstein, the fund divides up its investments into these five categories, starting out with about 20% of its money in each. Then, in response to changing business and market conditions, the fund invests more in one area than the others, or lightens up its holdings in an area. For example, in early 1999, he says, the technology fund pulled back from software investments because of concerns about a pre-Y2K slowdown of software purchases; meanwhile the fund went relatively heavy on Net stocks, which were coming off a good fourth quarter.

The vocabulary may be different, but other funds are doing the same thing. Chip Morris, manager of the T. Rowe Price Science & Technology fund, says he tries to have a "broad smattering" of companies across different segments such as software, hardware, and semiconductors. In general, says Morris, semiconductors, software, and communications have been the three biggest segments in the fund, each representing about 20 to 25% of the fund's assets at any time.

Of course, not all of us get paid to follow the tech market full-time, moving in and out of subsectors with agility. In that case, the subsector diversification becomes all the more important—if one area wilts, you've got others to make up the difference.

"By having this diversity," Loewenstein says, "you won't get killed in a down market."

In general, the greater percentage of your money you invest in tech, the more diversified you should try to be within it. There are arguably about a dozen major sectors in technology (though many more subsectors), as I listed beginning on page 76. If you are putting all your eggs in the tech basket, you should try to be in at least half of these—about 15 to 17% of your portfolio each, consistent with Loewenstein and Morris's approach.

If tech represents even half your portfolio, you should stay well diversified. But once you're down to 15% or less, then you should probably take Bob Turner's approach and try to pick a few great winners. If you're not banking on tech, you can afford the extra risk.

Online Tech Investing Information

The Internet isn't just a product of technology's progress; it's a chronicler of it too.

Here's an opinionated guide on where the layperson can go for technology information on the Internet.

ZDNet (www.zdnet.com)

The Internet offspring of the Ziff-Davis publishing empire, ZDNet is one of several good general news sites devoted to tech—computing and the Internet in particular. Start at ZDNet News (www.zdnet.com /zdnn). For investor-focused news, go to the Inter@ctive Investor part of the site (www.zdii.com). For insight into the business computing marketplace, go to the Web sites associated with Ziff-Davis magazines—eWeek, formerly PCWeek (www.zdnet.com/eweek), with news for corporate technology users; Sm@rt Partner (www.zdnet.com/sr), targeted at the middlemen of the business computing business; and Inter@ctive Week (www.zdnet.com/intweek).

CNET (www.cnet.com)

CNET, which has announced plans to purchase ZDNet, covers Internet and computing news with less of a bent toward tech professionals and more toward consumers and investors. Start at the news section (www.news.cnet.com) or go to the CNET Investor site (www.investor .cnet.com), which has been relying on feeds from Bloomberg (www .bloomberg.com), itself a news outlet with no slouch tech coverage.

The Industry Standard (www.thestandard.com)

The Web site of a fun, readable weekly magazine devoted to the business of the Internet and the culture of the Internet business. To get an overall sense of the coverage of each day's news, go to the Web site and subscribe to *Media Grok*, a daily review of how technology news is covered by other news outlets.

Semiconductor Business News (www.semibiznews.com)

Part of CMPnet (www.cmpnet.com), the online arm of technology publisher CMP Media, this site is a good place to keep abreast of—you guessed it—the semiconductor market.

Redherring.com (www.redherring.com)

This is the online arm of *Red Herring Magazine*, a publication whose traditional strength has been covering the technology venture capital markets. The site, which contains news about the IPO market and publicly traded companies as well, is a good place to get ideas about forthcoming developments in the tech market.

Whatis.com (www.whatis.com)

This guide for the perplexed is an online dictionary focusing on computers, the Internet, and other information technology subjects. If you have no clue about the technical expressions you're hearing, head here for the quick briefing.

Comp.risks (www.CSL.sri.com/risks.html)

Formally known by the driest of tech labels—"ACM Forum on Risks to the Public in the Use of Computers and Related Systems"—this long-running Internet newsgroup is one of the funniest, most fascinating technology newsletters you'll ever read. Moderated by computer scientist Peter G. Neumann, comp.risks is a compendium of news, anecdotes, and commentary about how computers fail, or how humans fail to use computers correctly.

Here's where you'll read stories about how supposedly erased data on a company's computer network is actually available to anyone on that network. Or—true story!—how a Scottish woman's phone call complaining about a spoiled sausage accidentally got forwarded to police headquarters and beepers all across Scotland. Regular reading of the newsletter (go to the above site to find out how to subscribe by e-mail) is a good inoculation against trusting rosy outlooks about the wonders of technology.

5

Finding and Researching Great Stock Ideas

We all know many of today's great stocks, the Ciscos, AOLs, and Intels that over the past decade have grown (and grown and grown) into behemoths with market caps exceeding the GDP of many countries. The problem is, knowing them today isn't nearly as useful as it would've been to know them before they started their amazing runs. Why didn't we know them long ago? More important, how do we find tomorrow's Cisco?

Beyond finding the next ten-bagger, how about pinpointing solid core performers? These are stocks that have matured but should nevertheless continue to serve investors well. Is McDonald's still an interesting stock to own, or has growth of the fast-food giant peaked in the United States? Can entertainment giant Disney be a real contender in this world of new media? Will the tobacco stocks like Philip Morris ever emerge from the litigation scourge to deliver any kind of return to investors?

These aren't the kind of questions you can easily answer on your own. But they're the kind you want to be thinking about in the search for good stock ideas. That's what this chapter is about—finding and researching stock ideas. There's certainly no shortage of stock information out there, especially online these days. The challenge is to know both the kind of stock ideas and information you're looking for, and the best places to find it.

As for the kind of ideas, think first about the ground we covered in the diversification and technology chapters. Before hunting for stock ideas, you need to consider the kinds of stocks you're looking for. Are they high-octane stocks? Core performers? Income engines? Are you hunting for tech names? Or is your search broader?

You need to ask yourself what types of investments are already well represented in your current portfolio, if you have one, in the form of either individual stocks or mutual funds. Compare your actual portfolio to your goals. Can you afford a little more risk? Do you feel comfortable with the risk profiles of the stocks you have but simply need more diversification into other sectors? Maybe you've cashed out on a high-flying stock that actually flew pretty high and you're ready for a lesser-known name with similar big potential. Or perhaps you're nearing or have just entered retirement and are ready for some more conservative plays.

Having an idea of what you're looking for in a stock is much more important than it was, say, 20 or even 10 years ago. Back then, more people relied entirely on a broker; investors basically didn't find their own stocks. They listened to their broker's recommendations and took it from there. These days, with more folks on their own for at least a portion of their portfolio, there's a great temptation to jump into the first attractive stock you read about. And with all the information out there for do-it-yourself investors, there's plenty of reading to be had.

But that kind of read-and-click behavior is not investing. It's indulgence. It's impatience. And it can be quite costly. That's why we urge you to have an idea of what you're looking for *before* you deluge yourself with stock ideas.

This chapter will help you sort through that deluge. I will walk you through the various sources of information out there and suggest ways to use them most effectively. To help me sift through those sources,

I've turned to John Rubino, a columnist with *TheStreet.com* and a former equity and bond analyst who wrote the book *Main Street, Not Wall Street*. We've come up with a wide variety of places to look for and vet promising ideas. After that, the legwork to decide if these ideas are worth your money begins—the subject of subsequent chapters about fundamental and technical analysis, and when to buy and sell.

The Information Food Chain

Most every investor is looking for an "edge." It's that insight that prompts him or her to get in on a good idea—to buy a stock—before others realize its potential and follow along, thereby bidding up the price. For some investors, that insight is firsthand experience with a niche product that you believe will develop mass market appeal. An example would be very early users of AOL (AOL:Nasdaq) or Yahoo! (YHOO:Nasdaq). For others, the insight is appreciation of the capabilities of a new CEO and the belief that he or she will be able to breathe life into an ailing stock. For yet others, it's application of some quantitative formula (e.g., low price-to-earnings ratio plus large market capitalization) that yields a list of promising stock ideas.

In all of these cases, the investor believes that he or she has a better idea of a stock's potential than the market does as a whole. It's the edge that gives you the ability to "beat the market."

Some investors presume that unless they have inside information—significant information about a company that's not yet been disclosed to the public—they can never get an edge. They dismiss all widely known information as useless on the theory that it's factored into the stock price already.

To a certain extent, they're right. Especially given the way stock information now travels at Internet speed, it's nearly impossible for an individual investor to get ahead on any immediate price shift in response to news and announcements.

But while public information releases may not be able to give you an edge in the short term, they can help you piece together a picture of a company. And if you get good at putting those pieces together and evaluating what makes for a strong company, and stock, you'll boost your odds of beating the market—or achieving whatever portfolio goals you might have.

The Mass Business Media

Some of the best places to start are the most prominent and popular: CNBC, *The Wall Street Journal, The New York Times, Barron's, Fortune, Business Week,* and *TheStreet.com.* These and other major business publications regularly detail industry trends, sector shifts, and corporate strategies, as well as stock-specific news like analyst actions.

Sure, this information can get factored into a stock's current price almost instantly. Most Wall Street professionals, for example, read the weekend financial publication *Barron's* in part because its articles tend to influence stock moves come Monday morning.

But those quick hits are just that—quick hits. You can take that same information and use it to help you understand a company, an industry, a macroeconomic change. You can study debates about the future of e-commerce and what it means for companies like auction site eBay (EBAY:Nasdaq). You can evaluate the pressures that Medicare policy changes could impose on pharmaceutical stocks like Pfizer (PFE:NYSE). You can learn of a chief financial officer's sudden departure from a company whose stock you had been considering. These are all examples of information that, albeit widely available, are nevertheless valuable to you as an investor.

The upshot: The first and most accessible place to get information about stocks is in the general publications that cover them.

The Specialized Business Media

Just as the mass business media is valuable, the specialized media can offer choice morsels of information that, as a bonus, are not as widely known. These publications are especially good for identifying high-octane stocks, companies under Wall Street's radar screen whose success is mostly known only to customers, employees, and others in the industry.

One way to catch tomorrow's stars is to dig into these trade journals—these narrow-gauge magazines and/or Web sites designed for an industry's insiders—and see what kinds of trends they're uncovering. Computer culture magazine *Wired* (admittedly the most mainstream of "trades"), for example, is generally a better source of emerging tech stock ideas than *The New York Times* or Merrill Lynch. Whereas mainstream reporters and analysts wait until a revolution is under way to report it, *Wired* thrives on ideas that *might* be revolutionary.

To take two examples, in May 1998, long before the rest of us understood the implications of unlimited bandwidth, *Wired* ran a feature on Qwest Communication's (Q:NYSE) efforts to build the world's biggest fiber-optic network. In the next 18 months, Qwest's stock price almost tripled, while all kinds of similar companies (which readers of the article would have been actively seeking) were up even more. The magazine's October 1997 article "Dawn of the Hydrogen Age" opened with a look at fuel cell maker Ballard Power Systems (BLDP:Nasdaq), which ran from 17 to 114 in the next two-plus years.

Most trade journals are a lot less fun to read than *Wired*, but whether their beat is hospital management, chain stores, or biotech, they all work pretty much the same way, ferreting out trends and interesting variations on themes before the rest of the world catches on. And where it used to be impossible to keep up with more than one or two trade journals, the Internet now makes it much easier.

It's now possible to pursue an idea or company from one end of the trade press to another. Type, say, "optical switch" into the search window of infotech journal *ZDNet,* and you get several articles, along with suggestions for other search terms like optical core switch, optical fiber, and optic mirror switch.

Or go to a meta-search engine like Electric Library (www.newsdirectory.com), described more fully on page 109, for a multiple-source search. In the meantime, here are a few trade sites to get you started:

Computers/Internet

Upside Today (free)
www.upside.com
Silicon Valley's business magazine, it's well written and sharply focused on the computer/Internet business and its movers and shakers.

Good Morning, Silicon Valley (free)
www.mercurycenter.com/svetch/reports/gmsv
*The San Jose Mercury News'*s online tech section is the Valley's hometown paper, offering an inside look at the infotech world.

Wired (free)
www.wired.com
Again, less revolutionary than it once was, but still an interesting source for technological trends.

Industry Standard (free)
www.thestandard.com
The leading magazine of the business of the New Economy, *Industry Standard* gives a good sense of which business models actually have a shot at making it.

CNET (free)
www.cnet.com
More focused on technology news than technology *investing* news, CNET is nevertheless a good place to find out what's going on with companies, which generally translates into action in stocks.

Networking and Internet Infrastructure

Business Communications Review (free)
www.bcr.com/bcrmag/default.asp
Here you'll find articles like "Can Fiber Make It Down the Last Mile?" and "The Death of Digital Telecom."

EETimes (free)
www.eetimes.com
If you have an engineering background, then you'll get the gist of things like "Silicon nanoparticle research heats up," and "Inova crafts Gbit serial link."

America's Network (free)
www.americasnetwork.com
All about telecommunications technologies.

Biotechnology

Biotechnology Industry Organization (BIO) (free)
www.bio.org
The industry's trade organ, BIO is a site that's rich in background on issues ranging from cloning to gene therapy to transgenic crops. It also offers an alphabetical listing of over 70 biotech journals with Web sites, as well as other countries' biotech sites. Use this as a starting point.

Genetic Engineering News (partly free)
www.genwire.com
The Web site has only abstracts of print articles, plus a daily news brief. But it's a decent place to start.

BioWorld Today (free)
www.bioworld.com
Features fresh company and financial news for the industry.

Columnists and Pundits

Beyond publications, there are certain individual columnists who stand out in offering great investing ideas—ideas both to gravitate toward and steer away from. Some of today's best online stock columnists draw on contacts and training to find hot and/or troubled stocks and pass their insights on to readers, laced with varying amounts of analysis, humor, and wisdom.

That kind of reportage is part of the founding vision of *TheStreet.com*. It should come as no surprise that we advocate following as many top columnists, with as many diverse points of view, as possible. The trick is to separate the brilliant few from the wanna-bes, has-beens, and never-weres. So before you put your money where a columnist's mouth is, go through their archived writings and look for:

- *Clarity of thought*
  Do you understand the whys behind their advice?
- *Documented results*
  Do they reveal their record and admit mistakes?
- *Willingness to be negative*
  Are they willing to discourage you from a stock as quickly as they are to sing one's praises?

Columnists who get high marks on all counts are rare, as you'll find out once you start surveying the field. We think *TheStreet.com*'s Real-Money.com, a subscription site, features the most impressive array of columnists out there. Herb Greenberg, for example, has made his name unearthing accounting problems and financial woes at companies with seemingly hot stocks.

Below, we've listed a handful of additional writers we find worth watching.

Harry Aloof, Wall Street Traders
www.wstraders.com (subscription)
Aloof is an old-school technical analyst (a chart user) who follows volume and price "momentum" or sharp movement. Each night Aloof screens for the stocks with the highest volume and then applies a series of other tests to get at the stocks with both liquidity—lots of shares that are actively traded—and momentum. Then, around 6 A.M., he publishes his list, offering subscribers (it's a paid site) an entry point and an exit price. His main column, in which he profiles the day's best bet, is available on more than 50 sites throughout the Web, many of them free.

Richard Hefter
www.America-iNvest.com (free)
Hefter's beat, via his "Editor's Choice" column, is growth—stocks whose earnings are propelling forward, along with the price. "I look for stocks in interesting, trendy industries and then see which analysts are getting behind them." The column includes some other writers as well.

Robert Green
www.Briefing.com (subscription)
To fill his three weekly columns, Green haunts technology conferences, listening to the speeches and buttonholing CEOs. His quarry: companies with "a sustained competitive edge in a growing market." Over the past couple of years, Green has found plenty. Two early picks—Cree (CREE:Nasdaq) and Metromedia Fiber Network (MFNX:Nasdaq)—quintupled in the ensuing 18 months.

Jon Markman, MSN MoneyCentral
www.moneycentral.com (free)
Markman is the polar opposite of the caffeinated, in-and-out trading guru. In fact, he offers his readers the prospect of market-beating returns in *one hour a year*. His secret: precisely crafted screens that turn up companies with great year-ahead potential. Sound good? Then visit Markman's SuperModels page at moneycentral.msn.com/articles/invest/models/5216.asp.

Steve Harmon
www.SiliconInvestor.com (free—this column)
A former Jupiter Communications Internet analyst who now runs his own Internet investment company, Harmon pops up all over the Net. But he's easiest to catch at Silicon Investor, where his "NetStocks" column is one of the site's top draws.

Bob Gabele
www.thomsoninvest.net (subscription)
Each day Gabele highlights a stock with exceptional insider buying and selling activity. For an annual subscription, his *Insider Chronicle* newsletter cooks the various kinds of insider activity down to one rank for each company, offering an important extra indicator to go with your fundamental and technical analysis.

David Smith
www.Worldlyinvestor.com (free)
Managing director of financial research firm Grayling Management, Smith specializes in Asian stocks, offering insight into a hyper-growth market that's undercovered by the United States media. As more Japanese and Chinese IPOs start acting like their United States counterparts, we'll all want to know what this guy is turning up.

Message Boards and Individual Investor Research

So far we've talked about sources of ideas from professionals—mostly journalists—who individually or through a publication have become accessible online. But the Internet has unleashed an entirely separate arena of stock ideas: those of individuals. The most common platforms for individuals to share stock ideas has been stock message boards. But more recently, investors have gravitated to sites that let them post their own research on companies, for sale to other individual investors.

Some investors rely heavily on message board and individual research sites for finding stock ideas. I don't recommend that. Though I'll detail ways in the following pages to help sort out valuable from lame "posts," I think there's too much dreck on the boards for investors to depend on them.

What I think *is* valuable is for an investor to check out the message board chatter on a stock you're already thinking about buying. Sometimes posters will link to interesting articles. Or they'll discuss business issues that you'll be glad to have known about. It's another source of information, but it shouldn't be your main source.

That said, here's some suggestions on how to approach these sites.

Message Boards

Boards generally feature five kinds of posters:

Who Can Ya Trust?

Newbies (thumbs down)
Meanies (thumbs down)
Pump and Dumpers (thumbs down)
Operators (thumbs up)
Industry Insiders (thumbs up)

Newbies Newcomers to the stock, the subject, and/or investing in general. Newbies make statements like "We just bought 2,000 shares. I researched a little, I hope I was right, we are very gun-shy and have been out of market for a month due to big loss on penny stock. Now with the little we have left, I was going to try and recover our past losses. . . . This looks like a great stock to keep. All Strong buy recommendations throughout the Web . . . What is the projected high for this stock in near future?" (This is a verbatim quote from a small-cap stock's message board. Sadly, as this is written, the stock is underwater.)

Meanies Meanies are disturbed individuals who have chosen this forum to battle their inner demons. Their trademark is the personal attack, generally laced with capitalized profanities. No need to supply examples here; you'll find more than enough if you start frequenting the boards.

Pump and Dumpers These are traders who have a position and are trying to move a stock's price, often with false, misleading, pseudo–inside information about upcoming announcements, new products, or lucrative contracts. The dreaded pump-and-dump artists pump up a stock's price with a lot of cheerleading and then dump their position. Because most bulletin boards allow users to hide their identity behind multiple aliases, even one of these bottom feeders can create the illusion of widespread interest in a small, thinly traded stock, simply by posting numerous messages under various names. Be wary of someone who seems just a tad too energetic about a position.

Operators Operators are savvy players who understand the market in general and have taken an interest in this particular company or subject. They tend to be much more balanced—and in turn trustworthy—than the pump and dumpers.

Industry Insiders Industry insiders have a grasp of the field and/or specific knowledge of a company and its prospects. There was, for instance, the time when CMGI (CMGI:Nasdaq) chief executive David Wetherell spent a week's vacation logged onto Yahoo!'s CMGI message board, which *Business Week* likened to "Mark McGwire taking a seat on a plane filled with rabid baseball fans."

On most boards—like elsewhere in life—the first three personality types outnumber the last two by approximately a hundred to one. But the last two are worth paying attention to, because they bring an expert's perspective to a stock and, unlike most other informed sources, share their insights free of charge. You'll know the good guys by the following:

How to Rate 'Em

Familiarity
Identity
Expertise
Popularity

Familiarity If someone's posted frequently and intelligently in the past, that's a good sign. Pump and dumpers, as the name implies, tend to wreak their havoc and move on. So if a post gets your adrenaline flowing, check the poster's record by clicking on their screen name to pull up their other recent posts and/or a profile. Silicon Investor's StockTalk Section (it's subscription for posters), for instance, has a PeopleMarks function that lets you search by screen name. A few minutes of this kind of digging, and you'll be better able to place the poster in his or her rightful personality slot.

Identity If posters use their real name, that implies an intent to stand behind their words. (Unless they're lying about their name!)

Expertise If a poster brings something of value to the table, beyond an opinion, that's a good sign he knows what he's talking about. Something from the trade press, or, better yet, a peer-reviewed journal, might be news to 99% of the world, giving it some potential predictive value. It implies that the poster knows the subject well enough to find and judge technical ideas.

Popularity Popularity is about as valuable as it was in high school. It tells you who's well liked but not necessarily much more. Still, several boards offer participants the chance to rate the quality of posts. These are cooked down into a score for each screen name, which gives an instant guide to the poster's credibility among his or her peers. Raging Bull (ragingbull.com), meanwhile, tracks the number of times a poster has been bookmarked by other members.

Most people tend to visit the individual stock boards, like the Gateway (GTW:NYSE) board or the Lands' End (LE:NYSE) board. This is unfortunate, as those are the haunts the newbies, meanies, and pump and dumpers tend to frequent most. On *topic* boards, people tend to be more engaged on a general subject. They're a place where you can really learn something.

For stock ideas, try the boards dedicated to subjects that you either understand or would like to. Silicon Investor's biotechnology thread, for instance, involves a lot of philosophizing and technical arcana and can be maddeningly stream-of-consciousness at times. But it features some great minds on the topic and will help you identify some of the hottest emerging companies in their fields. And check out the many "Gorilla Game" threads, based on the best-selling book of the same name that lays out a system for finding "gorilla" (i.e., dominant, standard-setting)

Stock Screens

Let's be clear about what you're doing when you collect lists of stocks from trade journals, pundits' columns, and message boards: You're looking for stock ideas from someone else. But you can skip the indirect approach. With a good stock screening service, you can input criteria and get your own list for further research. In subsequent chapters about fundamental analysis of stocks and when to buy, we'll talk about the various criteria you can employ. For now, keep in mind these stock screening sites:

StockScreener (free)
www.stockscreener.com
Drawing on data provided by Hoover's Online, StockScreener presents you with a page of categories like Ratios and Growth Rates, where you define the ranges, as in "price-to-earnings ratio between 5 and 15." You just fill in the boxes that matter to you and leave the rest blank, click on Go, and there's your screen. Some other tools have more bells and whistles, but this one has a nice combination of power and simplicity. As such, it's a great place to start.

MoneyCentral Investment Finder (free)
moneycentral/investor/finder/welcome.asp
Not easy to find, but once you're there, this is one of the most powerful free screening tools in existence. It lets you create just about any screen you can think up, while offering two levels of preset screens, simple and advanced.

CNBC (free)
www.cnbc.com
This site offers both preset screens and the ability to build your own screens. And—this is really cool—it instantly tests a given screen against historical markets.

Quicken (free)
www.quicken.com
Quicken has a very accessible stock screener in its investing section. Its "EasyStep" feature helps novices figure out how to select criteria by giving helpful explanations of terms like "price-to-book" and "market cap" along the way.

Zacks (free)
www.zacks.com
The focus here is on earnings, with screens geared to letting you slice and dice analyst estimates and earnings surprises/disappointments in ways that aren't possible anywhere else. But user beware. This software has the highest learning curve—and the highest frustration quotient—of any we tried. Be prepared to read the instructions patiently.

companies like Cisco Systems (CSCO:Nasdaq) and Microsoft (MSFT: Nasdaq). Motley Fool (www.fool.com) and Silicon Investor are good sources for these.

Investor Research Sites

The most recent step in message-board evolution has been the sites that feature individual investor research. This stuff is supposed to be akin to the stock research that Wall Street analysts do. But rather than being created by professionals, it's generated by individual investors.

Sites like www.iExchange.com enable investors to post their own written research on a stock and sell it to other site members. The site managers rate these industrious individuals on the track record of their stock picks, so that other readers can better judge which research is worth purchasing. Soapbox.com, from the Motley Fool, has a similar offering.

These sites are relatively new, so their worthiness remains untested. Still, the idea of injecting some accountability into the posting process is a good one. And better to have written support behind an idea than the typical "it's going to the moon" message-board post. At this point, I recommend you use these sites to see if there's anything helpful available about a stock that you're considering. Since you often have to pay up, check that the researcher has a good rating!

Databases

Since the Internet's arrival, raw data of all kinds have flooded the network. Thousands of documents pour into databases each day, creating the ever-expanding needle in a haystack for investors. Because of their volume, databases are not ideal for finding ideas from scratch (though we suggest a few ways to do that). Rather, it's helpful to know how to use these sources once there's a stock you're interested in. Here I review the electronic database of documents filed with the Securities and Exchange Commission, the EDGAR database, as well as news databases.

EDGAR Database

Public companies are required to file multiple forms each year with the SEC. Some of these forms are standard, like annual and quarterly reports and proxy reports, for shareholder votes. Others are more event-driven, reflecting, say, sales of stock by an insider or some special event affecting a company that requires notification.

Until the mid-1990s, these documents were filed by paper with the SEC's Washington, D.C., office. But since then, the agency has required that most documents be filed electronically. The SEC collects these forms in its Electronic Data Gathering, Analysis, and Retrieval (EDGAR) database, which is available to the public at www.sec.gov and other Web sites. Below we list the most useful SEC forms.

The Search Engines

Beyond the government's EDGAR site, other private sites with high-powered search capabilities include EDGAR Online (www.edgar-online.com)—the fancy search functions are subscription only—and 10-K Wizard (www.10kwizard.com), which is free. They can do things such as:

- Pull up all the instances where a given person or company appears in an SEC filing.
- Narrow the search to specific forms, e.g., 13D, 8-K.

Key SEC Forms

10-K/10-Q: These are the annual and quarterly reports. The annual report is a comprehensive overview of a company's business. The quarterly report includes financial results for that quarter.

13D: Form 13D has to be filed by an investor who buys more than 5% of a company's stock.

13G: 13Gs are like 13Ds, but they're filed by institutions like mutual funds, which do not intend to influence control of the company.

144: 144 is filed by insiders and some others who intend to sell a company's stock.

8-K: 8-K is mandatory when a company discloses a "material" or significant event. This can run the gamut from the CFO running off to Jamaica with all the company's money, to a big new order, to personnel changes at the top. Think of it as the anti–press release, where, after a company spins the public, it has to tell the real story to the SEC. To take just one of hundreds of recent examples, when wireless phone pioneer Iridium ran into credit problems in 1999, they first surfaced in an 8-K filing.

13F: 13F is a quarterly filing made by mutual funds and other large institutional stockholders of their holdings. If, say, Fidelity has changed its stance on a stock you're watching, you'll find it here.

14A: Proxies are the richest documents for data about a company's top five officers and board of directors. Here you'll find their base pay, bonus, stock options, and the other boards on which they sit.

- Set up "alerts" that e-mail you when the object of your interest appears in a filing.
- Search by keyword or concept. Type in something like "stock option repricing" or "changes in credit facility," and you can find out which companies are flying these red flags. "Personal aircraft" will show you which CEOs are taking full advantage of their lofty positions.

Arcane Databases

Lists and speeches and transcripts, oh, my.

They sound like the stuff of a political campaign. But actually, for the patient and industrious, lists, speeches, and transcripts can be tremendous sources for stock ideas. And unfortunately, the mainstream online search engines will get you only so far with this stuff. That's because search engines, no matter how sophisticated, can bring back only what they can access, and huge sections of the Web are closed off to them. There are other specialized databases that proactively compile, catalogue, and make available otherwise inaccessible information. Here are three worth checking out:

- Direct Search (free)

  This site (http://gwis2.circ.gwu.edu/~gprice/direct.htm) is run by George Washington University librarian Gary Price. One subsection of his site stands out.

  List of Lists, as the name implies, culls lists from magazines and organizations around the world. These lists—top 100, best of the breed—are gold mines of ideas, because 1) the people producing the magazines tend to know their territory, and 2) they often highlight companies that have yet to make it to Wall Street's radar screen.

  Unless you have a preternatural combination of free time and disposable income, you probably won't be subscribing to or even visiting the Web sites of more than a handful of these obscure publications. But move a couple of mouse clicks within Gary Price's List of Lists and you can access hundreds. Here are the top-10 companies from two randomly chosen 1998 lists from the site, along with their 1999 performance:

Deloitte and Touche 1998 Technology Fast 500
Company/ticker/52-week return
from Dec. 31, 1998 (or first day of trading)–Dec. 31, 1999

Advanced Fibre Communications (AFCI:Nasdaq)	307%
ICOS Corporation (ICOS:Nasdaq)	flat
OmniCell Technologies (Not yet public)	
SeaChange International (SEAC:Nasdaq)	767%
Incyte Pharmaceuticals (INCY:Nasdaq)	61%

Insight Technology (Not public)
Alpha Technologies Group (ATGI:Nasdaq)   292%
Yurie Systems (acquired in 1999)
Applied Digital Solutions (ADSX:Nasdaq)   111%
OrthoLogic (OLGC:Nasdaq)   −23%

Red Herring's 1998 10-to-Watch List
Company/ticker/52-week return
from Dec. 31, 1998 (or first day of trading)–Dec. 31, 1999

Copper Mountain Networks (CMTN:Nasdaq)   42%
Critical Path (CPTH:Nasdaq)   43%
Dragon Systems (Private and subsequently acquired)
EToys (ETYS:Nasdaq)   −66%
Extreme Networks (EXTR:Nasdaq)   51%
Informatica (INFA:Nasdaq)   262%
Maker Communication (MAKR:Nasdaq)   89%
Rhythms Netconnections (RTHM:Nasdaq)   −55%
Scient (SCNT:Nasdaq)   430%
Starmedia Networks (STRM:Nasdaq)   54%

These were pretty promising lists. But unless you were a reader of Deloitte or Red Herring, you might not have known they existed.

- www.NewsDirectory.com (subscription)
  This site offers searchable archives of 4,000 newspapers, magazines, books, trade journals, and other media grouped according to geography and subject matter. It also features a truly awesome search engine called Electric Library, which lets you search through multiple sources for mentions of a given company or technology. To see the difference, try entering the name of a favorite company (the more obscure, the better) into a standard finance site's "news" window and compare it to what you get here.
  We tried this with emerging biotech firm Gliatech (GLIA: Nasdaq) and found that Yahoo! and MSN yielded long but repetitive lists of company press releases and analyst upgrades and downgrades, while the Electronic Library search brought

up mentions of the company in newspaper articles, books, trade journals, and even a transcript of its CEO being interviewed on CNBC.

- **www.InvisibleWeb.com** (free)
  This is a directory of more than 10,000 databases, archives, and search engines that contain information that traditional search engines have been unable to access. Unlike Price's more bookshelf-like presentation, Invisible Web offers structured searches, where you input, say, "investments," and get back subcategories like "finance > stocks." Then you drill down further subcategories, until you find the specific thing you seek.

To combine these sites into a coherent program, try using Direct Search to generate undiscovered stocks, and Invisible Web and News-Directory.com to research them.

6

Figuring Out the Financials

The financials. We've talked about where to find good ideas, but even a good stock hunter needs to know the basics of how a company does business. Unless you're a hunch player (not a recommended strategy) or a pure chartist (see Chapter 7), you should be able to understand a company's financials. And thanks to some super tools on the Internet, it's easy for even a numbers rube to get the basics needed to help make a good investment decision.

The financials are, or should be, a bread and butter tool for most investors. Those who study the financials are often referred to as fundamentalists, or "fundys." But even chartists—those who rely primarily on charts to make their investment decisions—will peek at the financials, just as a fundamentalist will sneak a look at a chart.

Fundamentalists judge businesses by objective financial measures such as revenues, operating margins, and cash flow. For different industries, and for different stages in a company's life, certain measures carry more weight than others. For fledgling companies getting established, for example, the focus tends to be on revenue or market share. But soon enough it turns to profitability. No matter what the industry, eventually a public company will be expected to produce earnings—income. Ultimately, every company is measured by its success at meeting and enhancing profitability. That's why fundamentalists pay attention to the numbers.

In the late 1990s, old-school fundamentalists found themselves seething with disgust and frustration over what they saw as a rejection of these basic tenets of valuing a stock based on its profitability. Hundreds of so-called New Economy companies raised multiple millions of dollars selling new stock in the public market before they were even close to profitability. The fundys chalked up the bidding to mass hysteria, calling the phenomenon a "bubble" and predicting its swift and painful demise. "Valuations are too far out of whack!" they cried.

To a certain extent, the fundys had a point. Plenty of investors jumped into stocks of tantalizing new companies they knew nothing about just because they thought the price would keep rushing up.

But at the same time, much of what was happening in the Internet stock frenzy of the 1990s was fundamental in the purest sense. New businesses were being born. Investors needed to evaluate them—to decide which had the best chances of becoming leaders in their fields, be it e-commerce, Web content, Internet wireless, networking infrastructure, handheld electronic devices, or any other emerging industry. It's a lot tougher to size up these nascent industries than it is, say, to judge age-old businesses like restaurants or footwear.

The nature of these New Economy businesses was *new*. And so while many investors studied them as rigorously as they did any other company, they had to take more chances and make more leaps of faith in selecting the players they thought would survive and thrive. The idea was that it was better to be early, and risk being wrong, than to miss out on a great opportunity altogether.

Of course, that calculus works best—if at all—when the risks of being wrong are greatly diminished. And that's what this chapter is all about: How to figure out which acorns and saplings have the best chance of growing into a sturdy oak; how to figure out which established companies will be toppled by encroaching competitors; how to figure out which market leaders will lose their perch.

The best place to begin is with the company's financials. The principles we review apply to new and mature companies alike. Because of the Web, financial statements of public companies are now available to individual investors easily and free online. Better yet, many of the choice morsels from the financial statements are already broken out for you—complete with industry and historical comparisons—on investor Web sites, so you don't have to trudge through the actual documents on your own.

Strollers and Trollers

To help guide you through the process, I've enlisted the help of Tracy Byrnes, our resident tax and accounting columnist and an alum of accounting giant Ernst & Young. We've approached the material on two tracks: one for the "strollers" and one for the "trollers."

The strollers among you are probably somewhat new to investing, or you just don't have the time or inclination to tackle financial details. To help you, we've culled the most important numbers you'll need to know to at least give you some protection in your investing choice. You won't even have to read the main financial statements.

The trollers are more ambitious about data detail. You've got more patience for this stuff, and are willing to make more time for it. For such readers, we will give you the unabridged version of rigorous financial analysis.

Whether you're a stroller or troller, whether you're investing in new or old economy companies, this chapter teaches you the numbers you can rely on to reduce your risk and make smart investing decisions.

One note: There is no magic formula with these numbers. No single figure or ratio makes a stock a buy, or even a sell. Rather, together they help paint a picture of a company's health. If you see enough separate signs of infirmity, it's time to move on. If you see a relatively healthy company with seemingly strong prospects, then it's time to decide whether or when to buy. You might find a good company but decide that its stock is far too overpriced. That kind of valuation decision is addressed later in Chapter 8: "When to Buy."

Why Not Rely on Stock Analysts?

Before you begin to delve into the world of stock analysis, you may be asking, Why not rely on the people who get paid to do this: stock analysts? Stock analysts' reports, available at sites like Multex.com or Zacks.com, *can* have some helpful research on corporate financials. But there are limits. For starters, Wall Street analysts just haven't kept pace with the spate of newly public companies. Nearly 550 companies went public in 1999—on top of 375 in 1998. Tack on the existing 10,000 public companies on the NYSE, Nasdaq, and Amex, and you've got a lot of companies that go wanting for good stock analyst coverage.

Also, much analyst coverage is not exactly objective. Analysts' primary responsibilities include helping brokers get clients to buy stocks, and currying favor with companies to get their investment banking business. For more on analysts, see our discussion in Chapter 9, "Earnings, Splits, Buybacks, and other Events in a Stock's Life."

While you can certainly use analyst research to supplement your own, never rely on it alone.

Getting Started and the MD&A

There are four main financial documents from a company's annual report that will tell you most of what you need to know: a company's balance sheet, income statement, cash-flow statement, and Management's Discussion & Analysis (the MD&A), which basically reviews material elaborated on in the other three. For the trollers, there's also the treasure trove of the footnotes to the financial statements. Most financial analysis books focus on the balance sheet and income statement. But in our view, the MD&A and the cash flow statement are more important.

Throughout your financial analysis, it is important to keep in mind the value of relative comparisons: How does this company's performance compare to that of its industry peers? Revenue growth of 10% might be strong in one industry but weak in the next. For instance, a 5% annual revenue growth may be about all that's expected from a food products company like Bestfoods (BFO:NYSE), maker of Skippy peanut butter.

But you'd be disappointed if a computer hardware company like Compaq (CPQ:NYSE) wasn't seeing at least 20% revenue growth. An operating margin (the percentage of revenues a company keeps after paying operating expenses) of 8% may be impressive for a construction and mining equipment manufacturer like Caterpillar (CAT: NYSE) but weak for a beverage company like Anheuser-Busch (BUD: NYSE) or Coca-Cola (KO:NYSE), whose margins typically hover around 14%.

Fortunately, plenty of Web sites provide that kind of industry comparison in simple tables.

Finding the Financials

Start by pulling up the 10-K of a stock you own or have been watching. The 10-K is the official document that companies must file with the Securities and Exchange Commission 90 days after the close of their fiscal year. Within the 10-K you'll find the financial statements, footnotes, and a report from the auditors—precisely what you need to start your investigation.

Also pull up all the 10-Qs filed since the last 10-K. The 10-Q is essentially a quarterly update to the 10-K.

Financial Statements—They're All Over the Web

Company's homepage—investor relations section
www.edgar-online.com
www.freeedgar.com
www.rapidresearch.com
www.sec.gov

The MD&A

Once you've got the 10-K, strollers and trollers alike should scroll to Management's Discussion & Analysis. It comes right before the actual financial statements. Management has a story to tell, and the MD&A is where you hear it. It's a narrative introduction of the company's operating results and current outlook. The finance department generally pens this section, so don't expect a Grisham novel. You'll find a good overall explanation of the numbers here, and that's about it. For instance, there was no mention of Microsoft's (MSFT:Nasdaq) antitrust trial with the Department of Justice in its 1999 MD&A. There was a big footnote about it after the financial statements, but apparently the finance guys didn't think you needed to know about all that up front.

Still, the MD&A is worthwhile in that it provides a solid overview of the company and what's going on in the industry. MD&As have umpteen subheads, so we recommend that you jump to the ones suggested here. Take notes as you read. You might even consider keeping a Word document or notebook open so you can jot down questions that you'll want answers to from the main financial statements and know which numbers you need to compare to the industry averages.

Revenue Here you should find a detailed summary of revenue results over the last three years. Were there material increases or decreases in sales? If so, what explanation does management offer? Jot it down in your Word file or notebook to make sure the verbiage coincides with your subsequent analysis of the numbers in the financials.

Material World

"Material" is accountant/lawyer speak for any information that would affect the stock price were the public to find out about it. For instance, a $2 million expense is not material to Disney's (DIS:NYSE) $1.19 billion bottom line. So management may not even tell you about it. But a $2 million expense would be extremely material to Juniper Networks (JNPR:Nasdaq), the Internet infrastructure provider, since it reported negative net income of $9 million in 1999. Juniper's management would have to tell you about it. Disney's wouldn't.

Look for consistency in the percentage change in sales from one year to the next. Granted, hindsight is always 20/20, but when Sunbeam (SOC:NYSE) announced double-digit sales growth back in 1997, that should've been a red flag to anyone who had been following the stock, since it was operating in a single-digit growth industry (as you could have seen by looking at the growth rate percentages in the "comparison" section of investor site marketguide.com). It's one thing to strive to be an industry leader, but the company produces barbecues and irons. So when all its peers were reporting 9% growth rates and Sunbeam reported a 22% rate, it should've raised eyebrows. Are more people having picnics? Are shirts more wrinkled than usual? If so, then why weren't Sunbeam's peers reporting similar growth rates?

As it turns out, Sunbeam was allegedly playing accounting games and creating fictitious sales. The company was forced to redo its financials for 1996, 1997, and the first quarter of 1998 to reflect the true numbers. The stock paid for the trouble, falling some 90%.

Expenses Expenses generally are detailed next. Here you find out what the company spends to operate the business. If you're looking at a company like the Gap (GPS:NYSE), expect to see money spent advertising its brand. If you're researching a pharmaceutical or tech company, you probably should see a huge chunk going to research and development. As you would expect, one third, or $3 billion, of Microsoft's total operating expenses was spent on R&D in fiscal year 1999. Trollers, note any big expenses. They will be detailed later in the footnotes to the financial statements.

Liquidity and Capital Resources Next, there generally will be a discussion of the liquidity, or financial condition of the company. You'll get a detailed description of what you'll later see in the cash flow statement. You'll see what kind of debt it currently has and any future commitments it expects to take on going forward. Debt can be in the form of bonds, notes, or mortgages that must be paid by a specified date, a.k.a. maturity.

Having debt is not a bad thing. A company needs cash to run and grow its business. For instance, in 1998 the Gap incurred debt to open new stores. But since the company eventually has to repay these outstanding loans, owing too much stifles cash flow. So while taking on debt may be necessary to expand operations, managing its repayment is very important.

How much debt is too much? Later in our analysis we'll look at the debt-to-equity ratio and how it compares to those of industry peers. This section of the MD&A helps put that purely financial ratio in some context.

Segment Reporting While the SEC rules require that management discuss the company's different business segments, it leaves it up to the discretion of management as to whether it should break all the numbers down by segments in the MD&A. You'll find those details in the footnotes to the financial statements.

At a minimum, you'll get a detailed description here of the different businesses the company has its hand in.

For instance, if you read Sara Lee's (SLE:NYSE) 1999 MD&A, you'll learn that not only does the company make frozen pies and Jimmy Dean sausage, they also own the original Wonderbra and Hanes panty hose.

M&A Activity   Pay attention to the details of the company's acquired or "disposed of" operations. Understanding recent mergers and acquisitions (M&A) activity helps you understand the company's strategic direction.

As an example, PepsiCo (PEP:NYSE) spun off its restaurant business, Tricon (YUM:NYSE), back in September 1997, so it could focus on its main fare—soda and chips (they own Frito-Lay). PepsiCo contended that the disposal of that segment allows them to compete more effectively with its competitors (read: Coke). The logic has seemed to have helped. Since the spinoff, PepsiCo is up 27.5% through August 1, 2000, while Coke has seen only a 5% price rise over the same period, although they're both way off the S&P 500's rise of around 54% for that period.

On the flip side, is the company you're researching on a buying spree? How well do these additional businesses fit in with its core competencies? The Seagram Company (VO:NYSE) was a great example of acquisition confusion. Hankering to be a Hollywood mogul, the company's CEO, Edgar Bronfman, Jr., brought the distilled spirits and wine company into the media business with the purchase of a controlling stake in MCA, parent of Universal Studios, in 1995.

At that time, shareholders had no idea what type of company they were investing in. And it hasn't become any clearer. Seagram has since announced plans to merge with the Paris-based utilities company Vivendi to create a merged company called Vivendi-Seagram. But, as reported in *The New York Times* on July 31, 2000, analysts are confused as to what the combined company will do. "Analysts are still trying to figure out what Vivendi is—or at least what it is up to with Seagram," the article said. When Wall Street analysts can't size up companies, they often don't pay them much attention in the form of research and positive ratings. Even if you have the patience to dissect a complicated company, Wall Street confusion does not bode well for a stock.

Future Plans Now you know how the company did. Look out for what it expects to do in the future. Granted, you can't take its plans as gold, but you should know what management views as its strategic next steps. If, for example, the company has a burgeoning Net strategy, this is where you may find it.

Wrap-up You may be the type to dissect other sections in the MD&A. But if not (we're not), you're done. You should now have a good feel for the numbers—where sales and expenses are going, where the company allocated its money in the past, and what its plans are for the future. It's a good basis for your analysis going forward. And in case you came across any red flags, you've noted them as you were reading. Now you can focus your investigation on finding answers to your questions.

The Financial Statements

So you've read the company's story in the MD&A and now have a notion of how the company attempts to make money and what it sees as its niche. But does the story make sense? Is it logical?

That's where the financial statements come in.

There are three main financial statements—the balance sheet, the statement of earnings, a.k.a. the income statement, and the cash flow statement.

The balance sheet is a summary of a company's assets and liabilities at a specific point in time, generally the last day of the fiscal period (quarter or year). Assets are what the company owns and what it has a right to—like cash, property, and inventory. Liabilities are what it owes. Subtract liabilities from assets, and anything left is net worth, or shareholders' equity, in accounting speak.

Assets – liabilities = shareholders' equity

The income statement shows sales and expenses over a period of time, like a quarter or a year. Sales less expenses yields income (or lack thereof).

The cash flow statement—the most valuable of the three—mea-

For the Trollers: Comparison Trick

Since the finance folks write the MD&A, it's generally a templated document. That is, each year it basically says the same thing with different numbers. So, if you want to determine if, say, M&A activity is higher this year or if the company is fulfilling expectations it set in last year's MD&A about future expansion, compare this year's MD&A to last year's.

Microsoft Word can help you track the changes in this year's MD&A against last year's.

Here's how. First, go to your company's current 10-K filing and save the MD&A section in a Word document. Do that by using the cut and paste function under Edit. Select the MD&A and copy and paste it into a Word document. Save the file, let's call it "MDACurrent," and close it.

Then go back to an earlier filing, say the previous year's 10-K. This time you copy and paste the same section into another new Microsoft document. Call this one "MDAPrevious." Save the document and close the file. There should now be two files on your hard drive: MDACurrent and MDAPrevious.

Comparison of Microsoft MD&As, 1998–99

Microsoft develops, manufactures, licenses, and supports a wide range of software products for a multitude of computing devices. Microsoft software ~~products, including~~ includes scalable operating systems for intelligent ~~devices,~~ devices, personal ~~computers~~ computers (PCs), and servers; server applications for client/server environments; ~~environments; business and consumer~~ knowledge worker productivity applications; ~~software~~ and software development tools; ~~and Internet and intranet software and technologies.~~ The Company's ~~interactive~~ online efforts include ~~entertainment and information software~~ the MSN Network of Internet products and ~~programs; MSN, the Microsoft Network online service; Internet-based services;~~ services; e-commerce platforms; and alliances with companies involved ~~with~~ with broadband access and various forms of ~~digital~~ digital interactivity. Microsoft also ~~sells personal computer input devices and books,~~ licenses consumer software programs; sells PC input devices; trains and certifies system integrators; and researches and develops advanced ~~technologies~~ technologies for future software products.

Now you can compare the documents. Go to File and open MDACurrent. Next, while leaving MDACurrent open, go to Tools and click open Track Changes. Then click on Compare Documents and choose MDAPrevious. This will open MDAPrevious on top of the MDACurrent document.

A red strike-through line will highlight the old text; blue lines will highlight new text; and regular black type shows the text common to both filings. (If these colors do not show up, adjust your settings by clicking, in this order, Tools, Track Changes, Highlight Changes, and then the Options button.)

Tracking changes will help you get a good feel for how things like revenues and expenses have changed (or not) over the last year.

Note that this very helpful exercise works for any other section of the financial statements as well.

sures cash inflows and outflows over a given period. It's one of the most important measures of a company's financial health. That's because it tells you where the company is getting its money from and where it's spending it. It's like the company's checkbook. It basically tells you whether the company is getting enough money (in actual payments or IOUs) day-to-day and month-to-month to pay its bills—a key sign of a healthy company.

These financial statements are presented in the 10-K or annual report in the order just described. But that's not how you should read them.

Here's our plan of attack: After a stop at the income statement, we'll move to the cash flow statement, where the trollers will spend most of their time. We'll all do a quick visit to the balance sheet, then leave the trollers to tear up the footnotes.

For strollers and trollers, you will need to do some ratio comparisons—for example, looking at the revenue growth rate and the debt-to-equity ratio. We'll explain what the ratio is and what it's showing, but you won't have to get out the calculator. Web sites we'll point you to figure out the ratios for you.

Along the way, you can record information in a copy of one of the financial statement checklists presented in this chapter. Once you unearth and record your company's relevant numbers, your checklist will serve as a one-page snapshot, allowing you a quick overview of the company's financial health.

Before we dive into the numbers, get into a skeptical mind frame. Go in looking for potential problems that would cause the stock's future price to tank. If you look for those, and find a clean bill of health, then you should have the confidence to buy. It's a smarter approach than going forward cheerleading your way into a mistake.

Quick Stop at the Income Statement

Your investigation begins at the income statement (or statement of earnings). It generally comes after the balance sheet, which follows the MD&A. You need to focus only on two numbers on this statement, and both can be found broken out on financial analysis Web sites. You don't even have to look at the actual statement.

Revenues First, the revenue number. Revenues are the company's sales, so you may see "sales" as the section head instead. Revenues/sales represent the total money the company collected for the products it sold or the services it performed. No matter how large or new the company is, you've got to look at its sales.

To start, are there any?

Second, have they increased since last period? Companies are required to report numbers from the current year plus the previous two years in the income statement. So if the company is well established, compare its current revenues to last year's. If you're looking at a company that's less than a year old, pick up the financial statements and compare them to last quarter's. Since quarterly reporting is not required in the income statement, you may have to dig back in the MD&A for these numbers.

Either way, you're looking for an increase—read: growth. It's also good to see projections—which are derived from Wall Street analysts' estimates—of continuing growth. (These aren't in the companies' own statements but can be found on many financial analysis Web sites.) The percentage change in sales from one period to the next is the growth rate.

This information is all available free at a good financial analysis site. Our favorite is marketguide.com. But there are others. *TheStreet.com's* columnist Herb Greenberg, for example, likes stocksheet.com.

Stroller's Financial Checklist

	Company's Number	Up/Down from Prior Period	Industry Comparison	Your Opinions or Questions	Grade +/−
Revenue Growth Rate					
Operating Income (EBIT)					
Operating Margin					
Cash from Operations					
Total Net Cash					
Debt-to-Equity Ratio					

Troller's Financial Checklist

	Company's Number	Up/Down from Prior Period	Industry Comparison	Your Opinions or Questions	Grade +/−
Revenue Growth Rate					
Operating Income (EBIT)					
Operating Margin					
Cash from Operations					
Total Net Cash					
Accounts Receivable Balance					

	Company's Number	Up/Down from Prior Period	Industry Comparison	Your Opinions or Questions	Grade +/–
Accounts Payable Balance					
Receivable Turnover					
Inventory Turnover Ratio					
Debt-to-Equity Ratio					

For this chapter, we'll use marketguide.com. Go to the site and plug in your stock symbol at the upper left. Under "Highlights" in the left-hand navigation bar, you'll find a company's revenue and the growth rate of that revenue over time. If you go to "Comparison," you'll see the company's growth rate compared to its industry, sector, and the S&P 500.

Both marketguide.com and stocksheet.com list industry ratios, so you can do a good comparison of your stock to its peers. Let's assume your company's revenues are down. Did the industry see a drop in revenue too? If so, it may mean the entire sector is having trouble. Or, on the flip side, did the industry have a great year while your company's sales sunk? That could mean specific problems.

Take Lucent (LU:NYSE), the communications equipment company. In summer 2000, the revenue growth year over year was positive. However, analysts were predicting a mere 14% revenue growth at Lucent over the next five years, while its communication equipment peers were looking at around a 46% revenue growth, according to marketguide.com. Just doesn't seem right when selling networking equipment is one of today's hottest businesses. Perhaps that's one of the reasons the stock was trading at about 40, its 52-week low point.

Jot down anything that seems fishy in the questions column of your checklist.

Operating Income   Now you want to move to operating income. This is the "what's left" number after the company pays its operating bills. This number tells you how the company is financially managing the ins and outs of its day-to-day business. At a minimum, you're looking for a positive number. That means it has enough money to support its daily business. Ideally, you'd like to see that your company's operating income is higher than that of its peers. You'd also like to see it increasing over time. Record it in your company checklist.

Operating income is also available on sites like marketguide.com and stocksheet.com, where they break out the income statement for you.

Why aren't we looking at net income? you ask. Because net income—the equivalent of earnings—does not tell you if the business is making money from its actual operations. Net income has other stuff in it that distorts the true picture.

For instance, operating income, commonly dubbed EBIT—earnings before interest and taxes—is pretax money. A company's tax bill can vary drastically from one period to the next, so for comparison's sake, it's better to use pre-tax dollars.

Net income also gets clouded by investment income. Companies, like individual investors, don't like to leave extra cash lying around when it could be invested in the market or private companies, making more money. Actually, that's good money management. But that's not money it made selling its product or services. Whether the company makes good investments with its excess cash does not help you determine if it knows how to run its core business.

Operating Income v. Net Income

Operating Income	Net Income
just income from operations	more than operations
pre-tax money	after taxes
pre-interest money	after interest
no investment income	includes investment income

Microsoft is a great example of a company with huge income from investments, though its core business is also making money. Of the company's $2.44 billion net income in its fiscal second quarter, ended December 31, 1999, $436 million was from investment income. Analysts estimate that extra investment income bumped net income, or earnings, by about 4 cents to 44 cents per share. That's up from 36 cents in the prior year's corresponding quarter.

The Earnings Game

And speaking of earnings . . .

These days, for purposes of financial analysis, earnings are not very helpful. Earnings is another word for net income, or profits. It used to be what determines a stock's price. In the long run, that's still true.

For a stock, though, what's more important than what the earnings are is what Wall Street analysts expect them to be. Analysts come up with an estimated earnings number prior to the end of the company's fiscal period. If management doesn't hit or, in some cases, exceed that magic number, the stock stands to get slaughtered. (See our discussion of analysts and earnings in Chapter 9.)

Because of this pressure from Wall Street, there's plenty of incentive for management to manuever their numbers to make their earnings match or beat the expected figures. As money is shuffled around, "aggressive" accounting and "irregularities" fill the news headlines.

But playing with the numbers just to meet expectations is only a temporary fix. It's like using tape on a window crack—fine for now, but the next gust of wind will shatter the glass. That's why operating income is much more important to you as an investor trying to understand a company. It tells you how the business is doing, not how the company's executives are juggling the analysts.

The same goes for the corresponding price-to-earnings ratio. The P/E ratio takes the stock price and divides it by the last four quarters' worth of earnings per share. A high P/E reflects high expectations for earnings growth. If a high P/E company misses Wall Street's earnings expectations, the stock will likely plunge.

So, how do you judge a P/E? P/E is a valuation method that will help you decide whether or when to buy or sell a *stock,* which to a certain extent is a separate inquiry from whether you think the *business* is solid. That's why P/E is treated separately in Chapter 8, "When to Buy," and Chapter 9, "When to Sell."

Operating margin is a key measure related to operating income. It measures the *percentage* of revenues remaining after a company pays all operating expenses—basically, how much of what a company takes in does it get to keep? Margins are shown as percentages. Again, you're looking for the percentages to be besting the competition and increasing over periods. Analysts call this margin *expansion.*

You might also come across the term *gross margin.* Gross margin is a more product-specific measure. It tells you how much money the company keeps on each item it sells, based on the product costs. The basic ratio is sales less the cost of purchasing raw materials and manufacturing the finished products (i.e., "cost of goods sold") divided by sales. If a mouse pad sells for $10 but costs $5 to make, the gross margin is 50%.

Sale Price $10 – COGS $5/Sale Price $10 = 50% gross margin

If gross margins are expanding (going up) that could mean revenue is increasing, or the cost of making the goods is going down. Both are good things. If the sale price jumps to $15, the margin jumps to 67% ($15 − $5/$15).

But if the margin is declining, sales may be slipping, prices may be dropping, or the cost to make the product may be going up. These are bad things for the future earnings of the company.

While gross margin helps you understand how much a company takes home on each product, operating margin is ultimately a more compelling figure because it indicates how the company is profiting overall. It measures how much the company has left after it pays *all* its operating bills—not only product development and marketing, but also payroll and utilities, for example. Operating margin is calculated by dividing operating income (EBIT) by revenues.

Take Procter & Gamble (PG:NYSE), for instance. Its gross margin was around 45% in summer 2000. For every dollar the company took in as revenue, P&G kept 45 cents before basic expenses. Its industry peers keep around 50 cents. So that means its peers keep more of the profits on product sales.

However, P&G's operating margin was about 16%. After everything was paid—like utility bills and administrative costs—16 cents goes to the company's pocket. Its peers kept only around 14.7 cents at the end of the day, so the company appears to be running a bit more efficiently.

Operating margin is also available on ratio sites. On market-guide.com, you'll find it in the "Comparison" section. Jot down your company's operating margin percentage in your checklist, as well as an industry comparison.

Hellooo—Cash Floooow

Now that you understand ratios like revenue growth rate percentage and operating margin, you begin to have a feel for whether the company's business is making money, how its efforts are improving over time, and how its peers are doing in comparison. Now it's time to flip to the cash flow statement, or the quick-and-dirty equivalent on the ratio Web sites.

The basic value of the cash flow statement is that it tells you where the company is getting its money and how it's using it. It basically shines a bright light on the day-to-day operations of the company, giving you a sense of whether the business has the oil to run smoothly day to day. If it can't do that, then there's trouble in River City.

And cash, as you surely know, is just a good thing to have around. It helps companies get through the inevitable rough times; it helps them make acquisitions. Indeed, it can even make them a more attractive acquisition target.

A company's cash flow is its cash receipts—inflows—less its cash payments—outflows. The cash flow statement is divided into three parts: cash flow from operations, cash flow from investing, and cash flow from financing. Each section has inflows and outflows of cash.

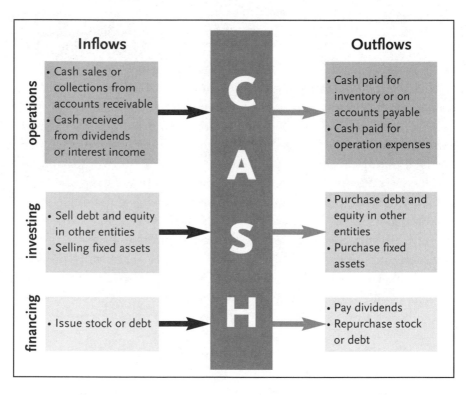

The cash flow statement basically works off a simple formula:

$$
\begin{array}{l}
\text{Cash from operations} \\
+\ \text{Cash from investments} \\
+\ \text{Cash from financing} \\
+\ \text{Beginning cash balance} \\
\hline
\text{Ending cash balance}
\end{array}
$$

Ideally, you don't want to see negative cash flow in a well-established company. That's a sign that the company is not making money from its product or service or that it doesn't have enough support from financing activities.

In a New Economy newbie, though, you could make the opposite argument regarding cash flow from operations. Arguably a company should be cash-flow negative from operations at the outset to get itself established.

Take Red Hat (RHAT:Nasdaq), the Linux operating system developer. You'd think the company was named after some of the red numbers on its cash flow statement. Yet, when it went public in August 1999, no one seemed to care. Investors were much more focused on their notions about Red Hat's future prospects. The stock soared 271% on its first day of trading. But in early 2000, fickle Wall Street turned hot on profitability. Negative cash flow turned into a negative on the stock. Red Hat lost 80% of its value from its December 1999 high.

Red Hat's operating cash flow number has been negative and is growing more negative. Its cash flow from financing, however, is very positive, thanks to money raised during the initial public offering. So there's plenty of funds to help finance its ventures—giving the company a lifeline to execute on its strategy for profitability.

But while the beefed-up financing makes the total net cash positive, you still need to be wary. There's more money going out the door than there is coming in from the sale of its products during its day-to-day operations.

Unless you're contending with a fledgling New Economy exception, where you feel such "bleeding" is acceptable, you want a company to be cash-flow positive in all areas.

Strollers: Go to marketguide.com and click on the cash flow statement. Go to the "A cash flow" down the left-hand navigation bar. That's the bare-bones version of the annual cash flow. (The "Q cash flow" is the quarterly cash flow statement.) Look up "net change in cash" on the annual statement. Hopefully, it will be black.

What if it's not? Scroll up the statement. Look at "total cash from operating activities." If it's negative, that means the company doesn't have enough cash coming in to run its day-to-day business. That's a concern. Next, scroll on to "net cash from financing." If that's positive, it means you've got some investors backing the firm. At least you know now where the money's coming from. Fill in total cash from operating activities on your checklist and the total year-end cash-flow number. Be sure to check out your company's cash situation over the last few periods. You'd like to see cash on the rise. Also, look at the industry comparison to get a better feel for where your company stands. And that's it. Strollers, you're done with the cash flow statement. Next, jump to the balance sheet section of this chapter.

Trollers: Let's drill down into the different aspects of cash flow.

Cash Flow from Operations   Cash flow from operations tells you about the cash flow surrounding the sale of a product or service. Like operating income, cash flow from operations is a clear view into the company's business. But cash flow from operations goes one step further. It includes money that's owed to the company from customers, for example. It also details money the company owes out to, say, suppliers. Operating income, in contrast, counts only what's actually in the coffers.

Inflows of cash from operations includes paid sales and accounts receivable collections (money owed the company). Outflows are anything that the company needs to pay for, like inventory or accounts payable (money the company owes). In addition, outflows include the cash to pay for day-to-day operating expenses—like the heating bill and employees' salaries. These are all outflows from operations. You can find the cash flow from operations number right on the cash flow statement, but it's important to understand its makeup. The components of operating cash flow help you understand a lot about management. We'll go through them now.

Accountant Speak

- **Accounts receivable** is the money the company is owed for goods and services it's provided.

- **Depreciation** is an accounting notion. Over time, natural wear and tear brings down an asset's value. So accounting folks deduct a portion of the asset's cost each year as an expense. After the full period of depreciation, the asset will eventually be worthless on paper.

- **Amortization** is the same as depreciation, only it pertains to liabilities and intangibles, like a mortgage or goodwill—a company's brand value. An amortized liability is gradually eliminated over a specified period of time.

To get the cash flow from operations figure, you start with the net income number. But as we explained earlier, net income is not as pure a figure as operating income. You'll see on the cash flow statement that "non-cash" expenses like depreciation and amortization are added back to net income.

Many companies carry big depreciation and amortization charges. With every merger and acquisition, the amounts get higher and higher. So operating income could be growing, but if amortization and depreciation charges keep skyrocketing, net income keeps dropping. With those charges added back, we can better understand the heart and soul of the daily business.

The next thing you'll see is the change in working capital. Working capital is current assets less current liabilities. You see your own changes in working capital when you balance your checkbook; it's the money you've taken in and are owed less the bills you've paid and

Getting to Cash Flow from Operations

Consolidated statements of Cash Flows YAHOO! INC.
(in thousands)

	Years Ended December 31,		
	1999	1998	1997
CASH FLOWS FROM OPERATING ACTIVITIES:			
Net income (loss)	$61,133	$(12,674)	$(43,376)
Adjustments to reconcile net income (loss) to net cash provided by (used in) operating activities: **Add back the fluff!**			
Depreciation and amortization	42,230	16,472	4,644
Tax benefits from stock options	37,147	17,827	—
Minority interests in operations of consolidated subsidiaries	2,542	(68)	(727)
Purchased in-process research and development	10,975	17,600	—
Other non-cash charges	2,985	2,429	23,041
Changes in assets and liabilities:			
Accounts receivable, net	(20,272)	(19,596)	(8,524)
Prepaid expenses and other assets **This is your change in working capital!**	(21,219)	2,308	(7,239)
Accounts payable	1,700	1,141	4,700
Accrued expenses and other liabilities	49,953	22,667	9,347
Deferred revenue	49,062	34,126	3,395
Net cash provided by (used in) operating activities	216,336	82,232	(14,739)

still have to pay. What's left determines what you can do this weekend.

Same goes for companies. Good cash management attempts to accelerate cash inflow while slightly delaying cash payments.

After you've adjusted net income for noncash charges and working capital, you get cash flow from operations.

There are two things trollers should look for with working capital. First, a decrease in the accounts receivables balance from the prior year. That would mean the company is collecting the money it's owed faster than the previous period (assuming revenues remain constant or increase). And second, a slight increase in accounts payable. Your initial reaction might be that the company is dragging its feet to pay its bills. But that's not necessarily true. Let's take an example: Dell (DELL:Nasdaq).

Dell is renowned for its quality cash management. In 1999 it took Dell 36 days to collect on a sale but 54 days to pay its bills. Let's assume Dell sold a computer and bought a chip on the same day, all on credit. They'll collect $2,000 on the computer and they owe $800 for the chip. Thirty-six days later the company gets its $2,000, but they wait another 18 days to pay the bill on the chip. Dell collects on its sales of its product far before it needs to pay for its supplies. That's an extra 18 days to keep that money in short-term investments, and the interest adds up.

Why do you want to see a decrease in the accounts receivable balance from the prior period? That would mean that there should be some extra cash on hand because the company collected more. Let's assume last year's accounts receivable balance was $1,000 and this year it's only $600. That extra $400 will be shown as an addition to the overall cash balance. If the receivable balance went up to $1,200, you would instead see a subtraction of $200 on the cash flow statement, since there's $200 less to use this year.

Just the opposite occurs with the accounts payable. Let's assume the prior year's payable balance was $1,500, and this year it went up to $2,000. That means there's an extra $500 on hand this year. That $500 increase would be added to the cash flow statement. If instead the company pays $300 to a supplier, the accounts payable balance will decrease to $1,200. That $300 decrease is subtracted from total cash.

So what's the state of your company's working capital? Did receivables go up? If so, maybe the company's having a hard time collecting on the money it's owed. That doesn't bode well for the future. Are payables up from last year? A slight increase could be good, indicating the company is managing its cash flow à la Dell. But too steep a rise may mean the company is having a tough time paying its bills. Any big swing either way should be addressed in the "accounting policies" footnote.

If you're not face deep in your company's financials, market-guide.com does all the dirty work for you. Click to the cash flow statement, and there's your working capital number.

Generally, you want to see that number decrease. That would mean receivables are decreasing over time and the company is managing its cash collections. On the flip side, too much of a decrease could mean that payables are increasing too much. Look at the industry standard for guidance.

Now you've got an understanding of cash flow from operations. Once net income is adjusted for non-cash items and any changes in working capital, you can tell how much cash the company receives and uses just in conducting the day-to-day activities of its business.

EBITDA vs. Operating Cash Flow

Operating cash flow gets us pretty close to "EBITDA"—Earnings Before Interest, Taxes, Depreciation, and Amortization—an analyst favorite.

There is a big difference, though, between operating cash flow and EBITDA. The taxes a company has paid along with the interest paid on outstanding loans are included in operating cash flow. Why? Because the company paid cash for them, so they affect overall cash flow. Generally, they reduce the operating cash-flow figure.

But some analysts think that paid interest and taxes have nothing to do with the actual operations of the company. By adding paid interest and paid taxes, along with depreciation and amortization expenses, back to net income you get EBITDA. Some analysts believe this is the true operating cash number. No more fuzzy nonoperating accounting charges to cloud the waters, this is their pearl in the oyster.

EBITDA has come under attack because it ignores changes in working capital. And, as you now know, working capital is key to a company's financial health. That's why we don't like to rely solely on EBITDA.

Cash Flow from Investing Activities In this section you'll learn where the company is investing any excess cash and how it's expanding its business. Expanding the business includes things like buying property, plants, or equipment. For instance, in 1998 the Gap opened more stores. That cost is in this section of the cash flow statement. If you look at Microsoft's cash flow from investing, you'll find details of the outside investments that created its excess investment income.

Finally, you might also see information on loans made or collected from related parties. Sometimes companies have policies that allow them to offer loans to executives and shareholders, mainly in correlation with stock purchases or buybacks. That's reported here too.

Cash from Financing This is how you find out how the company comes up with the extra money to grow the business. If you're looking at a young company with no sales and overall losses but the cash flow from financing is high, that should make you feel better. It's a sign that someone out there, including other public shareholders, thinks this company has what it takes to make it. At the least, it's got some cash to sustain it for a while.

Cash Flow Summary So now you understand cash flow from operations. That helps you understand how the business is running. You've got a feel for how much it's selling, how fast it's collecting the money it's owed, and how well it's paying its bills.

You understand the difference between cash flow (pure) and net income (adulterated). You also know what the company is investing in and what it does to raise money. You're well on your way to deciding whether this is a company you'd want to own.

Balance Sheet

Next, flip to the balance sheet. For strollers, the key thing you need to know here is the debt-to-equity ratio. Trollers will look at that ratio, but we're also going to work the balance sheet in conjunction with the footnotes to the financial statements.

Debt-to-Equity Check the total debt-to-equity ratio. On marketguide .com, you'll find it under "Comparison." Total debt-to-equity is the total liabilities divided by the total net worth (total shareholders' equity).

Basically, if the company were sold today, could it pay off all its debt? If the ratio is under 1, it probably could. If the ratio is greater than 1, then the company might not have enough money to pay its creditors. That's cause for concern. As a shareholder, if all goes badly, you're last in line for a payout *behind* creditors. Before you jump to conclusions, though, check for an industry comparison, as some industries, like the construction industry, understandably carry more debt. Enter that debt-to-equity figure into your checklist. Strollers, you are now done with your data gathering. Flip to the end of this chapter, where we'll pull it all together.

Trollers: The Footnotes to the Financial Statements

With the debt-to-equity ratio done, it's time to dismember the footnotes: a pro-style treat. Hedge fund analysts and short sellers revel in the footnotes to the financial statements. Many will tell you it's the first place they turn when reading the 10-K. If you're looking for chicanery, or even just an ailing business, you've come to the right place.

While management can choose to include only the good stuff in the MD&A, it's required by the SEC to tell you the whole story in the footnotes. The footnotes intimidate most investors. But if you can forge through, you can find red flags that will help steer you away from bad investments.

We'll give you an overview about which footnotes are key, and what to look for to help you spot irregularities.

Summary of Significant Accounting Policies

Understanding a company's accounting policies has come into vogue over the last few years, as everyone wants to unearth the next Cendant-style (CD:NYSE) accounting disaster. (That big company, involved in real estate, travel, and other businesses, reported major accounting problems in 1998 that crushed its stock.) While we can't guarantee that result, we can help you determine if a company is being aggressive or conservative in its accounting practices. Being aggressive is good on the football field; on financial statements, it's like throwing away the game.

The "accounting policies" footnote, the most important of the footnotes, is broken down into subsections. Here are some highlights:

Revenue Recognition   As we said earlier, revenue is the company's sales. The sooner the company records a sale, the sooner revenues go up. But recording a sale before the item is actually sold is just bad accounting.

Most companies consider an item a sale at the time of shipment. Even more conservative would be to recognize the sale at the time the good is actually placed in the buyer's hands.

On the flip side, recording revenues too soon is very aggressive and, in some instances, just plain inaccurate. But aggressive revenue recognition has even plagued some New Economy companies.

For instance, back in March 2000, MicroStrategy (MSTR:Nasdaq) recognized millions in revenues too soon. The business-to-business software provider was booking revenue immediately for sales of software packages that included a long-term servicing element, instead of booking the revenue over the life of the deals. The accounting rules say that if you're providing a service over a period of time, you have to spread out the revenue recognition accordingly. The company was later forced to defer revenue over the span of a contract, which meant it had much less revenue now than it originally stated. The stock fell 61.7% on March 20, 2000, the day it announced the change.

Another hot issue in the technology world is the debate over reporting gross revenue or net revenue. Priceline.com (PCLN:Nasdaq) was a much-talked-about practitioner of the gross revenue style in early 2000. For example, the company buys an airline ticket from a carrier for $100 and sells it for $150. It makes $50 on the deal. But the company records $150 as revenue and the $100 as a cost. Granted, the net effect is still $50, but that's inflating the much-watched revenue line. Technically, only the net amount of $50 should be reported as revenue, many analysts say. The SEC had not forced any changes at the time of this writing.

But priceline's revenue recognition method is explained in its 1999 footnote: "With respect to airline ticket, hotel room, and rental car services, the Company recognizes as revenue the amount received from the customer, net of taxes, and records as the cost of revenue the amount that the Company pays the respective airline or hotel."

There are some industry standards that make certain practices more acceptable. But be concerned if the policies, such as those described above, seem unusually aggressive.

Accounts Receivable   If a sale is made on credit, a corresponding accounts receivable account will be created on the day of that sale.

The accounts receivable balance is the total money owed to the company by customers. The sooner the company collects, the better. The longer it takes someone to pay, the greater the chances of default.

Yet, often companies just won't give up on older money still due. An unusually big A/R balance may mean that the company is not writing off older receivables. If a customer bought an item on credit four months ago and still hasn't paid for it, it may be time for the company to accept that the money just isn't coming. But companies are hesitant to write them off because it's an expense to its bottom line. By "uncounting" a sale that was not collected, you lower net income. A big A/R balance also can signal a cash management problem in that the company is having problems collecting the money it's owed.

Click to your ratio analysis Web site again. Check the "receivable turnover" ratio. It'll tell you just how quickly a company collects its money. The ratio is total annual sales divided by the average of the most recent two years' accounts receivable. As an example, Compaq's receivables turnover ratio was 5.69 in summer 2000. But what does that mean?

Nothing until you divide the ratio into 52 weeks (52/5.69). (Okay, we fudged, you have to do one little calculation on your own!) Now you can tell how many weeks it takes the company to collect its receivables. You've actually just calculated a version of the company's "days sales outstanding," which is a big favorite metric of the short sellers and hedge fund managers.

It takes Compaq about nine weeks to collect its outstanding receivables. That's a bit longer than its peers. The industry ratio was 6.48, around eight weeks. While a ratio of 13 is considered standard—that's a four-week turnaround—it varies with each industry. Again, check the company's competitors.

Record this ratio in your checklist.

Property Plant and Equipment You're looking for the company's depreciation method in this section. Over time, natural wear and tear bring down an asset's value. So, accounting folks deduct a portion of the asset's cost each year. On paper, the asset will eventually be worthless. So, the longer it takes to depreciate an asset, the lower the annual expense. And the lower the annual expense, the more income each year.

Compare your company's depreciation method to a competitor's, looking at its financials. Be concerned if your company is taking an extra-long time to depreciate its assets, especially a technology company. If it's depreciating computers over ten years, shake your head. You know firsthand that your PC is outdated within two to four years after you purchased it. So it's good to see that About.com (BOUT: Nasdaq), the Internet service, depreciates "using the straight-line method over three years" for PCs.

But Deere (DE:NYSE), the heavy equipment manufacturer, can take a long time to depreciate its assets, since good trucks can last years. The company depreciates "using accelerated depreciation methods" over longer periods of time.

Be aware of changes in depreciation methods. (Remember the Microsoft Word "compare" trick we talked about earlier? That would work well here.) Companies can pull a little extra money into income by changing the depreciable life of an asset from, say, 25 years to 30. If a company is struggling to produce pretty numbers for the analysts, this is a trick they sometimes pull.

Inventory Method Inventory is the goods that are held for sale in the ordinary course of business, including raw materials and factory supplies. Too much inventory can be a bad thing. If the stuff doesn't get sold, it means lots of expenses without corresponding revenue.

Compare the inventory balance to the prior period's. If it's much higher, that may mean that the company is accumulating too much inventory too quickly before an actual sale is made.

The revenue number may help you figure out what's going on. If sales were up over the last period, that would mean that the company sold a ton of merchandise. So inventory should be pretty low. But if the inventory number still is relatively high compared to the prior period, even with good sales, it might mean that the company is holding too much inventory. If instead sales were down, that would explain the higher inventory number.

You should also check the inventory turnover ratio. That's the "cost of goods sold" (on the income statement) divided by the average of the current year's and prior year's ending inventory balances. This will tell you how quickly items are created and sold. A company should try to produce as close to the amount sold as possible. Storing too much inventory is costly and another telltale sign of mismanagement.

Inventory problems have plagued Lucent. The company reported record earnings in the first half of 1999 as its cash flow from operations had plummeted. A big reason for the company's negative operating cash flow: Lucent's receivables and inventories had soared, a sign that the company might have been overestimating underlying demand for its product.

Record this ratio in your checklist.

Commitments and Contingencies

This note is a must-read. You'll learn about the company's long-term debt and contingent, or possible future liabilities, here. What are you looking for? Whether the company is taking on more debt than it can afford. This information may be all in one footnote or divided into two, depending on the amount of information.

Commitments, like rent payments and leasing agreements, are things the company is already locked into owing. Contingent liabilities are things the company *may* owe. These bills are conditional on, say, an upcoming transaction or a lawsuit.

So while Microsoft's finance folks decided not to mention its Department of Justice trial in the MD&A, you'll get all the details here, including how much it may owe when the whole mess is over.

If you're investigating a chemical company, pay attention to environmental liabilities. They can be mammoth. Does *Exxon Valdez* ring a bell? In 1994, a federal jury ordered Exxon, now ExxonMobil (XOM: NYSE), to pay $5 billion in punitive damages for the 1989 *Exxon Valdez* oil spill—the worst ever in the United States—in Alaska's Prince William Sound.

But that's nothing compared to what the tobacco companies are up against. Legal liabilities have risen to such a level as to threaten the ability of big tobacco companies to even survive as businesses. So it's no surprise that Philip Morris (MO:NYSE) has a huge contingency footnote.

On July 14, 2000, a Miami jury ordered America's big cigarette makers to pay $145 billion in punitive damages, a stunning penalty for blue chip corporations held responsible for injuring hundreds of thousands of smokers—half of that amount to be paid by Philip Morris. Assuming no change on appeal, look for that information in the commitments and contingency footnote of its 2000 10-K.

Stock Options Plan

Current accounting rules give companies the choice either to expense the fair market value of the stock options outstanding or just include an explanation of that figure and its effect on net income in the footnotes. (We're not kidding here.) So companies either can show a really big expense on the income statement, which will no doubt eat up revenues, or they can write up a footnote, essentially sweeping under the rug the amount of the real compensation expense they're incurring to hire talent.

Which would you pick?

Accounting boards are fighting to make the fair market value of stock options a required compensation expense on the statement of earnings. But until then, the information is buried here.

While this outstanding options number might not be very helpful to you now, be aware that if the accounting rules change, your company's numbers may change as well.

Risks and Uncertainties

Sometimes labeled "concentrations," this section is another important one. If the company is dependent upon a particular supplier or customer, you'll find that information here. Be wary of this stuff. If one customer makes up 50% of the company's sales, and the customer chooses another vendor, that's not good.

For instance, Coca-Cola Bottling (COKE:Nasdaq) is almost totally reliant on its parent, Coke, for sales. If you didn't surmise that before reading the company's financials, it's stated in this footnote. "Approximately 90% of the Company's sales are products of The Coca-Cola Company, which is the sole supplier of the concentrate required to manufacture these products. The remaining 10% of the Company's sales are products of various other beverage companies."

Pulling It All Together

Congratulations. You're basically done. You've got your checklist filled out. You'll see we put a +/− column at the end of each line. That provides a shorthand way of judging how your company stacks up on the key fundamental factors.

You'll rarely get all pluses. But if, overall, things look positive, and there are no major red flags, you can consider buying the stock with confidence. As for minor red flags? Now you know what to keep an eye on if you go ahead and buy the stock.

Before making a final decision, though, consider some intangible fundamentals: your view of the company's business strategy and its management. By reading news articles, listening to company conference calls and reviewing other data sources, you can get a sense of these things. (For more on researching stock ideas, see Chapter 5.)

7

How to Read a Stock Chart

Many investment pros prefer a numbers-crunching fundamental approach to deciding whether to buy, hold, or sell a stock. Today, however, many individual investors—and some pros as well—either rely on or consult stock charts before making an investment decision. Charting, or "technical analysis," is about using charts of past performance to make predictions about future performance of the market or an individual stock. The practice goes under many names, including the acronym TA.

When I was undergoing my own education of the market, the sages offered few books on TA. Wall Street, like everywhere else, works in hierarchical ways. Fundamental analysis is seen as academically interesting and worthy. TA, on the other hand, is seen by some of the Street's snootier aces as a kind of trailer-park alternative to real investing.

Burton Malkiel, in his book *A Random Walk Down Wall Street,* depicts chartists as poorly dressed purveyors of investing elixir. But that kind of exclusion is less common today. For all the "fundy" snobbiness, charting has a time-honored position in the investing pantheon. Even the "pure" fundamentalists will, on the sly, glance at a chart when making investment choices.

At *TheStreet.com*, we've got several top-notch chart pros. Helene Meisler, who helped in writing this chapter, trained at places like Goldman Sachs and has developed her own brand of studying the charts. Helene has a near cult following of readers who hang on her every interpretation of the charts.

Why? Because history repeats itself. This is the basic premise behind technical analysis. Charts show historical patterns. And more than that, charts in many ways illustrate human nature. Even with a New Economy, human nature remains much the same, and that nature is reflected in stock-trading patterns that can be illustrated in charts. We can use charts to forecast future patterns based on past actions.

Charting has a rich history. The venerable Dow Jones Industrial Average, for example, was created by Charles Dow more than 100 years ago as part of his own, home-grown version of charting. He used the industrial stocks and transportation stocks as the heart of his Dow Theory. The Dow Theory, simply put, contends that the industrials and transports "confirm" whatever trend the market exhibits by moving in the same general direction. It's a crude measure based on the idea that what the industrials make, the transports must take.

As for investors who use technical analysis to purchase individual stocks, the strict adherents rely entirely on charts to make their buy-sell decisions, so much so, in fact, that they often don't even know the name of the company they're buying, let alone what the company does. It's got a symbol, it's got a chart pattern, and that's all they need. *TheStreet.com* columnist Gary B. Smith is a great example of this type of investor.

While I have enormous respect for investors who feel confident enough to invest solely based on charts, theirs is a very particular type of investing. You need to have a methodology—an approach to studying the charts and making decisions based on them—that is worlds away from traditional fundamental investing. It's more about math, statistics, and probabilities than about whether a CEO of an Internet company has a viable business strategy or whether retail stores will have a good season.

Indeed, unless you're really the TA type (and you can get a sense of them by reading the columns of folks like Gary B. Smith and Helene Meisler), I recommend that investors conduct some hearty fundamental analysis like what we reviewed in Chapter 6 and complement that with charts. Investing is a volatile mixture of art and science. You should use as many tools available to you as possible, and charting is one of the most valuable.

This chapter contains a basic introduction to charting—enough fodder for the investor just getting started with charts. It then gets into some more advanced material, for the budding and veteran chartists among you. If you find the material a little overwhelming, take a break, fold the page, and come back when you're ready.

Individual Stocks

Charting is helpful both for investigating an individual stock and analyzing the broader market. A stock chart—depicting the movement of a stock's price—shows us what the stock has done in the past, and in so doing, provides clues as to where it might go in the future. We can find "support" levels—prices at which investors have bought the stock before—that suggest good entry points to the investor, as well as "resistance" levels—prices at which sellers have appeared—which may be a good spot to sell, or "exit" a trade.

The use of the word *trade* here is important. Quick-draw traders, especially in places like the currency markets, will almost exclusively rely on charts. Same goes for many individual day traders, who buy and sell numerous stocks in the span of a market session. Longer-term investors, like disciples of Warren Buffett's buy-and-hold strategy, largely eschew charting. That contrast is something to bear in mind as you develop your own investing style.

The Broader Market

Technical analysis can also help you understand the psychology of the broader market in order to predict which way the market is headed. One key method is to focus on the market's "internal" movements. That is, even if one can surmise the direction in which the market is heading, it's just as important to know how many shares are participating in that move. The more shares, the more forceful the move.

"Breadth" of the market is a concept that reflects market internals.

Breadth is measured by advancing issues vs. declining issues, or in today's newer, faster-paced market, advancing volume vs. declining volume (more on that later). It also helps us determine the underlying trend of the market.

Sentiment

Charting also helps us measure investor sentiment. Are there mostly bulls out there or mostly bears? Whenever investor sentiment tilts too far to one side, technicians say, it is bound to correct that extreme. If there are too many bulls, who will be left to buy? If there are too many bears, who will be left to sell? Think of the market as a pendulum— when it goes too far to one extreme, its sheer weight brings it back to center. That's why sentiment indicators are considered "contrary" indicators. If the sentiment is highly bullish, it's time for a shift toward the bearish, the technicians say.

How high a sentiment is too high? Since technicians believe history repeats itself, they are always searching for the direction the market took at prior peak readings. They read charts that offer tangible statistics measuring that sentiment, some even with a history of being right!

The accompanying chart shows the extreme lack of bullishness in the market that accompanied both the October 1998 and October 1999 lows in the market. Investors had turned their backs on equities, just as equities were bottoming, giving us one of the best contrary indicators we have. Investors who followed such charts might have put some cash to work at quite an opportune time.

Percentage of Bullish Investors

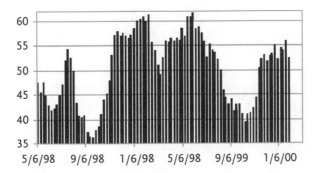

Source: Investor's Intelligence

In sum, this chapter is intended to help you learn to use charts in your buy-sell decisions on particular stocks and show how they can help you grasp the trends in the broader markets. So it's helpful if we know in which direction the trend is heading.

Whether you're looking at the overall market or the movement in an individual stock, technical analysis is a useful tool in forming an investment decision. As we all know, a picture is worth a thousand words.

Trends

There is an old adage on Wall Street that says, "the trend is your friend." But saying the "trend is our friend" is like saying an object at rest tends to stay at rest. What does that mean?

The trend is the general direction of the market or a stock. Since markets rarely move in a straight line, it's helpful before buying or selling to have a sense of whether the forces moving the market are pushing higher or lower or even sideways.

Uptrend

In an "uptrend," there are three things you want to see. First, are stocks making higher highs? A "higher high" means that each upward jaunt in the stock pushes it higher than the move before. Second, are they making higher lows? A "higher low" means that the dips don't fall quite as low as the stock had been before. The third thing you want to see is expanding volume—an increase in the number of shares trading—indicating that other investors want to get in on a good thing. Setbacks in an uptrend are generally short-lived (and low volume) and the stock price usually doesn't drop significantly below the previous rally peak.

Downtrend

In a downtrend, volume picks up on the declines and is somewhat lighter on the rallies. Just as we see buyers come in on dips in an uptrend, in a downtrend we see sellers come out on rallies. Every up move is met by eager sellers hoping to get out while they can, giving the rallies a fragile feeling.

An Uptrend

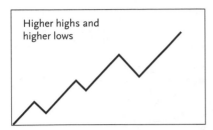

Higher highs and higher lows

A Downtrend

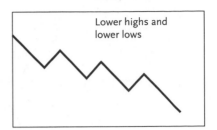

Lower highs and lower lows

Support and Resistance

Technicians have names for the peaks and troughs that create these trends: *support* and *resistance*. The idea is that investors are supporting, or buying, a stock around a certain price, and are resisting an upward move, or selling, around a certain price.

Let's use the hypothetical example of XYZ stock. Let's say it's been trading between 40 and 60 for quite some time. Thus far, the pattern has been that if the stock dips as low as 40, the buyers emerge. But if the stock starts trading as high as 60, the sellers take the opportunity to unload. In this case, we would term 40 the *support* level and 60 the *resistance* level.

If, one day, XYZ trades through 60 and goes to 70, that 60 level now becomes a *breakout*. We have broken out of the 40–60 trading range. This breakout tells us that the sellers who were there at that 60 resistance have stepped aside—for whatever reason—and are no longer present.

The breakout tells us the demand for the stock at 60 has finally outweighed the supply, which means we now have quite a number of investors who we can assume bought the stock around 60. And if they thought 60 was a good price once, it's likely they'll think it's a good price again, so 60 now becomes the new support level. An investor wanting to own this stock should now view 60 as a good entry point. Think of it this way: Prior resistance, once broken, becomes support.

If we flip this trend around and begin seeing lower highs and lower lows, we're in a downtrend. Let's go back to XYZ stock when it was trading between support at 40 and resistance at 60. Let's say instead of breaking out to the upside above 60, it breaks out to the downside, below 40. In other words, it breaks support. The buyers who were reliable at 40 are all of a sudden no longer there.

Support and Resistance

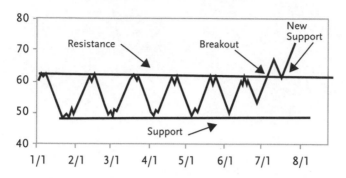

If you own the stock, breaking support is not a good thing. We all want to make money in the market, and if we buy a stock at 40 and it goes to 30 we are not happy. At that point, we are no longer thinking about making money. Now we're just thinking about not losing as much or getting back to even. For that reason, it's easy to understand why a stock that is bought at 40 and goes to 30 would find sellers again at 40: Folks just want to get out with what they paid for a stock. That's how prior support becomes the new resistance. Prior support, once broken, becomes resistance.

Entry and Exit Points

If you take nothing else away from this chapter, you've now gained an understanding of support and resistance. Let's talk about how to act on those important concepts.

In our first example, XYZ was making higher highs and eating through resistance levels, putting the stock clearly in an uptrend. In an uptrend, investors buy during those pullbacks—or dips—toward support, as they are good entry points.

In the latter example, XYZ was making lower lows and lower highs and was therefore in a downtrend. This is a stock we may want to sell when it reaches resistance.

Drawing in Trend Lines

We've talked a lot about the trend. How do you identify and follow the trend? You draw a line. Here's a rule of thumb for drawing in lines:

> ### Easy Way to Get Support and Resistance
>
> Don't want to read the chart, but want the benefit of it? Microsoft's moneycentral.com has a neat tool, the Stock Research Wizard, which you'll find under "Stocks." You just stick a symbol into the "Wizard," click along, and eventually it will just tell you its measure of resistance and support. *Voilà!*

Keep it simple. Two points make a line, a third confirms it. The trend line helps you identify points of resistance and support. The more points on the line, the more reliable the line is.

But keep this in mind: A very steep line is a dangerous sign. Just think of the stock price the way a fundamentalist might look at a growth rate. Earnings or revenue growth at 75% a year is great. But that's usually not sustainable for very long. A very steep trend line is the same way. It's generally not sustainable either, as almost nothing moves with that sort of acceleration or deceleration for extended periods. So, if the trend line you draw turns out to be very steep to the upside, it will likely get broken—that is, the stock will plunge. A steep trend line is not likely to give a very good signal to the chartist.

An uptrend line with a flatter angle is more sustainable. Look at the chart of Cisco Systems (CSCO:Nasdaq) as it traded from its 1998 low. At first its rise was sharp and steep, which is not the kind of uptrend that is generally sustainable for any length of time. Had the chartist rushed in to draw that uptrend line (line A), he would realize that this steep line is a short-term trend, not a long-term one.

Cisco Trend Lines

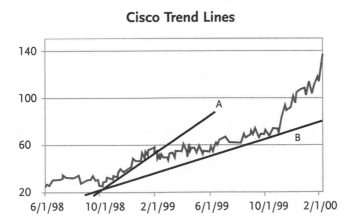

Exercising patience here is important. If the chartist had waited until the stock had corrected from that initial steep rise, and then drawn in the uptrend line (line B), which was much flatter, it would be clear this stock would be able to sustain higher highs and higher lows. Cisco was in an uptrend, and for TA practitioners, it was a stock to be bought on each trip back to the trend line, or support.

How would the chartist know when the trend changed for Cisco? First, the stock would begin to make lower highs and lower lows; that would be our first warning. But it's only a warning. Until the stock breaks that flat, very well confirmed uptrend line, any move down to that line should be viewed as just a correction in a long-term uptrend, and therefore a buying opportunity.

Volume

In our hunt for the friendly trend, a factor as important as price is volume. Volume might not have the glamour role enjoyed by price, but volume is vital when trying to identify a trend.

Volume is the number of shares traded in any given stock on any given day. One of the first rules an investor should remember is that *changes in volume generally precede changes in price.* In other words, the chartist can generally see volume expand before the price begins to move.

Volume: NYSE vs. Nasdaq

Volume is counted differently on the New York Stock Exchange (NYSE) than it is on Nasdaq. On the NYSE, if I buy 1,000 shares from you, the volume is 1,000 shares. However, on Nasdaq, it is more typical for that same trade to be counted as 2,000 shares. The reason is that on the NYSE the stock is traded only in one place: on the floor of the NYSE. But on Nasdaq, often each dealer (the buying and selling dealer) reports the trade. Thus, we get "double counting."

On a slow market day in August 2000, volume on the NYSE was 822.4 million shares, compared to an average volume of almost 1 billion shares per day. On the Nasdaq, it was 1.385 billion shares, compared to an average volume of 1.5 billion shares a day.

Most stocks launch their initial rise from a "base" formation. A base takes time to form, typically at least several months, if not years. A base generally forms when a stock has swung back and forth between support and resistance for an extended period of time—a kind of tug of war between the bulls and the bears.

As the base forms, and the price is basically in a trading range, you want to watch volume. Why? If new investors in the stock are anxious to buy, but there are still plenty of sellers present, you'll see a pickup in activity—in volume—prior to the actual price movement of the stock. Once those sellers have completed their selling and are out of the way, the stock can move through its resistance level with ease.

How do we know higher volume is bullish when a stock is emerging from a base? Because if there were no buyers, then the volume would be low. Sellers would just be waiting for buyers to appear before they could unload their shares. Think of a retail store in a mall. If they're offering merchandise no one wants, the SALE sign sits in the window with no customers. But if merchandise is hot, crowds appear, anxious to purchase, with or without a sale sign.

Volume can also accompany a selling panic. After a stock has been sliding for an extended period of time, you may notice a pickup in volume, leading to a very high-volume day when the stock practically collapses; this is typically a *selling climax*. A selling climax comes when investors can no longer stand the declining stock day after day. Rather than wait for a good price to sell, they decide this stock is never going to rally again. They just instruct their brokers to get them out. When all those sellers are washed out, that's when you know you're at the end of the decline.

The '87 crash was a great example of a selling climax. The market had actually been sliding since the end of August, when the Dow Jones Industrial Average made its high. By the time October 19 came around, most stocks had been sliding for some time. But that dreaded day saw the highest volume the NYSE had ever known at the time: just over 600 million shares. The next day the majority of stocks hit their lows, making the Crash of 1987 the end, not the beginning, of a major decline.

A good rule of thumb is to be cautious of stocks that are trading near their highs on high volume but are going nowhere. That's the equivalent of the retail store having enough merchandise to fulfill the crowds: The crowds still come, but there's plenty of supply. What happens when the customers stop coming and the supply remains high? You do not want to be a buyer when there is excess supply.

A stock in an uptrend will "pull back"—or fall—on lighter volume and resume the rise on renewed volume. Expanding volume on a rally is important to confirm the direction of the price movement.

How do you measure a stock's volume? Many financial Web sites, including Yahoo!, report a stock's volume for the day, as well as the "average volume" (which in Yahoo!'s case is defined as the daily volume averaged over three months). By comparing daily to average daily volume, you can get a sense of how high volume is on that day.

Volume ranges all over the map. A big, popular stock like America Online (AOL:NYSE) can trade more than 10 million shares a day. A smaller stock with less investor interest, like new media company I-Village (IVIL:Nasdaq), might trade only 300,000 shares a day, or even fewer.

Volume can also indicate general market health. Technicians calculate "upside volume" and "downside volume." This is the volume in all the stocks that were up on the day and the volume in all the stocks that were down on the day. It is a way of measuring market breadth or overall participation in a market move. Upside and downside volume information is available on some financial Web sites and in daily newspapers, including *The Wall Street Journal* and *The New York Times*.

Volume is yet another tool in determining the trend of the market. When the market or a stock is in an uptrend, volume should be rising along with it, as a confirmation of the uptrend. That is, it's not just that there are buyers, but that the demand for the stock far outstrips the supply. Should the volume not confirm a price rise, investors should be cautious, as there is a possibility supply has finally met demand.

Now, if you've come this far in the chapter, you know the basics of support, resistance, and volume, all of which help make up the "trend." These factors alone should be a big help to you in gauging the movement of a stock or the broader market. If you're still hungry for more, stay with me.

Basic Chart Patterns

There are a lot of terms technicians use to describe certain chart patterns—too many, if you ask me. The world of technicians sometimes feels like a massive glossary contest. But don't fret. I'm going to review a few quirky terms that describe "patterns." The idea here is that if you can identify a pattern, you will be better able to make an informed prediction about where a stock is headed.

Most stocks launch their initial rise from a base formation, which can develop over quite some time. Remember, a base generally forms when a stock has swung back and forth between support and resistance—a kind of tug-of-war between the bulls and the bears.

If an uptrend is defined by higher highs and higher lows, then the first sign of an uptrend comes when we get a higher low. The next move the technician looks for is a move through the resistance, with volume confirming (that is, higher than average daily volume). That move through resistance is called a breakout, and when it comes on increased volume, it is the recipe for a further move upward.

It is common for a stock to break out and then come back and retest the breakout level. As prior resistance becomes support, this is simply a test to determine the new support level or the level at which the stock should now be bought.

To come up with a price target, a general rule of thumb is to take the high of the pattern and subtract the low of the pattern, then add the difference between them to the breakout level to get your target price. In the example below we would take 62 minus 48 to get 14; we add 14 to 62 to get a first target price of 76. The target price is the point at which a trader might be expected to take profits. A buy-and-hold investor, on the other hand, might simply regard it as a rest stop before a correction and then a resumption of the uptrend. In either case, the target price should be used as a guideline; often it is the general area where the stock will take its first rest.

Base Building

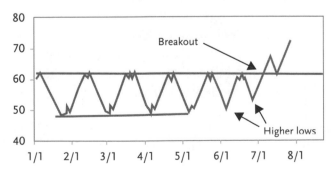

Head and Shoulders: A Reversal Pattern

The "head-and-shoulders" pattern is a reversal pattern, not a continuation pattern. That is, it is a pattern that suggests when a stock is changing course.

Head and shoulders is characterized by a rally on high volume (the shoulder) that retreats, only to re-rally to a higher high (the head). The pattern begins to develop when the rally to the higher high comes on lighter volume than the previous rally. Since this rally is not confirmed by the volume, it will likely retreat back to support, which happens to be approximately the same level it just came from. The chartist can now draw in an "LS" (left shoulder) on the first rally and an "H" (head) on the second rally. At the same time, you can draw a flattish line connecting those two support levels. This line is called the neckline, or "NL."

Head and Shoulders

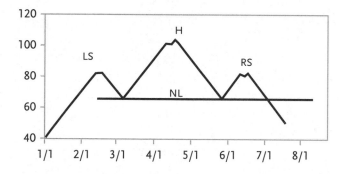

From this neckline we then see a rally, once again on light volume, only this rally stops short of the previous one, giving us a lower high. We can now term this rally a right shoulder, or "RS." The pattern is not confirmed until it breaks through the neckline. It is important to watch volume at this point, as the volume must confirm the break. Just as volume must confirm an upside breakout, it must confirm a downside breakout as well. How much volume do you need to see? There's no set number, but it should amply exceed average daily volume. The measurement for this head and shoulders pattern is similar to that of a base: The high minus the low, subtracted from the neckline, gives the target.

Let's look at an example of a head and shoulders chart of Finnish telecom powerhouse Nokia (NOK:NYSE).

Nokia's Head and Shoulders

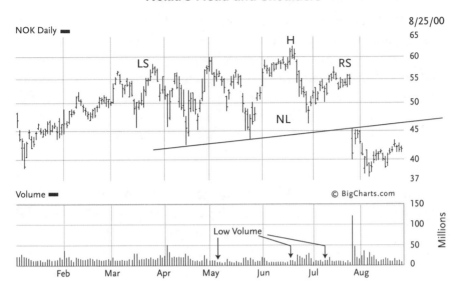

Nokia had a very good rally on increasing volume to the 55–60 area between March and May. But after a mid-April decline to 43, the uptrend looked shaky; the subsequent rally to 60 in early May was on less volume than in previous rallies.

The decline in May brought us back down to the mid-40 level, but did not break the previous low. So now we have a confirmed support level, which becomes the neckline (NL). A rally to a new high in mid-June follows, but it's on very light volume, and the decline from that high has a significant increase in volume. At this point, we might pencil in that March–April period as the left shoulder (LS), and the high in mid-June as the head (H).

From that high-volume decline, Nokia rallies in mid-July, but this subsequent rally is on extremely light volume. At this point, we can begin to suspect this rally will fail to make a new high (the volume is the best clue we have for this) and call this rally a potential right shoulder (RS). For those who wish to anticipate the head and shoulders, this is the time to sell the stock. For those who would prefer confirmation, they can wait for a break of the neckline (around 46) to sell. (However, in this case, the stock opened on a gap and you would not have had a chance to sell at 46.)

Flags and Pennants: Consolidation Patterns

In this Internet economy many stocks move faster than they used to. It used to be that you were doing well if a stock you owned was up 25% on the year—even two or three years! But today stocks move 25% in a single day! With the advent of these kinds of trading moves, consolidation patterns have become the norm. A consolidation pattern is the point at which a stock takes a rest after a big run. Often it is like a weigh station where the stock catches its breath before pushing higher (or lower) again. If you are anxious to buy or sell this stock, this is usually a good time to do it.

In this pattern, the stock will "consolidate its gains (losses)" along the way, without retesting support. Many of these patterns come in the form of flags or pennants. As the name suggests, there is a rather sharp move that comes very quickly (that's the flagpole). Rather than coming back down to retest the support or breakout level, the stocks simply weave back and forth (forming the flag). The stock will often fluctuate a bit, but usually within parallel lines—thus defining the flag. The key to this consolidation pattern is volume: It drops off markedly while the flag is forming.

The pattern will typically last only for a few days to a few weeks before resuming its upward (or downward) run.

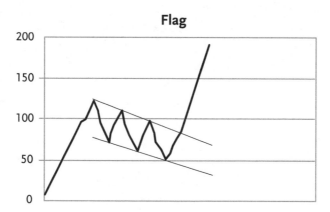

Flag

The pennant is almost exactly the same as a flag except that the consolidation pattern will have lines that converge rather than parallel lines, making the pattern look more like a pennant than a flag.

The same rules of time and measurement apply to the pennant as the flag. Often after the rally resumes, the flagpole will duplicate itself, giv-

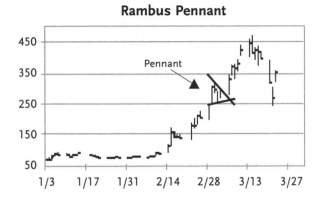

ing the chartist a new measurement for an upside target. For the Rambus (RMBS:Nasdaq) chart above, for example, the stock moved 175 points, from 75 to 250. It then emerged from the pennant around 275. Add on that first 175-point move, and you get a target price—to sell—of 450.

While it is helpful to recognize a pattern when it occurs, it is also important not to manufacture one that isn't really there. When the pattern is genuine and is behaving the way it should, it is a useful tool to know that specific pattern's characteristics. However, when investors look for patterns that may or may not be there, it's as if they are trying to get the stock to do what they want it to. And we all know that the market is willfully independent.

Types of Charts

Some people look only at the basic charts—bar charts. But this book is about the basics and beyond, so we're going to stretch a little bit and give you more than that. Don't get frightened, however, and if this stuff seems too wacky, just come back later when you're ready.

Bar Charts

Bar charts are popular primarily because they are very simple. All you need is the high, low, and close (sometimes the open is used as well) for an individual stock. This chart requires a posting each and every day, regardless of the action on that particular day.

The vertical line represents the high and low of the day. The horizontal tick mark to the right represents the close, and if the open is

Bar Chart
Dow Jones Industrial Average
High-Low-Close

used as well, you will find that marked horizontally to the left of the vertical line. Bar charts are the most common form of charts.

Point-and-Figure Charts

Point-and-figure charts have been used in the United States since the late 1800s. Sometime in the 1930s, chartists began using the letter x to replace the actual price, or figure. The x was called a point. Somehow the two names stuck and these charts became known as point-and-figure charts.

On a point-and-figure chart we study price movement, but not time. The point-and-figure chart is plotted with a series of x's and o's, with x denoting rising prices and o representing falling prices. Each box is given a predetermined dollar value. For example, if each box is "worth" 2, the stock must move at least 2 for it to be posted that day. If it moves only 1½, there is no posting for that day. So, if the stock was up four on the day, then it gets an x in each of 2 boxes.

Point-and-figure charts have an advantage over bar charts in that they rarely give false signals. It takes so much price to move one of these charts that the stock is typically well into its trend by the time the point-and-figure charts show the emergence from a base or top. Thus, breakouts and breakdowns are quite easy to see. The disadvantage is that they do not show time. If the stock is consolidating for an extended period, but does not trade outside the predetermined trading range, then it is not posted for that period of time. Helene and I both believe that time heals all wounds (or at least most of them), and for that reason don't prefer point-and-figure charts. Quite often a stock will mark time without

Point-and-Figure Chart

		X					
		X	O				
		X	O				
		X	O				
		X	O				
		X	O				
X		X	O				
X	O	X	O				
X	O	X	O				
	O		O	X			
			O	X	O		
			O	X	O	X	
			O		O	X	O
					O	X	O
					O	X	O
					O		O
							O
							O
							O
							O
							O

making progress in either direction, which can make the chartist think there's nothing going on when, in fact, a base or top is being built.

The best place online to see good point-and-figure charts is www .dorseywright.com.

Candlesticks

The candlestick chart, used by Gary B. Smith, another chartist who writes for *TheStreet.com,* is posted much in the same manner as the bar chart, in that each day is posted with an open, high, low, and close represented on the page.

The major difference is that in candlestick charting, the vertical line is called the body, and the color, size, and shape of the body represent the day's action. The body in a candlestick represents the open and close of the session. If the body is empty (i.e., not filled in), it

DJIA Candlestick Chart

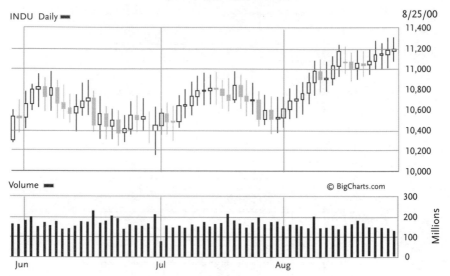

means the close was higher than the open. If it is black, or filled in, it means the close was lower than the open. The thin lines above and below the body represent the high and low of the day.

Candlestick charting takes considerable effort to study and understand, as there are many, many patterns, each with different names and meanings. However, the main difference between this method of charting and bar charts is the emphasis these charts put on the relationship between the open and close of the day. It is believed that these two periods are the two most emotionally charged periods of the day and, therefore, should be given prominence in the recording.

Arithmetic vs. Logarithmic

Every time I see Arith- and Log-, I start to glaze a bit, but we promised you some grad-level stuff. These issues address the scale in which a chart is plotted. The majority of computer-generated charts are plotted on an arithmetic scale.

An arithmetic scale accepts all point gains to be similar, with equal distances between the prices, regardless of the actual price of the stock. For example, two stocks that rally 10 points each will look similar on an arithmetic chart, whether it is a $10 stock or a $100 stock. In both cases, it will look like a big move.

A logarithmic scale will space the prices according to percentage moves. In the above example, the $10 stock has doubled and would be shown as a large move on the chart, whereas the $100 stock has only moved 10% and, thus, the move on the chart would look small in comparison. Both stocks have gained $10, but the return on your investment varies tremendously.

Qualcomm Arithmetic Scale

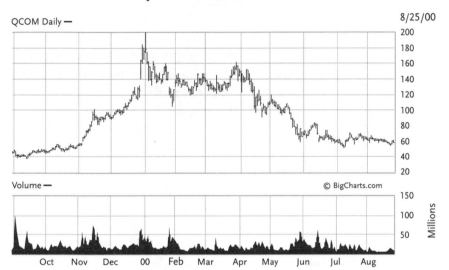

Qualcomm Logarithmic Scale

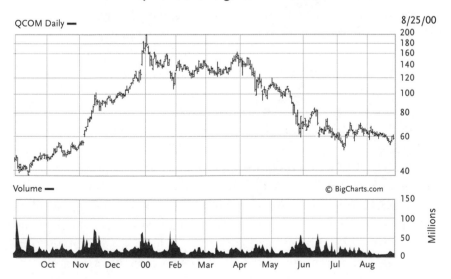

This difference is important, especially in this New Economy where stocks make big price moves on a daily basis. Many stocks are so high in price that these daily price changes sound enormous, when in percentage terms they're more modest. A logarithmic scale puts these moves in perspective. Helene prefers to plot all stocks, but especially these high-priced New Economy stocks, on a logarithmic scale, as it helps the investor better see that the wild intraday swings are often not quite as wild as they seem.

Here are two charts of the same stock, Qualcomm (QCOM:Nasdaq), 1999's big winner. On both charts, it's easy to see the 60-point move from 40 to 100 back in the third quarter of 1999. But notice how you must squint to see the 60-point move from 140 to 200 in late December of 1999 on the logarithmic chart? That's because you added 150% on the first move but only 43% on the latter move.

The Market Internals

Market internals provide an X-raylike view of the market. Internals are vital to understanding the market, because most of the time all you hear about are the major indices. The indices don't always give you a complete story.

Take the Dow Jones Industrial Average (DJIA). This average has a mere 30 stocks. Critics have long complained that it receives too much attention for its narrow base. Add to that, the DJIA is price-weighted. That means if a high-priced stock in the index goes up one dollar, it has the same impact as a low-priced stock that goes up a dollar. This may seem logical, but a one-dollar move on a $10 stock is 10%, while a one-dollar move on a $100 stock is only 1%. With the Dow, either movement would contribute the same number of points to the calculation of the index.

In addition, when the average was created, the Dow Jones folks picked the thirty stocks and divided by 30. However, over the years stock splits and readjustments have essentially turned the divisor into a multiplier. Now a one-dollar move in a stock adds approximately four dollars to the DJIA.

The S&P 500 and the Nasdaq Composite are market-cap weighted (market capitalization is the price of the stock multiplied by the number of shares outstanding). The largest capitalized stocks are given the most weight in computing the average. Sometimes this means that the largest capitalized stocks can swing the average in one direction while the majority of stocks are moving in the other direction.

Because all of these indices are limited, technicians prefer to look at the market's internals. Included in the internals are the breadth indicators—how many stocks are participating in a move. Tools for measuring the internals include the advance/decline line; upside/downside volume; and the list of stocks making new highs and new lows. The advance/decline statistics tell us the number of stocks that were up or down on the day. In an uptrending market, we want to see more stocks advancing than declining. When advancing issues outweigh declining issues, we say the market has positive breadth.

The same can be said for volume. In a rising market, up volume, or volume in stocks that are up on the day, ideally should be greater than down volume, or volume in stocks that are down on the day. This is also positive breadth and is therefore bullish.

The "New High" and "New Low" list, which indicates the number of stocks hitting new 52-week highs or lows, is a breadth indicator. In a rising market, an increasing number of stocks making new highs is bullish, as it shows the rally expanding or broadening out.

Recently, much has been said about the advance/decline line not mattering anymore. On the Nasdaq, the advance/decline has never been a good indicator. Nasdaq is where the majority of IPOs (initial public offerings) wind up, and many of these companies never become great stocks. They simply languish and go nowhere, or even worse, go down. But while investors may forget about these stocks, they don't vanish. They hang around on the Nasdaq, including themselves in the statistics, making for a generally negative advance/decline line. These stocks typically trade on very little volume. For this reason, the up/down volume—reflecting the shares where the trading action is—is a better breadth indicator for Nasdaq.

On the NYSE (New York Stock Exchange), breadth is a better indicator, although it does have its flaws. There are a great many stocks listed on the NYSE that are not pure common stocks. They are preferred stocks or closed-end bond funds, which are highly correlated to interest rates. Therefore the a/d statistics on the NYSE are heavily skewed toward interest rates. When interest rates are declining, these rate-sensitive stocks do quite well and can mask what the majority of common stocks are doing. In an environment when interest rates are rising, these stocks will likely suffer, causing this statistic to be quite negative. This is just one of the reasons a declining interest rate environment is bullish for the NYSE stocks.

One of the purest breadth indicators, used by chart guru Helene Meisler, is the unweighted average. This is one of those indicators you will not find readily available. It is derived from QCHA (for the NYSE) and QCHAQ (for the Nasdaq). That stands for "quote change." It is provided by a financial services company called Quotron and it is the *average percentage change for the average stock* on the specific exchange.

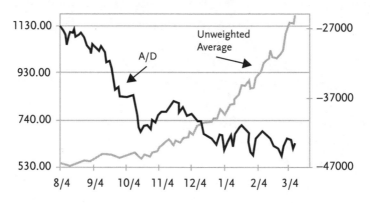

Nasdaq Unweighted Average (left scale) with Nasdaq Cumulative A/D (right scale)

This chart shows the difference two breadth indicators can have. It is important to know which one represents what the majority of stocks are doing.

The number provided by Quotron is the actual percentage change, so if the number says +35 then that means the average stock was up .35% on that particular day. You can pick a random number to begin with for your unweighted average, perhaps 500. You would then figure out the point change by using the percentage change that you are provided. For example, a QCHA of +35 on a 500 unweighted average would add 1.75 points (500 x .0035 = 1.75) to the "index," moving the unweighted average to 501.75. This actual percentage charge number can be found in *Barron's* Market Laboratory section each week.

This unweighted average provides a very good snapshot of what the majority of stocks are doing, without skewing the data by market capitalization or price. And since as investors we are buying individual stocks, it is quite important for us to know what individual stocks are doing. When market breadth is positive, the underlying trend of the market usually is as well. It is always best to buy when breadth is positive, as a rising tide tends to carry all ships.

Summing Up

A working understanding of charts can help an investor in numerous ways. Just understanding the basics of support and resistance, trends, and volume can help you avoid buying at the top, or selling at a bottom. Being able to discern specific patterns like "head and shoulders" can help you set price targets. And knowing a bit about market sentiment and internals can help you gauge when the market is on your side—when that trend is your friend.

Now, if you're a hard-core buy-and-hold fundamentalist investor, you might be saying, "Why do I need to bother with this stuff? What does it matter where I get in if I'm holding for the long haul?"

It matters as much as money matters. Think of it as buying a house. You may well plan to live in a house for 30+ years, but you still want to pay the least amount possible when you buy it. That extra money you save can help you redo a kitchen, or pay some college bills. Why spend more than you have to?

That's the same theory behind seeking good "entry" and "exit" points on a stock. Technical analysis isn't a guarantee. But some familiarity with charting can give you confidence that you've raised your chances of not spending more than you have to—and not hanging around longer than you should.

8

When to Buy

Now that you've searched for good stock ideas, and you've researched your company's fundamentals, and even checked out some charts to get an idea of how the companies you are interested in have been trading, is now the right time to buy? That's what this chapter is all about—the buy decision. Building on the material presented earlier, this chapter will help you decide whether a stock price is too rich or too risky, or whether it's an attractive investment opportunity.

If there were simple answers to evaluating stock prices, you wouldn't need this book. We'd all be geniuses—and rich. Not only are there no surefire tricks to valuation, but investors—especially professionals—hold a variety of philosophies on the best way to size up stock prices. Some will buy a stock only if they believe the rest of the market is vastly underestimating its potential value. Others shun "bargain" stocks and instead gladly pay up for expensive popular names if they are convinced there's more upward momentum in the price.

In this chapter, I review these different investment philosophies and walk you through the metrics that drive them. I also discuss how to use technical analysis to help your buy decision, as well as macro factors, like interest rates. Finally, I introduce you to some Web sites that provide easy access to these metrics, along with industry comparisons. This chapter complements much of the material in the "when to sell" discussion in Chapter 10, as you often need to go through a similar analysis for either decision.

I've turned to *TheStreet.com*'s metrics editor, Mark Martinez, for his invaluable insights on the valuation topic. While we can't give you one single answer, we can give you the factors to consider that will help you boost your odds of getting in at a good price. Boosting your odds of success is what smart investing is all about.

Different Strokes for Different Folks

Buying a stock is not that different from buying any other good or service. Take purchasing a home. Some people will move to an unpopular neighborhood where they can afford more space for their money, maybe even buy a "fixer-upper." Their hope is that they'll turn their rough gem into a diamond, and in the meantime others will begin to recognize the many benefits of the neighborhood. The buyer hopes that eventually his small investment will be worth many times what he paid.

Some home buyers do the opposite. They don't want to take the chance that a neighborhood will improve. What if it doesn't? They could be left with an eyesore in a bad location. Some bargain that would turn out to be. These wary buyers would rather pay top dollar, even for a smaller place, in an already chic neighborhood. So chic, in fact, that they are convinced that their already-expensive purchase will get even more pricey.

The same spectrum of "value" philosophies applies to stock investing. Some investors like to buy the market's downtrodden stocks, hoping for improvement, while others are willing to pay higher prices on the theory that they'll likely go even higher. Some prefer to mix up their portfolio with a combination of bargain and pricey stocks.

Stock valuation can generally be divided among about five main styles along a spectrum:

The Valuation Spectrum

- Turnaround Investing
- Value Investing
- Growth at a Reasonable Price
- Growth Investing
- Momentum Investing

I'll take each one of these styles in turn. First, I'll talk about the qualitative nature of the different styles, the kind of thought process involved in sizing up a company. Then I'll talk about the different metrics, like price-to-earnings and price-to-sales, that you can use to make similar determinations. By getting a sense of the valuation process, you'll be better equipped to make a confident "buy" decision.

Turnaround Investing

The turnaround investor looks for down-and-out companies, sometimes at or near bankruptcy. What attracts the turnaround investor to the stock is the possibility of just that—a turnaround. After languishing for years, a company may have recently announced that it has a significant new customer that's going to buy lots of the company's product. Or maybe the company has recently hired a new CEO with a knack for pulling distressed companies out of the abyss. Whatever the reason, the turnaround investor is looking for a situation where a company that has been performing miserably appears to hold a better-than-even chance of turning things around—and with it the stock price as well. They'll pay bargain-basement prices for stocks that others wouldn't touch.

An example of a successful turnaround story is US Airways (U:NYSE). In 1996, the company was reeling; it was losing money and its prospects seemed bleak. Its stock was trading at around 12 a share; its price-to-earnings ratio was being compressed from about 25 in 1995 to 10 in 1996. Indeed, the two years prior to 1996 were horrendous. The company lost almost $500 million during 1994 and 1995 combined. Enter Stephen Wolf, the airline turnaround artist.

Wolf was brought in to do just what he had done at three prior companies: make significant improvements, and ultimately get the stock price up. If you knew Wolf's track record, you knew there was a pretty good chance that he'd pull it off. And while you may not agree with his turnaround tactics of coming in and cleaning house (layoffs, wage reductions, etc.), the chart doesn't lie: From 1996 to the middle of 1998, US Airways' stock went from the low teens to around 80, for a return of about 500%.

The airline has hit some turbulence since then, but the stock still remains much higher than when Wolf came on board. Indeed, in the summer of 2000, United Airlines (UAL:NYSE) announced plans to purchase the company, confirming the wisdom of investors who bet on a turnaround four years prior.

Not all turnaround stories have a happy ending. Sometimes a turnaround story stinks up the joint, taking investors right along with it. Take Sunbeam (SOC:NYSE), for instance. The day after Sunbeam announced that Al Dunlap was coming aboard as CEO in July 1996, investors cheered, sending Sunbeam's then-flailing stock soaring some 60%.

At the time, Sunbeam was a struggling company. Expenses were high, sales were declining, losses were piling up, and employee morale was low. But judging by the stock's rise, investors were confident Al Dunlap could pull off a turnaround. The thinking was that "Chainsaw Al," known for his relentless cost-cutting at other companies, would come in and work his magic at Sunbeam. For a while, that's exactly what seemed to happen. But not for long enough.

In an effort to make the company profitable, Dunlap was cutting jobs and product lines at a rapid pace. But because these kinds of measures can be taken only so far (you need products and people to make and sell them), the cruel realities of the housewares business finally began to take their toll on the company.

Investors who were getting accustomed to rapidly growing earnings (which took hold as expenses were being dramatically reduced) began to realize what a lot of other people already knew: It's difficult for a functioning housewares company to grow earnings by more than 5 to 10% a year, as the margins are just too small.

What followed for Sunbeam was a disaster. Not only was the company unable to keep up with the growth that it was forecasting for Wall Street, but in an effort to match Wall Street's expectations, the company allegedly turned to financial hocus-pocus. Without getting into all of the sordid details (you can read John Byrne's great book, *Chainsaw: The Notorious Career of Al Dunlap in the Era of Profit-at-Any-Price,* for those of you that are interested), suffice it to say that the company was forced to restate its financial results. The stock price plummeted. At the peak of Sunbeam's heyday—March 1998—its share price reached 53. In August 2000, shares were trading at about 3.

So you see, as an extreme form of "value" investing, turnarounds can be quite risky. If the company can't turn itself around, your investment could be futile. That's why turnaround investing tends to be the province of sophisticated professionals who specialize in the area.

Value Investing

Like the turnaround investor, the value investor is also looking for situations where other investors may be slow to realize the good things happening at a company. He's like the homeowner who buys a fixer-upper. This investor believes there is value in a company where others do not. That's why these types of stocks are often lower priced: Other investors have not piled into the stock because they do not see a good enough reason to do so.

The value investor, if correct, is able to get into a stock early and reap a windfall later on, when the rest of the market comes to see the company's worth and buys in. The value investor prides herself on being early but never late. The problem with value investing is when you're *too* early. While you wait and wait for the rest of the market to see the wisdom of your idea, other stocks can zoom ahead while yours languishes. Eventually, all that waiting time means missed opportunity for your portfolio. And there's no guarantee that other investors will ever recognize what the value investor believes to be true. Which means the stock may remain a perpetual "bargain."

Value investors tend to rely heavily on fundamental analysis of stocks. They try to ensure that there's enough "value" in the enterprise to support the stock price, ideally *more* value than the stock price currently reflects. They do not consider a high P/E ratio acceptable. They buy stocks that others would call "dogs."

Take the cigarette stocks. They've been perceived as value stocks for several years. Philip Morris (MO:NYSE), the poster-child stock for the value crowd, has traded under 40 for most of the time since 1997 (it briefly exceeded 50 in late 1998, and retreated quickly after that). It wasn't that the company's operations were suffering. In 1999, for example, the company did $79 billion in revenues, earned $3.20 a share, and had more than $4 billion in cash—all strong numbers. Yet the company couldn't rise above the specter of continuing lawsuits arising from the dangers of smoking. With the potential of crippling jury verdicts looming over the company, investors essentially stayed away from the stock. It lost more than 50% of its value during 1999.

Screaming bargain? Ask investors who got into the stock back in 1997, when they, too, thought the company was a steal. If you'd bought Philip Morris at the beginning of June 1997, when it traded at around 40, and didn't scoot out during the brief window of late 1998, you would have still been underwater in summer 2000.

Still, value players are continually on the lookout for the "catalyst" that will get a company's stock pumped again. An argument that Philip Morris fans were proffering in the summer of 2000 was the notion that the several states that had been suing the cigarette maker actually would back off, for fear that the company would go bankrupt and be unable to pay plaintiffs. It's a creative argument, the kind of contrarian thinking that value investors go through in deciding that a company's time has finally come.

Then again, some value stocks turn out to be great investments. Cable stocks are an example of this. Back in 1997, the performance of this group of stocks, including Telecommunications Inc.—it was acquired by AT&T (T:NYSE) in 1998 for $52 billion—Liberty Media (LMG.A:NYSE), and Time Warner (TWX:NYSE), which, in early 2000, announced it was being acquired by America Online (AOL: NYSE), was abysmal. But some value investors saw strength, notably fund manager Mario Gabelli. He believed in the group, and invested heavily in it. In 1998, he was vindicated. Cable proved to be one of the best investments that year.

Value investing is often said to be safer than growth investing—buying pricey stocks in the hope that they'll go up even higher. The idea is that you've already bought downtrodden stocks with real assets to back up the price. How much more bad news could there be to bring the price down any further? Indeed, value investors often claim to do better in down markets on the theory that their stocks don't fall as far as stocks with high performance expectations built into a steep price.

The problem is, this conventional wisdom about value investing just hasn't proven consistently true. Even low-priced stocks can fall lower. That's what happened in the 1997–98 Asian crisis meltdown. As the stock market fell, value mutual fund and stock investors alike expected their prudent style to help cushion their loss. But it did no such thing. Value funds everywhere got clobbered.

Consider Robert Sanborn, then the widely regarded manager of value fund Oakmark. His fund did poorly during this time period—a period when value investors probably thought a fund like this would thrive. In 1998, when the S&P 500 returned more than 28%, Oakmark returned a measly 3.7%. In 1999 it got even worse. Oakmark actually lost money that year, losing more than 10% of its value in a year when the S&P 500 was up more than 20%. Not exactly a safety play, let alone a bargain return. After years of bad performance, Sanborn resigned from the fund.

The moral: Buy a value stock because you think it's a good value, not because it's safe. And remember this: A good value stock doesn't— or, at least, shouldn't—remain a value stock forever. Ideally, it blossoms and starts to resemble a more pricey growth stock. (At the same time, a fallen growth stock can suddenly seem like a great value.)

Growth Investing

Next in line is growth at a reasonable price, or GARP. But it's easier to understand GARP if we understand growth investing first. So we'll come back to GARP.

The growth investor typically doesn't care about the value attributes of a stock. Growth investors are mostly concerned with a company's ability to continue growing its revenues and earnings. Loosely defined, growth investors seek companies whose annual revenues and earnings show sustained upward growth, both historically and in analysts' predictions for growth.

Take the PBHG family of mutual funds, a firm that made its name in growth investing. The fund managers of most of the PBHG growth funds specifically target small- and mid-sized companies with high earnings growth projections, typically in the high 20-to-30%-a-year range. When they find these companies, price is usually not much of an object. When the stock market is rewarding companies that exhibit this kind of growth, fund families such as PBHG are hugely successful—not to mention popular with investors. But when these stocks fall out of favor—look out below.

As for individual stocks, Dell (DELL:Nasdaq) is an example of a stock that was a favorite with the growth crowd when it first went public in 1988. The company was fairly small, but it had rapidly growing revenues and soon had rapidly growing earnings to boot. Since it had a small base from which to build, the company was able to show substantial revenue and earnings gains both on a yearly basis and a quarterly basis. As the company continued to exhibit these traits, adherents of the growth style stuck with the company and drove its price.

For Dell the growth trend continued unabated for most of the late 1980s and the '90s. Over that time period, its stock price zoomed from 9 cents (adjusted for splits) to 51, for an eye-popping 56,000% return (that's no typo).

Recently, however, it appears as though the law of large numbers has finally begun to catch up with the computer maker. It's easy to double revenues when there are only $2 million in sales per quarter. But try to do it when the company has more than $7 billion in revenue per quarter. That's the challenge Dell is now being confronted with. That's not to say Dell is a bad company. But it's difficult for Dell to grow at a torrid pace forever. As a result, investors seem to be taking a more conservative approach with Dell; its stock price, reflecting that sentiment, has retreated a bit, falling from 51 to 38 by mid-August 2000.

What's the biggest risk of growth investing? That the stock will fail to meet the high expectations for it that investors have built into its price. Dell continues to be a good example. In the summer of 2000, it declared second-quarter earnings that beat Wall Street's expectations by a penny. But it missed the revenue figure analysts had predicted by $200 million (about $7.7 vs. $7.9 billion). Investors sent the stock down 10%.

In general, growth investing can be more volatile than value investing. Which is not to say it's bad. You just need the stomach for it.

Growth at a Reasonable Price

The world according to GARP. Somewhere between value and growth investors are folks who adhere to the GARP philosophy, or growth at a reasonable price. GARP investors want to invest in growth companies, but they are not willing to mortgage the house to do so. These investors want companies with growing revenues and earnings but that are trading at reasonable valuations. What's "reasonable" for a GARP investor may be too pricey for a true value player. The pure growth investor, in contrast, is willing to pay a huge premium for a company if its earnings are consistent and ramping.

GARP investors sometimes get the rap of being wishy-washy—unwilling to go out on either the growth or value limb. Wouldn't everyone love some growth at a reasonable price? their detractors say. It sounds too good to be true. Perhaps that's why stocks with good growth prospects and reasonable valuations don't tend to go overlooked for too long.

As an example of a GARP play, homebuilder D.R. Horton (DHI: NYSE) probably would have fit the bill in early May 2000. The company's P/E was a very low 5. Meanwhile, its earnings had grown a nice 18% over the last year and 30% annually over the last five years. Analysts projected its earnings growth rate to be about 16% a year.

Those are the kinds of ratios that get the attention of GARP investors. There clearly seemed to be growth taking place at the company, but that growth could be had at a reasonable price. As a result—and not surprisingly—the company's shares jumped from 13 in May to 18 in August, for a gain of 38%. And even with the price appreciation, boosting the P/E to 6, the shares were still trading at reasonable levels—which means that investors who were looking for a stock that fits the GARP investing style could still find one in D.R. Horton.

Why doesn't everyone practice seemingly sensible GARP investing? Because sensible does not tend to produce outsized returns. GARP investors are more likely to match the market. So for the most part, you'd arguably do just as well in a mutual fund that tracked the broader market.

Momentum Investing

An extreme form of growth investing is momentum investing. Momentum investors don't give a hoot about anything other than upward mobility. They want to know one thing: Is the stock heading up? If a stock is moving up, and it looks as though it will continue rising for some time, a momentum investor will ride the stock for all it's worth. Think of the momentum investor as the person who goes from party to party on New Year's Eve. As long as the music's playing, this person is willing to stick around. But as soon as the music stops, that's it. The partygoer is on to the next party. The momentum investor operates in the same manner. As long as a stock is moving upward, all is well. But as soon as the stock peaks, or soon thereafter, the momentum investor bolts.

Some momentum investors are like growth investors in that they look for "earnings momentum." These investors study their own earnings projections on a stock or those of Wall Street analysts, and they look for companies with expectations of swift and substantial earnings growth.

Other momentum investors rely entirely on stock charts. Looking at past patterns, they try to predict when a stock is about to soar.

Still other momentum investors are entirely unquantitative. They might see the froth boiling for a stock on Internet message boards or in news reports and decide it's a hot story. They'll pile in, hoping to catch a price rise amid the mania surrounding the stock.

Take Internet Capital Group (ICGE:Nasdaq), a company that invests in other Internet companies in the business-to-business e-commerce field. This stock was a darling that appealed to virtually all types of momentum investors: In early 2000, the stock was expected to have swift and substantial earnings growth. And back then, business-to-business was considered the latest, greatest frontier of the Internet stock explosion. Indeed, during the height of the business-to-business (B2B) mania, Internet Capital was one of Wall Street's most beloved and most chatted-up stocks.

But as with many momentum stocks, ICGE took a fall, and it was brutal. After reaching an all-time high of 212 on December 22, 1999, after an IPO only four months earlier, Internet Capital finally ran out of gas. Initially, its fall from grace was metered. But within a matter of weeks, the downward spiral of the stock gained traction. By the end of March 2000, the stock was trading down 63% from its highs. By the end of the second quarter, it was down 84% from its highs. That kind of swift descent doesn't leave a lot of time for an investor to check out with much to show for himself.

And that's the problem with momentum investing. When you're ready to sell a stock and move on, it's not always easy to make a graceful exit. If a company surprises investors with bad news, like an earnings warning, momentum investors feel compelled to rush the gates all at once. The result is that a stock can suffer a sharp and swift decline, taking all investors along. Just ask momentum investors who tried to catch a ride on e-business software company MicroStrategy (MSTR:Nasdaq) during the first three months of 2000, when the stock soared from 52 to 333. When the company announced that it was changing its accounting policy regarding its revenues, switching to a more conservative method—which also resulted in the company's restating past financial results—investors bolted en masse. The stock went from 333 to 20 in a matter of eight weeks. Message for momentum investors? Live by the sword, die by the sword.

If you haven't met any momentum investors, don't be surprised. It's considered somewhat heretical in the investing world to be interested in the short-term moves of a stock rather than the long-term goals of a company. Momentum investors don't exactly wear the momentum moniker on their sleeve. They don't want to be dubbed un-American.

In our view, if you can make money from momentum investing, all the more power to you. It's not a moral issue. But momentum investing is not easy. If momentum investors are right, they are very richly rewarded. But if they're wrong, they can get seriously crushed.

Quantitative Valuation Metrics

Now that we've identified the prevailing investment valuation styles, let's look at some of the quantitative metrics that investors rely upon when making a buy decision. These ratios, like price-to-earnings or price-to-sales, are not exclusive to any one way of investing. Rather, different investors weigh the metrics differently, depending on their M.O. As for where to find the information? This chapter lists top sites for valuation ratios.

Price-to-Earnings Ratio

The price-to-earnings ratio is a staple among financial metrics. Taking the price of the stock and dividing it by the company's last four quarters of earnings per share gives you the company's trailing twelve-month P/E ratio. Take the stock's current price and divide it by what analysts are forecasting its earnings to be for the upcoming year, and you get the company's forward-looking P/E ratio. The trailing P/E ratio is considered more reliable because it's based on real figures, not projections.

The P/E ratio is available on almost any standard stock quote on the Internet. Unless the site indicates otherwise, the listed P/E ratio is generally the trailing P/E rather than the forward P/E.

The P/E ratio of a stock is not valuable in itself but is helpful as a comparative measure. You can use the ratio to compare a stock to competitor companies, an industry average, the stock market as a whole, or even nonequity investments like bonds. The P/E gives you a sense of how expensive the stock is compared to these alternative investments.

The strict value investor tends to use P/E to compare a stock to nonequity investments like a bond. They do this with a concept called "earnings yield," which enables an apples-to-apples comparison with bonds. The earnings yield is the reciprocal of the P/E ratio. So if the P/E ratio is 10, the earnings yield is $\frac{1}{10}$, or 10%.

Here's how the comparison works. Say a company is trading at 80 times earnings, or a P/E ratio of 80. Essentially, you are paying $80 for $1 worth of earnings. The earnings yield would be 1.25% ($\frac{1}{80}$). Essentially, this means that for each dollar you invest, you have claim to 1.25 cents of its current earnings. At the same time a bond will yield, say, 6%, or six cents on the dollar. An investor who buys a stock with a P/E ratio as high as 80 is essentially betting that earnings will soar, easily exceeding the bond's currently higher yield and attracting new investors along the way. Value investors are often loath to take the chance that such high hopes will pan out, especially when they can get a nice yield in a much safer investment, like a bond. (For more on the earnings yield concept, see our detailed discussion in Chapter 10, "When to Sell.")

Indeed, so few New Economy stocks have P/E ratios that compare favorably with the bond yield, investors who are interested in these stocks largely don't use the earnings yield comparison. Essentially, they have decided that the future for these stocks far exceeds the potential of bonds. They use the P/E ratio instead to compare these pricey stocks to *each other*.

Take Cisco Systems (CSCO:Nasdaq), the San Jose–based networking giant. It has typically traded at a premium to its industry peers. For example, in August 2000, it had a trailing P/E of 186, while the P/E ratio for the networking sector was 46.

Does that kind of sky-high P/E ratio mean you shouldn't own the stock? Not necessarily. The fact of the matter is that some companies deserve to have lofty P/E ratios because their earnings potential really is that tremendous. At least that's what the market seems to believe about Cisco.

Some companies, on the other hand, don't enjoy any kind of pre-mium. Computer Associates (CA:NYSE), a software company notori-ous for disappointing Wall Street, was sporting a trailing P/E of just 15 in late summer 2000. Meanwhile, its peers in "application software" had an average P/E of about 44, according to marketguide.com.

Investors clearly lacked faith in this stock for one reason or another. What they perhaps were saying with this lower P/E was that Computer Associates' earnings going forward are unreliable. After all, the com-pany has a history of letting Wall Street down. Why should Wall Street not price another letdown into the company's stock?

Essentially, you should use the P/E ratio like this: Compare a com-pany's P/E ratio to those of its industry peers. If it's more expensive, ask yourself if your research suggests that this higher valuation is jus-tified. If it's less expensive, ask yourself if your research indicated any black spots on the company's record that would urge you to stay away from the stock as well. It's a helpful check to give yourself the confi-dence that you're not overpaying.

Price-to-Sales Ratio

The price-to-sales ratio is a traditional valuation metric that has taken on more prominence in recent years. Until the New Economy boom, price-to-sales was just another way to value a company. But once the terrain was littered with companies without earnings, price-to-sales rose in popularity. Investors who adhered to traditional valuation met-rics to determine a fair price for, say, a company like community site TheGlobe.com (TGLO:Nasdaq) would likely have been unable to find one using the P/E ratio. So investors bent on getting in on the Internet craze turned to other valuation measures to help gauge their purchases.

An analysis of revenue growth, the price-to-sales ratio is market capi-talization divided by annual sales. (It's really no different from the P/E ratio in its basic calculation. With P/E the figures are all on a "per share" basis—price per share, earnings per share. Since revenues aren't typically divided "per share," the price-to-sales ratio is generally figured using mar-ket capitalization, which is price times the number of shares outstanding.)

Indeed, a host of Internet stocks that came to market in 1999 traded based on revenue projections instead of on earnings. The think-ing was that if companies were able to rapidly grow their revenues, earnings would eventually follow once companies figured out how to make money on the Web. For most of 1999, this kind of thinking prevailed on Wall Street. By late 1999, however, Wall Street started to get impatient.

What kicked off the change in part was interest rates. Interest rates began to head higher, with the Federal Reserve raising rates several times in 1999 and 2000. This ramp inevitably put pressure on growth stocks, including technology stocks.

At the same time, Wall Street started to doubt whether stocks that had promised eventual earnings would ever deliver. The flagship company for this phenomenon was Amazon.com (AMZN:Nasdaq). Amazon was the icon of Wall Street's "earnings don't matter, no, earnings do matter" 180-degree turn. For most of Amazon's existence since its May 1997 IPO, Wall Street was willing to let Amazon become profitable at its own pace. The story went like this: Wall Street would ask Amazon when it expected to be profitable, and Amazon would tell it that it would be profitable after it achieved critical mass. What that meant was that Amazon was going to spend its revenues and financing funds to get market share at the expense of any profits—for the indefinite future. Wall Street embraced the company's seemingly entrepreneurial flair and confidence.

But one day Wall Street said enough is enough. When the company, during its 1999 fourth-quarter earnings report in January 2000, told Wall Street that higher revenues during the quarter would not translate into earnings anytime soon, Wall Street grew impatient. The stock was hammered. "We'll wait no more, and we'll pound your stock until you show that you can be profitable" was the message that was sent to the company. By August 2000, the stock was down more than 70% from its all-time high of 113 in early December 1999.

Even if you're not a New Economy investor, price-to-sales is a helpful ratio. What the price-to-sales ratio shows is how much an investor is willing to pay for $1 in revenue. Consider this: A company that is doing $1 billion a year in revenues and trading at a market cap of $1 billion is said to have a price-to-sales ratio of 1.0. A company that has a market cap of $800 million but has annual revenues of $1 billion trades at a price-to-sales ratio of 0.8. A 0.8 price-to-sales ratio is telling you that an investor can get $1 worth of revenues for 80 cents. That's better than a ratio of 1.0 in terms of valuation.

Let's take Coca-Cola (KO:NYSE) as an example. In August 2000 it had a price-to-sales ratio of about 8. That means that investors were willing to pay $8 for every dollar of revenue that Coke brought in. PepsiCo

(PEP:NYSE), meanwhile, was trading at about 3 times sales; investors were paying only $3 to get $1 of revenues. All other things being equal, PepsiCo was a better deal.

Just as a point of reference, the S&P 500's average price-to-sales ratio was 8.7 in August 2000.

Price-to-Book Ratio

Price-to-book is market capitalization divided by the company's book value. Book value is a company's assets minus its liabilities. What you have left over is called shareholders' equity, or book value.

The theory behind price-to-book value is that it tells you how the price compares to the amount you'd get if you sold all the assets (after liabilities) of the company. It's a favorite measure of many value investors bent on assuring themselves that they're getting real value for their money.

In the New Economy age of intellectual capital, this particular metric has lost some of its luster. Price to book worked much better with companies that had lots of hard assets such as factories, heavy equipment, and the like. Look at steelmaker Bethlehem Steel (BS:NYSE). During the summer of 2000 it was sporting a price-to-book ratio of just 0.4. Microsoft (MSFT:Nasdaq), on the other hand, had a price-to-book ratio of 9. The lower the price-to-book ratio, the better valuation-wise. After all, would you rather pay $9 for $1 worth of assets or 40 cents for $1 worth of assets?

Based on those numbers, you can safely go out and buy Bethlehem, right? Not necessarily. Today, lots of companies—especially tech companies—do not have much in the way of hard assets, but they do have plenty of intellectual assets, namely their staffers and patents. Price-to-book ratios aren't especially useful when you're trying to compare technology or service companies with industrial firms.

But the ratio does work well when you're comparing businesses with lots of assets with other similar businesses. Take Ford (F:NYSE) and General Motors (GM:NYSE). The price-to-book ratio for Ford during the summer of 2000 was 1.44. The ratio for GM was 1.75. Ford's ratio was also lower than that of the car industry as a whole, GM's a bit higher. If all other things were equal, Ford would be a better deal.

The metric is also popular among investors in financial stocks, where the assets include loans and cash on the books. Take Wells Fargo

(WFC:NYSE) and Chase Manhattan Bank (CMB:NYSE). Wells Fargo in August 2000 had a book value of $14.42 a share, which gave it a price-to-book value of 3. Chase, meanwhile, had about $19.50 a share in book value, which gave it a price-to-book value of about 2.5. Again, all other things being equal—and they may not be—Chase would be the better value here.

PEG Ratio

Another useful metric in determining a stock's value is the PEG ratio. You get this ratio by taking a company's P/E ratio (preferably trailing) and dividing it by the company's annual earnings growth rate analysts expect for a company over a specific period (typically, three to five years). A company that has a P/E ratio of 40 and an expected earnings growth rate of 20% is said to have a PEG ratio of 2. A company that has a P/E ratio of 20 and an expected growth rate of 20 has a PEG ratio of 1.00. The lower the company's PEG ratio, the cheaper—or more reasonably valued—the stock is perceived to be. A PEG ratio of 1 is considered fairly valued for most industries. A PEG ratio of 1.5 is about average for technology companies.

Think of it this way: A higher PEG ratio means the market is more ebullient about the growth prospects of a company than are analysts. A low PEG ratio, meanwhile, indicates the opposite. Considering that analysts tend to be optimistic (see our related discussion Chapter 9, "Earnings, Splits, Buybacks, and Other Events in a Stock's Life"), a high PEG ratio is not a great sign.

The reason this ratio is important is that it allows an investor to see where the company's price-to-earnings ratio is in relationship to its expected growth rate. A price-to-earnings ratio by itself allows you to take a look only at its past earnings divided by its current price; it tells you nothing about whether the P/E ratio is in line with its expected growth rate. At the same time, many fundamental investors don't like PEG because it relies on analyst projections rather than actual company fundamentals.

As always, just because a stock has a low price-to-earnings ratio, or a low PEG ratio, or low ratio of any sort doesn't necessarily make the stock a screaming bargain. Sometimes stocks have low ratios because they deserve them. So, use the PEG ratio as yet another measuring stick in your arsenal of tools.

Price-to-Cash-Flow Ratio

Remember back in the financial analysis chapter when we said cash flow is more telling than earnings? Well, the same concept applies in valuation. This measure compares price to cash flow—how much cash a company is generating above its day-to-day expenses of doing business.

Bob Olstein, manager of the Olstein Financial Alert fund, considers this his most important valuation ratio, because while earnings can be finagled with, "cash is real."

Olstein says that companies that enjoy excess cash flow have an advantage over companies that do not. He offers five things a company can do when it has excess cash flow:

1. Raise the dividend

2. Buy back its own stock

3. Make acquisitions when others cannot—and at more opportune times

4. If problems do develop, it does not have to adopt short-term strategies that are not in the long-term interest of the company

5. It makes the company a more attractive acquisition target

The relevance of the ratio follows from the importance of cash flow itself. A company selling at a lower price-to-cash-flow ratio (all things being equal) would be more appealing than one that trades at a higher one.

In sum, no one ratio tells the whole story. Many investors rely just on the P/E ratio, and that's not so horrible, considering how widely used it is on Wall Street. Still, all ratios help paint a picture of a company's valuation. It's good to look over as many ratios as possible.

Web Sites with Valuation Metrics

Now that you know what things you are looking for when buying stocks, let's talk about good sites that provide this information.

MSN MoneyCentral
www.moneycentral.com
MSN MoneyCentral sports a feature in its "Investor" section under "Stocks" called "Research Wizard." Pop a ticker symbol into the research wizard, and, *voilà!,* out comes the price-to-earnings

ratio. Perhaps its best feature is a compare function that allows an investor to pit one stock against another. You can quickly compare P/Es of similar stocks.

Marketguide.com
www.marketguide.com
Marketguide.com has lots of good investment information as well. For valuation metrics, its strongest feature is the "comparison" section.

The comparison section compares a company—Yahoo! (YHOO: Nasdaq), for example—with the rest of its industry, sector, and the S&P 500. The beauty of this kind of comparison is that you can quickly find out where Yahoo! is relative to those other benchmarks. Its price-to-earnings ratio (on a trailing twelve-month basis) was about 400 during August 2000. The P/E ratios for its industry, sector, and the S&P 500 were 29, 46, and 35, respectively. Which just goes to show the kind of risk you're taking with a stock like that.

So while MoneyCentral does a nice job of a stock-to-stock comparison, marketguide.com serves as a second check with the industry comparison. Another nice feature of marketguide.com— it includes the price-to-cash-flow ratio.

Zacks.com
www.zacks.com
Zacks.com is a good place to help you figure out the PEG ratio. That's a ratio that seems elusive on the Web, so you need to do a little bit of math yourself. (Not a lot!)

At Zacks.com, you'll find the average annual five-year earnings growth rate for a stock. Grab that under "estimates," and then pick up a trailing P/E from most any financial site. Remember, PEG is the P/E ratio divided by the growth rate.

Let's use Microsoft to see how PEG works. Its trailing P/E ratio in August 2000 was 41; analysts surveyed by Zacks were projecting the company to grow by 21% annually over the next five years. So, doing the math, its PEG ratio is 41/21, or 1.95, a number that would indicate the stock's richly valued. Or, as we stated earlier, it's a stock that investors are more ebullient about than analysts are.

Using Price Charts to Determine Entry Points

Up to now we've discussed the tools that fundamental investors use in valuing stocks. But there's another group of stock pickers out there who don't care one iota about the fundamentals. The technical analyst is concerned only with a stock's price chart. The technician uses charts to pinpoint good buy and sell, or, as technicians say, "entry and exit" points for individual stocks.

Even if you aren't a pure technician, it's wise to look at a chart when you're thinking about buying a stock. Technical analysis is the study of past market performance, and because history often repeats itself, stock prices are likely to behave in a predictable manner.

The key concepts for buying and selling with charts are "support" and "resistance." A support line on a chart forms at the price that a stock tends to stay above. It may fall toward that price, say 20, but whenever it gets there, buyers come in and "support" the stock. At or near support is generally a good place to buy a stock because, if the chart is right, odds are the price won't go lower.

Resistance is the price that the stock just can't seem to reach. Just as the stock reaches resistance, the sellers come out of the woodwork, keeping the stock down. A stock approaches the resistance price but rarely exceeds it. When it does, that's a breakout. The resistance line is generally the place to sell, not buy.

(Here's a helpful hint: If you're really chartphobic, you don't even have to look for yourself. MSN MoneyCentral gives you support and resistance points in its Research Wizard.)

As an example, let's take a look at electronics manufacturing services company Solectron (SLR:NYSE) from August 1999 to August 2000. Each time the stock approached 32 per share, it held its own and moved higher. Its peak was predictable too. The stock chart shows that 48 consistently served as a resistance level. To the skilled technician, that kind of price action was money in the bank. When you know the general high and low for a stock, you can better time your purchases.

The point is that whether you're a technician who lives and dies by the charts or a fundamental investor looking at price-to-earnings ratios and other metrics, it's helpful to consult a stock's chart before deciding to take the plunge into an investment.

There's a lot more to technical analysis than I've looked at here. We addressed much of it in Chapter 7, "How to Read a Stock Chart."

Solectron: Support and Resistance

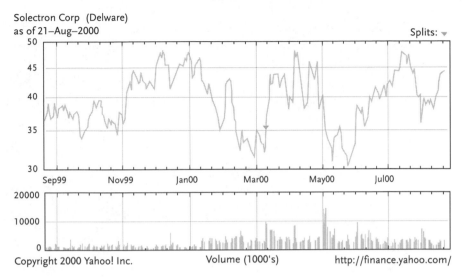

Solectron Corp (Delware)
as of 21–Aug–2000

Splits: ▾

Copyright 2000 Yahoo! Inc.   Volume (1000's)   http://finance.yahoo.com/

Data Source: Commodity Systems, Inc. (CSI) www.csidata.com

Macro Events Often Provide Buying Opportunities

Beyond the stock-specific issues to consider when buying (valuation ratios, support, and resistance), there are bigger-picture trends that can create opportunities for the savvy investor. Essentially, when the entire stock market is swooning or rising thanks to macro-type events, that could be a good time to buy or sell a stock that's going along for the ride.

Interest Rates

Take interest rates. As we detailed in the Chapter 2, interest-rate movements can be either good or bad for stocks. Rising interest rates for the most part tend to weigh on stock prices. But if the market as a whole is falling thanks to interest rate fears, and the stock you've been eyeing is dropping with it, that could be a good time to be a contrarian and buy.

At the same time, while rising rates are generally not good for the market overall, certain types of stock tend to thrive during a rising interest rate environment.

Food and beverage stocks often do well in times of rising interest rates. Sure, consumers might cut back their spending on more luxuri-

ous items—boats, jewelry, cars—but hopefully, they aren't going to cut
back on eating or drinking. That's why when interest rates soar, you'll
often see these kinds of stocks either maintain their levels or even rise.
Investors are looking for safety during times of turmoil, and these
stocks are seen as the place to be.

As interest rates rose throughout the first half of 2000, for example,
Anheuser-Busch (BUD:NYSE) thrived. Take a look at the chart. You'll
see that Budweiser's stock really took off in April/May, just about the
time that the Fed issued its big half-point rate hike.

BUD Enjoys Interest-Rate Hikes

That said, when the Fed stops raising rates, look for companies like
BUD to pull back a bit; they're generally getting the price appreciation
as a result of being in this kind of interest rate environment.

Drug companies are also popular in a rising interest rate environment. Most people are not going to curtail their spending on medica-
tions and analgesics that are essential to their everyday living. Pfizer's
(PFE:NYSE) chart illustrates the point nicely.

Macro-market Moves

Beyond interest rates, there are also other events that can often lead
to good buying opportunities. "Gray Monday" in October 1997 is an
example. As word spread that Asian markets were collapsing, stock

Pfizer Stays Healthy as Interest Rates Rise

markets around the world suffered huge downdrafts—the United States stock market included. But for those who had the stomach for short-term pain, this moment proved to be a great buying opportunity. Stocks—good, bad, and ugly—were all thrown out the window. Investors, though, who felt confident that Cisco, Microsoft, and America Online were worth much more than they were being traded for could have snapped up these shares and have been richly rewarded less than a year later. America Online, about a year after Gray Monday, was trading about 200% higher; Microsoft was up 65%; and Cisco was up about 75%.

The stock market crash on October 19, 1987, was also a great buying opportunity. Less than a year after the Dow Jones Industrials index crashed, the index was up more than 25% from the bottom.

There are plenty of other examples—overseas disruptions, political turmoil, to name a couple—that can serve as buying opportunities for investors as well. The only requirement for those would-be opportunists is that they possess a cast-iron stomach. Buying stocks on these kinds of "dips" is not for the faint of heart. You might buy in, only to see things get worse before they get better.

So whether you are looking for stocks that rise or hold their own during hostile interest-rate environments or looking for stocks that are being thrown out with the proverbial bathwater, the point is that macro-generated buying opportunities do exist, especially for investors who've done their homework ahead of the crisis du jour.

Putting It All Together—A Valuation Example

Now that we have discussed the various ratios and know where they are on the Internet, let's put it all together and try to analyze a stock.

Let's take a look at CEC Entertainment (CEC:NYSE). The CEC stands for Chuck E. Cheese, the pizza and entertainment company. This is a company that's been public for about ten years and has a market cap of $780 million. Its main business is operating restaurants and entertainment centers. Say you like the company's business model and its fundamentals. Now you're trying to decide whether to buy. It's time to conduct some valuation analysis.

CEC's trailing P/E ratio, according to marketguide.com, during the middle of August 2000 was 16. Its price-to-sales ratio was 1.7, its price-to-book was 3.4, and its price-to-cash-flow was 10.2.

Those numbers alone, though, don't tell us that much. We have no idea how they compare to those of CEC's peers. So let's find out.

The company's trailing P/E of 16 was much lower than the restaurant industry's 21.2, according to marketguide.com. Its price-to-sales ratio, price-to-book, and price-to-cash-flow ratios, meanwhile, were all lower than those of its industry peers as well, according to marketguide.com. That's a good thing. As for its PEG ratio (remember: expected 3-to-5-year growth rate divided into its trailing P/E)? I took the analysts' expected growth rate of 23% (grabbed it at Firstcall.com, a paid site; Zacks.com would have worked too) and divided that into the P/E of 16. The result was 0.7, a relatively low number.

How CEC Stacks Up				
Valuation Ratios	CEC Entertainment	Industry	Sector	S&P 500
P/E Ratio	16.01	21.22	34.40	34.01
Price-to-Sales	1.72	2.46	5.96	8.68
Price-to-Book	3.36	4.29	5.73	9.66
Price-to-Cash-Flow	10.28	13.64	20.16	26.66

Source: Marketguide.com (August 2000)

At this point, things look promising. The stock is relatively inexpensive yet has promising growth. How about the chart? According to moneycentral.com, resistance for the stock (where the sellers come out) is sitting at 36; support was at 27. During the middle of August the stock was trading at about 29, near the support level—another good sign.

Interest rates, meanwhile, have played a part in tempering investors' enthusiasm for restaurant stocks, but that would be yet another reason to be "contrarian" and buy now.

In some ways, CEC was the perfect example of a GARP stock. It's got some growth potential, and it looked fairly cheap versus its peers.

GARP investors looking for a company that was growing at a reasonable price would have done well to consider this stock during the summer of 2000.

As I said when we began this chapter: There is no easy answer to valuation. But this chapter should help give you the tools you need at least to understand the valuation process and increase your odds of not overpaying for a stock.

9

Earnings, Splits, Buybacks, and Other Events in a Stock's Life

Buying a stock is merely the first step in investing. As all of us who have spent a little time in earshot of CNBC know, a mind-boggling number of things happen to stocks—from workaday analyst actions and earnings releases to splits to buybacks and spinoffs. Each event in a stock's life marks a new opportunity to buy more, ditch the stock, or simply hold. At the very least, these events are moments that prompt investors to reconsider their positions—for better or worse.

This chapter aims to help investors who own stocks understand what is happening to them when they hear about things like a stock split or an earnings warning or a new tracking stock. While not specifically about *when to buy* a stock, the topic of Chapter 8, the information here can help you pinpoint opportunities to do just that. At the same time, while not specifically about *when to sell*, the topic of Chapter 10, much of what you learn here will help you make that tough decision.

In these respects, this chapter supplements material elsewhere in the book about analyzing stock fundamentals, charts, and valuations to decide when to buy and when to sell. The goal is to give you the confidence you need to make informed decisions in the haste of hot news. It will help ensure that fear and panic don't get the best of you.

To help elucidate these issues, I turned to Thomas Lepri, a seasoned markets and companies reporter at *TheStreet.com*.

Analyst Coverage

When you think about the people best positioned to influence a stock's price, you usually think of the CEO or the CFO or VP of sales. But actually, the folks who can really throw weight around a stock price are people who don't even work for the company: Wall Street analysts, or securities analysts.

Securities analysts supposedly do just that: serious securities analysis. The term "securities analysis" (or "stock analysis") sounds quite broad and academic. And it does flow from academic work. Benjamin Graham and David Dodd, authors of the 1934 classic *Security Analysis*, wrote and taught its fundamental merits. Famed investors like Warren Buffett worship the virtues of securities analysis: tireless and dispassionate scrutinizing of corporate balance sheets and industry conditions.

And to a certain extent that kind of study is what securities analysts, or Wall Street analysts, do. But analysts are far from academicians. Indeed, they're foremost salespeople—hawking stocks. Many of them probably don't even know about Graham or Dodd. No wonder, then, that securities analysts are the most prominent figures on what's known on Wall Street as the "sell side"—a world so named because it makes a chunk of its living off the stock research it sells to "buy-side" clients. Buy-siders are firms that buy stock, like mutual funds, pension funds, and hedge funds.

Analysts generally are responsible for a specific group of stocks, like food stocks or footwear or semiconductors. They relay opinions on these stocks in several ways. They issue ratings or recommendations, like buy, hold, and sell. They make earnings estimates for quarters and for full years. They set price targets—where the analyst expects to see the stock by a given date, say twelve months. They issue research reports with detailed analysis of a company or industry. They also issue shorter "notes" on companies, usually in reaction to news events.

Because these analysts have so much influence over a stock's price, it's helpful to get to know which ones cover your stocks, and what they have to say about them.

The Analyst's Dilemma

What analysts say, though, is rarely unadulterated insight. That's because of the conflicts analysts face. Their relationships with their employers can be tricky. Analysts are generally employed by investment banks and brokerages like Merrill Lynch, Salomon Smith Barney, and Morgan Stanley Dean Witter. These firms make much of their money by "underwriting," or helping to sell, stock of public and newly public companies, and by doing mergers and acquisitions work for them. To get that business, banks try to curry favor with the companies issuing stock or doing the merging.

Analysts are supposed to be separate from this side of the business—they style themselves as "independent" researchers who evaluate stocks on their merits.

But in fact there's little that is dispassionate about the business of securities analysis as practiced on Wall Street. Analysts have to consider the interest of many different groups when commenting on stocks. Perhaps most important, there are the firm's investment bankers and the companies whose stock the analyst covers—two groups whose interests are closely intertwined. Underwriting stock offerings is a very lucrative business, and investment bankers often feel they cannot afford to alienate potential clients with negative comments from their firm's analysts. To this end, many analysts are compensated partly by the underwriting deal flow they can deliver to the firm. A lot of negative ranting doesn't help the deal flow.

Then there's the sales staff—or brokers—at an analyst's firm, who largely work on commission and want to be able to move their product (stock) without the burden of an awkward "neutral" rating from the analyst.

Finally, there are the firm's big clients—like mutual fund and hedge fund managers. One would think these money managers would value the most honest assessment of a stock they could find. But if they already own the stock, they don't always appreciate it when their holdings get waylaid by a renegade analyst.

Conflicting Interests of an Analyst

The Ratings Game

With all that in mind, you should approach analysts' ratings—the buy, sell, and hold variety—with considerable skepticism. As in high school, there's a lot of grade inflation going on. Analysts sling "buys" around so much that they've taken on an almost neutral status. A "hold" or a "market perform" should make investors wary, especially when it comes from an analyst who works for one of the company's underwriters.

Think about it. Why would you hold on to a stock that's merely keeping up with the broader market, when there are so many "outperforms" right there for the taking? And a "sell" rating? You generally don't want to stick around long enough to find out what that rare rating means.

Investors can get frustrated trying to decipher analysts' ratings, primarily because different brokerage houses use different terms on different scales. For example, Everen Securities has three ratings—"outperform," "market perform," and "underperform"—while Deutsche Banc Alex. Brown uses a subtler scale of five. What Gruntal Financial calls a "strong buy" is on the "priority list" at Goldman Sachs, though each is the highest rating those firms give.

You'll find that if you want to compare one brokerage's "buy" with another's "accumulate," you'll first have to compare the terms and scales each uses. You may find that they're actually the same rating. On the other hand, if you're talking about a single firm's ratings, just compare their positions on whatever scale the company uses. To use an academic metaphor, on a scale of five, think of a "strong buy" as an A and a "buy" as a B. While both seem to advocate increasing your position in a stock, the "strong buy" suggests the more aggressive acquisition strategy.

Because of the conflicts of interest that plague the business of Wall Street securities analysis, you might find it useful to look at ratings as composites. For example, imagine that the ratings of the four analysts that cover a stock break down as follows: two strong buys, one buy, and one sell. Using a five-point scale in which a strong buy equals a 1, a buy equals a 2, and a sell equals a 5 (the third and fourth ratings could be market perform and market underperform—again, each brokerage has its own descriptions), you can calculate a composite rating of 2.25. On a scale of 1 to 5, 2.25 would be somewhere between a buy and a market perform.

$$(1)(2 \text{ strong buys}) + (2)(1 \text{ buy}) + (5)(1 \text{ sell}) = 9$$

$$(1)(2) + (2)(1) + (5)(1) = 9$$

$$9/4 = 2.25$$

Many Web sites, including *TheStreet.com,* Yahoo! Finance, and Marketguide, provide composite information for free—you don't need to calculate it yourself. By itself, though, that information is not very meaningful. You'll want to see how that rating compares with other stocks in the industry.

Who's Got You Covered?

In its "Research" section, Yahoo! Finance gives you a list of the brokerages that cover each stock. For example: biz.yahoo.com /z/a/i/ibm.html lists the analysts who cover IBM (IBM:NYSE). If you want the specific analyst's name, you can just call up the brokerage and ask. (First Call's site gives this info for a charge.)

Ratings are just one tool analysts use to evaluate stocks, and all in all, they're not a very controversial one. Generally, there's such ratings consensus among analysts that ratings don't precipitate much heated discussion.

Occasionally, though, an analyst will break ranks by going negative on a stock or group of stocks, as Michael Mayo did when he slapped a sell rating on four big bank stocks in the summer of 1999 while at Credit Suisse First Boston.

It's precisely because ratings are generally so effusive that individual investors do well to keep on the lookout for negative or neutral ratings. Such contrarian calls should be treated as red flags. And while you shouldn't automatically sell a stock when you see one of those flags, you should definitely take the time to think over the possible risks of your investment, especially if the analyst making the call is credible—an issue we discuss later in this chapter.

Take the case of Amazon.com (AMZN:Nasdaq). In late June 2000, a Lehman Brothers bond analyst came out with a searingly negative report about the company's creditworthiness. The analyst, Ravi Suria, called the company's credit "weak and deteriorating" and recommended that investors avoid the stock. The news helped send the stock down some 20%.

Displaying that kind of negativity toward a Wall Street darling is not an easy thing for an analyst to do, and in fact several equity analysts who cover Amazon did not have the gumption—or inclination—to follow suit. Until a month later, that is, after Amazon's earnings report indicated that revenue growth had fallen short of analysts' expectations. The day after *that* news, six equity analysts cut their rating on the stock, and it plunged another 13%.

Price Targets

Price targets are a lot more provocative than ratings. Indeed, price targets—an analyst's guess at what price a stock will reach by when—are the primary means by which analysts have acquired fame in the recent hyperbull period. In a bull market, the most difficult question to answer is not whether stocks will go up but how much they will go up, particularly in the technology and Internet sectors. More and more, if analysts want to make a stir in their industry and raise their profile and compensation, they do it with price targets.

Now, it would be nice if the price targets that analysts set represented their assessment of how much a stock is truly worth on a fundamental basis. But that's almost never the case. Price targets are being revised on Wall Street with increasing frequency. And the number of times those revisions are not accompanied by any corresponding revisions in earnings or revenue estimates makes it clear that analysts are essentially trying to keep pace with market speculation and momentum.

Take the example of Deutsche Banc Alex. Brown telecom analyst Brian Modoff, who raised his price target on momentum darling Qualcomm (QCOM:Nasdaq) to 250 from 225 (both pre-split prices) in early November 1999 after the company had beat earnings estimates and set plans for a 4-to-1 split. Qualcomm surged past 250 almost immediately, and two days later Modoff raised his target to 320 without revising his earnings estimates for the company.

Perhaps the most famous example of momentum analysis is the case of then–CIBC Oppenheimer Internet analyst Henry Blodget and Amazon.com. On December 15, 1998, Amazon closed at the then-stratospheric price of 242¾ (pre-split). The stock had enjoyed an incredible run over the last month, and the question on most observers' minds was when the stock would pull back. Surely it couldn't continue to defy gravity indefinitely.

The next day, Blodget grabbed Wall Street's attention by raising his price target on Amazon to 400 from 150, and the stock reacted with another rush of strength, jumping 46¼, or 19%, to 289. He wasn't able to make any upward revisions to the company's earnings estimates, since it didn't have any near-term prospects for earnings in the first place. In his research note, Blodget himself conceded that "Amazon's valuation is clearly more art than science."

Still, in a matter of a few short weeks, Amazon was trading at 480. (It later split.)

Unless you're into pure momentum trading—a game you probably shouldn't be playing unless you're playing with money you can afford to lose (see Chapter 8, "When to Buy")—don't bother trying to capitalize on a price target–infused run-up in a stock. You're likely to come too late to the party. Even in this democratized investing world, institutional investors still have a leg up when the information being distributed comes from analysts, their counterparts on the sell side. If you try to buy, you'll likely get an already very bid up price. If, on the other hand,

Amazon Sprinted with Blodget's Dec. 1998 Call

you've been thinking about selling a stock, you couldn't find a better way to unload it than into a frenzy of price-target buying.

The Ax

With that successful Amazon call under his belt, Blodget jumped to Merrill Lynch to replace Net analyst Jonathan Cohen, who, ironically, had gone sharply negative on Amazon by setting a price target of 50 one day after Blodget's infamous 400 target. The Amazon call made Blodget's career. Even more important, it elevated him to the status of "ax"—that is, an analyst so influential that he or she alone is capable of moving selected stocks and sometimes entire sectors with just a single positive or negative comment.

Analysts generally become axes by making a big, high-profile, and "right" call—whether a revision of a stock's rating, earnings estimates, or price target—before anyone else does, essentially "Blodgeting" the stock. An analyst's ax status is confirmed if the call is borne out by the market, or, as in the case of Blodget, the call itself proves a self-fulfilling prophecy, actually inducing the "correct" market reaction.

Ax status can emerge or fade in short order. But during the time an analyst carries the ax aura, it's worthwhile to follow what he or she says about your stock, as Wall Street will likely do the same.

Here's a list of analysts considered the ax on certain stocks in 2000. But don't rely on it indefinitely. Reputations can slide with one bad call.

Selected Axes, Summer 2000		
Analyst	Firm	Category
John Bensche	Lehman Brothers	Wireless Telecommunication Services
Henry Blodget	Merrill Lynch	Internet Software & Services
Amy Butte	Bear Stearns	Diversified Financial Services
Laura Conigliaro	Goldman Sachs	Computer Hardware
Mark Edelstone	Morgan Stanley Dean Witter	Semiconductors, Computer Hardware
Gregory Geilling	J.P. Morgan	Telecommunications Equipment
Jack Grubman	Salomon Smith Barney	Integrated Telecommunication Services
Ashok Kumar	U.S. Bancorp Piper Jaffray	Semiconductors
Steve McClellan	Merrill Lynch	IT Consulting & Services
Mary Meeker	Morgan Stanley Dean Witter	Internet Software & Services
Anne Meisner	Goldman Sachs	Systems Software
Steve Milunovich	Merrill Lynch	Computer Hardware
Dan Niles	Robertson Stephens	Semiconductors, Computer Hardware
Rick Sherlund	Goldman Sachs	Systems Software
Dana Telsey	Bear Stearns	Apparel Retail

Analyst Rankings

Axes aren't the only analysts who matter on Wall Street. In fact, there are many lesser-known analysts who are quietly respected, and others who enjoy celebrity status but actually are better at making TV appearances than analyzing stocks. Several Web sites and publications, including *TheStreet.com,* have ranked Wall Street analysts. *TheStreet.com*'s ranking, included in Appendix A of this book, judges analysts both on their popularity among influential institutional investors and the analysts' stock-picking abilities.

Credible surveys like these can help an individual investor decide which analysts are worth listening to. That doesn't mean you need to react to every upgrade or earnings revision the analyst puts out. But it can be helpful to pay attention to what the analyst actually says about a stock's business or the trends and trials facing an industry.

Earnings

Investing is largely a matter of keeping the proper perspective. In the short run, stocks—swayed by press releases, securities analysts, and market momentum—move up and down with seemingly random volatility. In the long run, as the great economist John Maynard Keynes said, everyone is dead.

But somewhere in between those two points, companies are forced to report their earnings. At root, the stock you own is nothing less than your stake in a business, the purpose of which is, ultimately, to make money.

So it makes sense for investors to be in a state of somewhat heightened awareness during those periods when companies give their shareholders a glimpse at the books. As we described earlier in our treatment of fundamental analysis in Chapter 6, earnings can be convoluted and won't always give a clear picture of a company's actual operations. But at the end of the day, earnings do represent a company's profits—or lack thereof—and are therefore investors' ultimate measurement.

Earnings Seasons

Just like the meteorological seasons, earnings reports come in seasons. These seasons tend to ebb and flow along with the fiscal calendar, which varies from company to company. The United States government's fiscal year ends September 30. But in the private sector, companies determine their own calendars, with many seasonal businesses staggering them to match their business cycles.

Fiscal calendars aren't completely without pattern. If they were, it would be impossible to refer to anything like earnings seasons in the first place. You'll find that the most common fiscal year is one that matches the calendar year, with quarters ending March 31, June 30, September 30, and December 31. Though companies have up to 45 days to report quarterly earnings, and up to 90 days after the fourth quarter, most reports cluster in the second and third weeks after the end of the quarter.

You can determine a company's fiscal calendar by looking at its government filings, which you can access free of charge at Web sites like freeedgar.com, or sec.gov, the Securities and Exchange Commission's site.

Expectations

Knowing when a company reports is one thing. But judging the quality of those reports is something else entirely. If, like most investors, you're not employed as a securities analyst at a major brokerage firm (or even if you are), you'll probably find yourself watching the opinions of others, at the very least to compare them to your own research.

The investing public knows those opinions collectively as "expectations"—as in "Intel today released first-quarter earnings above expectations" or "analysts expect Wal-Mart to earn 36 cents a share for the second quarter." But what does that mean? Who's doing all this "expecting"?

It's the securities analysts from banks like Merrill Lynch, Goldman Sachs, and Robertson Stephens who "cover," or follow, that stock. Though the financial media usually report earnings expectations as a single figure—e.g., 23 cents a share—the estimates you read on *TheStreet.com* and hear on CNBC are actually averages of a number of analysts' forecasts, or what's known as the "consensus estimate."

"Consensus" is actually a misleading term, because often analysts' views on a stock are anything but a consensus. That's why it's important to know as much information behind consensus expectations as possible. For example, how many individual estimates make up the consensus? The more analysts, the more reliable the estimate tends to be. What are the high and low ends of the range of expectations? The larger the gap, the greater the likelihood actual earnings will diverge from the consensus.

Have analysts recently been generally revising their estimates higher or lower? That's a sign that either expectations are very high (and an earnings report that misses expectations could bring on a big selloff) or much lower (so the stock is not likely to drop much on a report and could even bounce).

Earnings Info Available Online

DoubleClick Inc. (Excl. GW) (DCLK: NASDAQ)			31 $^1/_2$	▲
07/12/00 04:15 PM EDT			DCLK	3

Consensus Earnings Estimates	Year Ending		Quarter Ending	
	12/2001	12/2000	9/2000	6/2000
Current Mean EPS	0.41	−0.06	0.04	−0.05
Number of Brokers	22	22	21	22
Year-Ago EPS	NA	−0.24	−0.07	−0.07
Current High	0.55	0.05	0.08	−0.03
Current Low	0.31	−0.19	0.00	−0.10
Median	0.41	−0.06	0.04	−0.04
Standard Deviation	0.06	0.05	0.02	0.02
Current vs. Year-Ago	NA%	−75%	−157%	−28%
Report Date	0	0	16 Oct. 2000	18 Jul. 2000

Earnings Estimate Revisions and Trends	Year Ending		Quarter Ending	
	12/2001	12/2000	9/2000	6/2000
Current Mean	0.41	−0.06	0.04	−0.05
7 Days Ago Mean	0.41	−0.06	0.04	−0.05
10 Days Ago Mean	0.42	−0.24	−0.04	−0.05

Source: TheStreet.com, data from First Call

Unfortunately, most retail investors do not attempt to answer these kinds of questions about the stocks they own. If you do, however, you'll have an important edge. And there's lots of information online, in the "research" sections of sites like *TheStreet.com* and Yahoo! Finance, to give you that edge.

Generally speaking, the larger and more high-profile the stock, the more analyst coverage it will have. And stocks with heavy coverage tend to produce consensus estimates that are more reliable and representative of the entire range simply because their data sample is larger.

There are exceptions, though. Relatively large companies can sometimes produce results capable of utterly confounding the consensus. Just look at the case of Advanced Micro Devices (AMD:NYSE), a major semiconductor manufacturer with annual revenues of more than $2.8 billion. Early in 2000, AMD released 1999 fourth-quarter earnings of 43 cents a share. That was well above the penny-a-share consensus estimate reported by the newswires—about 4,200% above, to be exact—despite the fact that some 20 analysts, a respectable number, were covering the stock.

The market had clearly been betting on a strong quarter from AMD, as the stock ran up about 30% in the two weeks preceding its report. But was there any other way investors could have been ready for such an upside shock?

A quick glance at the individual estimates within the consensus would have made it clear enough that the analyst community didn't have much of a clue where AMD was headed. Those estimates fell as low as a loss of 11 cents to as high as a profit of 26 cents, a wicked spread usually reserved for the forecasting of emerging economies' gross domestic product figures. The width of the range of estimates was largely a factor of AMD's recent troubles—the firm was coming off a string of particularly tough quarters, and rebounding companies produce volatile comparative results, especially in rambunctious sectors like semiconductors.

Bottom line: Be sure to give any stock with a wide range of earnings estimates extra scrutiny. If its median estimate—the middle point of the range—is a wide margin from the mean estimate—the average—don't be shocked if a company's actual earnings results deviate from expectations by a similarly wide margin. That's not to say you should automatically buy such a stock. Nor does it mean you should necessarily unload it, since earnings surprises can be positive as well as negative. But a wide range of estimates indicates a degree of uncertainty among the analyst community about where a quarter is headed. Ultimately, in such cases, you'll have to use your own judgment—relying in part on the analysis and valuation tools we discussed in Chapters 6, 7, and 8—to gauge the company's prospects.

Now, in the example of AMD, you could also blame AMD for doing a poor job of providing guidance to the analyst community. A wide range of estimates is often a sign of loose guidance. Guidance, in essence, is how the company's chief financial officer manages the company's relationship with Wall Street. For instance, a company like

---

The Earnings Conference Call

Another evaluation tool at your disposal—post-earnings announcement—is the earnings conference call. These calls are a chance for professionals to grill the CEO and CFO about the company and its earnings report. As important as what the company says is what the analysts and big shareholders ask the company about.

Once these calls were strictly the province of institutional investors and Wall Street analysts. Nowadays, these calls are almost universally open to individuals on a "listen-only" basis over the Internet. On the call, you can get a strong sense of the confidence and conviction of the company's top executives as well as an idea of the biggest issues they are facing.

For example, when so-called dot.com companies started to suffer in late 1999/early 2000, an increasingly common question among analysts for companies reliant on advertising revenue was "How many of your advertisers are dot.coms?" (Read: Who might end up as bad debts?) An investor hearing that question would be keyed off to an important industry threat. He or she could scan the site or station of any company—from network CBS (VIA:NYSE) to women's media site iVillage (IVIL:Nasdaq)— and sense for him- or herself how reliant that company was on tenuous Net-firm advertising.

Most companies now provide links to conference calls from their Web sites. Also, they're often available at sites like broadcast.com or bestcalls.com. If you're uncertain, call your company's investor relations department and ask.

General Electric (GE:NYSE), whose actual earnings rarely deviate more than a penny from the consensus, keeps Wall Street well abreast of its wide array of business lines. That sort of guidance inspires confidence in a stock by making it easy to trust its earnings estimates.

But loose guidance and analysts' inability to identify upturns in profit cycles aren't the only thing that can cause companies to beat expectations. There's a practice on Wall Street that's euphemistically known as "managing expectations," and it involves nothing less than a concerted effort to guide analysts to artificially low earnings projections.

Funny enough, many companies and analysts are complicit in this game. They get together and manufacture an artificially low estimate so that the company can "surprise" Wall Street with strong quarters. Of course, nobody would ever admit as much. But the numbers do tell a compelling story of consistent lowballing, as quarter after quarter the number of companies beating expectations continues to far exceed those disappointing. According to First Call/Thomson Financial, over each of the last five years, on average 56% of S&P 500 companies have beaten their quarterly earnings expectations, whereas 26% have missed. And the figures are even more dramatic in the recent past. In the four quarters of 1999, 65% exceeded while just 14% fell short.

Whispers

This predictable earnings performance pattern hasn't gone unnoticed by the market. How could it? According to the strict "efficient market hypothesis," an efficient market prices into itself all present knowledge and all future expectations. And the understanding that companies massage earnings is pretty widespread. Even the casual observer not digesting every last bit of market information could hardly fail to miss the regularity with which companies beat earnings expectations.

So with the market well aware, the game changes. Bets are placed not on whether companies will meet expectations—increasingly a given—but on the margin by which they'll exceed them. People speculate, rumors circulate, and therein is born the "whisper number," the common term for the rumors that are said to originate with industry analysts or a select group of savvy market participants.

Some would argue that whisper numbers are nothing more than rumor-mongering and stock-hyping, and that may well be the case. But regardless of the reputability of those who traffic in them, whisper numbers on earnings exist. They're one reason you'll sometimes see a company's stock slump when it meets or even beats the consensus estimate.

The problem with whisper numbers is that they fall victim to the same pressures as the earnings estimates themselves. That is, even if they were a reliable guide to the margins by which firms will beat their estimates—and there's no evidence that this is the case—it's nearly impossible to make any money from them.

Efficient market theory makes the catch-22 clear: You could capitalize on a piece of information only if it's not yet in the market, for if it were, the market would have already priced it into the stock. And if you've seen a whisper number on a Web site, or heard it from a broker, it's likely making its way into the market and the price of the stock.

That's still not to say that whisper numbers have no purpose. They can be very useful as composite sketches of the most bullish camp on a given stock. Use them as such, and measure them against your own estimation of a company's performance, and you'll do well.

For example, imagine that a company called Kansas Milling Co. has a whisper number that puts its fourth-quarter earnings solidly above consensus estimates. Moreover, imagine that Kansas Milling has been able to generate, and largely meet, such lofty whisper numbers for several quarters running. What does that information tell you? Should you automatically assume Kansas Milling will beat expectations? Should you call your broker and load up on the stock in anticipation of a big upside earnings surprise?

Not at all. What the whisper number is telling you is that there is an extreme and sustained bullishness in the marketplace concerning Kansas Milling's fundamentals. Now, that's not a bad thing by any stretch for Kansas Milling's shareholders. The positive sentiment on that stock is usually a by-product of its history of consistently beating earnings expectations. For a stock like Kansas Milling, or for a real-life example, Yahoo! (YHOO:Nasdaq), the bullishness indicated by whisper numbers can create a lot of momentum ahead of an actual earnings release. If you can stand the risk—which is to say, if you can afford to lose such a bet should things turn out badly—that momentum can create huge opportunities for nimble investors.

The problem is that whisper numbers effectively raise the bar for companies. Say the market expects Kansas Milling to beat expectations by a nickel, and it ends up beating them by only 3 cents. The stock may not get as favorable a reception as it would have if those increased expectations weren't already embedded in it. In addition, momentum can disappear very quickly after a company reports. By definition, a pre-earnings run will end once earnings are out. This is the case with a number of New Economy companies, including Yahoo! at times, which tend to rally strongly ahead of their earnings releases and sell off immediately after. Another example: Intel (INTC:Nasdaq), which before its second-quarter 2000 earnings rallied for several days. Then it fell the day of and after its report, when it beat expectations.

A number of Web sites—www.streetiq.com and www.whispernumber

.com are a couple—publish whisper numbers, though they don't always make clear who's doing the whispering. Treat the information as you would just about anything being gingerly whispered into your ear: with caution.

Missing Earnings Expectations

In heady economic times like those we have enjoyed over the last decade, and with firms devoting so much energy to the successful management of expectations, it's easy to lose sight of those companies that actually do fail to meet Wall Street expectations. Surely it can never happen to companies you've invested in, can it?

It can, and it will. And when it does, you'll have to face one of the toughest dilemmas of investing: whether to dump a stock along with the panicking masses, or to stay the course.

It sometimes takes courage and conviction to do the latter in an environment where professional money managers, judged by their quarterly, if not daily, performance won't hesitate to pull the trigger on a fallen angel of a stock. In the performance game, says one money manager, "the minute a problem comes up, you shoot first and ask questions later. If your performance is going to be affected by it, don't take the chance."

A company doesn't need to actually miss its earnings to cause professional managers to start bailing. All it needs to do is "warn" or "preannounce" to the market that its earnings, or even just its revenues, won't be as impressive as Wall Street expects. The main difference between a miss and a warning is slight but important. Unlike a miss, which is final, a warning can be a second chance at guidance. Companies that warn tend to give a new, lowered range of possible earnings. So it's possible that if a company is able to guide analysts sufficiently lower, it will be able to exceed lowered expectations when it finally reports.

Anticipating earnings warnings, however, is difficult. Companies generally follow patterns in their preannouncements, tending to time them a certain number of weeks before they report. And while traders often refer to the couple of weeks before the end of the quarter as "preannouncement season," there's no law that says a company can't preannounce after the quarter is over too. Strictly speaking, preannouncement season lasts until the moment a company has reported its earnings.

Preannouncement Policies

Preannouncements don't violate any sort of regulatory quiet period. Unlike IPO quiet periods, earnings season quiet periods are self-imposed and vary by company, more a matter of practice than of regulation. Companies can preannounce with absolute regulatory impunity if there's a considerable discrepancy between forecasts and their actual earnings.

When it comes to earnings misses and warnings, individual investors have a definite edge on the professional: You don't have to report your results at the end of each quarter to clients and bosses who look very unkindly on subpar short-term returns. You are your own boss. You set your own time frame and decide whether it's worth it to hang tough or even buy on an earnings blowup. In the short term, stocks that warn or miss can come under heavy selling pressure, especially if they've been momentum darlings in the past—driven up by institutional investors' enthusiasm. But in the long term, you'll have to follow your own assessment of the company's prospects. There's no single right response.

Take Charles Schwab (SCH:NYSE), the discount broker. Back in late 1997/98, Schwab made a business decision essentially to remake itself into a Web company, enabling all of its customers to trade stocks online at discounted prices. Those discounts, though, meant less commission revenue. The company was convinced the change would be just a short-term hit to its bottom line. It believed that customers were gravitating to the Net, and in the long term they would make up in volume what they lost on the discounts.

But Wall Street wasn't thinking long term. In April 1998, Schwab missed Wall Street's earnings expectations, partly because of the dip in commission revenue. The Street crushed the stock. But anyone who understood Schwab's strategy, believed in it, and bought on that dip would have been rewarded. The stock was up 141% from that warning until the year's end, as the strategy was vindicated.

Some stories aren't quite so rosy. In August 1999, Bank One (ONE:NYSE) warned Wall Street that it would miss estimates due to losses in the company's credit card division. The warning, which came out of nowhere, proved to be anything but a buying opportunity. In

November, the bank warned *again*, once again citing continued problems in the credit card division. The stock, which dropped 23% on the first warning to 43, was down another 19% to 34⅝ after warning number two.

What's the difference between the two tales? In Schwab's case, the losses were generally expected as the short-term by-product of a revamped business strategy. If you believed in that strategy, the dip represented a chance to get in on it. In Bank One's case, there was nothing but trouble to blame. The company cited slower growth and more competition in the credit card industry, exacerbated by interest rates. Those were not "good" problems to have.

Thus, the specifics matter. But keep this general notion in mind: Guiding and meeting Wall Street expectations has essentially become a necessity for any viable public company, particularly a large, established company. Failure to "make the number," or a key part of the earnings report—like the revenue figure—indicates either some real problems in operations, or some serious blunders in managing analyst expectations. Neither is generally good, so don't take an earnings warning or shortfall lightly. (It's not good for a smaller, younger company either, but it is more understandable, especially for a company trying to establish its business model.)

Stock Splits

If any other piece of property we owned carried the potential to be arbitrarily divided into pieces, we'd be more than a little concerned. Yet when a stock splits, it's usually good news. In theory, a stock split should have no impact on the price of a stock. In practice, however, it has become common wisdom that stock splits benefit investors. Most people think that having twice as much stock, even at half the price, is unequivocally a good thing.

When a stock splits, the number of shares that you hold changes but the value of your position stays the same. In a 2-for-1 split, for example, if you had 100 shares, each trading at $10, you'd now have 200, each worth $5. Generally, companies split their stock when they feel its price has risen above the level at which the investing public feels comfortable buying it, somewhere north of 100. In such cases, splits help bring a stock's price roughly in line with the price of stocks in the broader market.

Splitsville

The 2-1 Split
100 shares at $10 = 200 at $5

The 3-1 Split
100 shares at $10 = 300 shares at $3.33

The 3-2 Split
100 shares at $10 = 150 shares at $6.66

The mechanical device by which companies distribute splits is a dividend payment. When a company's board sets a split, it establishes both a "record date" and a date of distribution. Being a registered owner of a stock on the record date entitles you to the dividend, which comes in the form of a split certificate mailed on the split's distribution date. Trades generally take three business days to settle—that is, for ownership to officially transfer from seller to buyer—so if you haven't bought the stock two days before the record date, you won't get that certificate.

Stock-Split Specifics

Record Date	All registered owners of a stock on the *record date* are entitled to a dividend.
Distribution Date	Split certificates are mailed on the *distribution date*.
Ex Date	The stock price changes to reflect the split on the *ex date*.

When does the split actually show up in the price of the stock? That happens on what's known as the ex date, which generally comes one day after the distribution date.

This all might sound a bit overwhelming. But you needn't spend any time worrying about mechanics. In practice, it's impossible to miss out on a split no matter when you buy the stock. If you were to buy it after the ex date, the question would be utterly moot, since you would be buying the already-split shares. And if you were to buy a stock in the period between the split's record date and its distribution date, the purchased shares would come with a "due bill" attached to them, stipulating that you receive the additional shares.

Do splits matter? Not in any fundamental sense. No matter how you slice it—2-for-1, 3-for-1, 3-for-2—a split does nothing to change the value of your equity stake in a company. A 2-for-1 split will yield shareholders twice as many shares but at half their former value.

Still, there's no denying the existence of a school of trading that tries to capitalize on anticipated run-ups in stocks that are expected to announce splits. One theory behind that trading strategy is that splits make stocks go up because the reduced price of a split stock makes it more attractive to investors who previously thought they couldn't afford it. A second, more tenable explanation is that enough people believe in the first theory to make pre-split momentum a self-fulfilling prophecy.

One thing that makes it difficult to cash in on splits is that stocks tend to get the biggest rush before the split is actually announced. There's no reliable way to know whether a split is on the way, although an intense escalation in a stock's price can only make a split more likely. At any rate, regardless of a split's likelihood, the moment it looks like investors are betting on it, the split momentum becomes a market fact. And like all momentum trends, it's as potentially lucrative as it is dangerous.

Stocks that enjoy big run-ups on this sort of speculation typically give back some of those gains after a split is announced. This post-split depression is really just a case of investors' "buying on rumors and selling on news."

We don't recommend playing splits as an investment strategy. Remember, splits have no fundamental impact on the value of a stock, and it's entirely too difficult to develop a consistent game plan based on when pre-split runs will start or finish.

If our warnings don't dissuade you from playing splits, there's no shortage of Web sites devoted to the practice: Sites like splittrader.com and stocksplits.net send out e-mail bulletins when companies announce, or are expected to announce, splits, while many financial information sites offer free calendars of record and distribution dates.

Sites with Splits Calendars

www.theonlineinvestor.com
www.quote.yahoo.com
www.e-analytics.com
www.siliconinvestor.com

A couple of practical things you should be aware of: First, because they don't change the value of your overall position in a stock, splits have no tax consequences. Second, be sure to find out whether your portfolio tracker automatically accounts for splits. If yours doesn't have that feature—and many don't—you'll either have to switch trackers or be prepared to monitor yours extremely closely and enter the necessary changes on your own.

Spinoffs

Imagine that you're a company focused primarily on one type of product—automobiles, for instance. You're a large firm. Just huge. So massive, in fact, that you can lose track of entire businesses within yourself, businesses that don't have a whole lot in common with your main focus.

The tragedy of it all, from your perspective, is that these internal businesses have actual earnings and growth potential that aren't reflected in the price of your stock simply because Wall Street isn't paying attention to them. Presumably, Wall Street is so focused on the core business, it doesn't recognize and value all these other endeavors.

What could you do? Well, you—call yourself General Motors (GM: NYSE)—could spin off an underappreciated unit—call it Electronic Data Systems (EDS:NYSE) or Delphi Automotive (DPH:NYSE)—and start reporting those earnings separately.

That's the general logic behind spinoffs. Though they're often characterized as a way to allow companies to focus on core operations, that's rarely the only reason. Instead, spinoffs are increasingly about the magical process of "unlocking hidden value" in the eyes of Wall Street. It's a task companies can accomplish with both real, neglected subsidiaries and with Web sites whose value couldn't be hidden any better by Houdini himself.

A spinoff creates a separate stock, which immediately gives the newly spun operations a market value that is often in great excess of what may have been implied within the valuation of the parent corporation. In the process, the spun-off company gets a currency—its own stock—with which to expand through acquisitions.

One typical way that spinoffs proceed involves the parent company's floating a minor portion of a subsidiary via an initial public offering. The parent will usually follow up that IPO by distributing the remaining shares as tax-free distributions to its shareholders of record. Mechanically speaking, the process is just like the payment of a dividend, except instead of getting a dividend, you get shares of the newly issued stock. And as with dividends, the value of the parent's stock will decline by the value of the distribution. For example, the day that GM spun off its remaining 80.1% of Delphi to shareholders, GM shares fell by about $14 each.

What's in it for the parent? The strategic payoff is that both companies will, ideally, run better—management-wise—as separate entities. Investment-wise, the parent becomes an owner in a newly liquid company, and the value of its stake can rise in proportion to the market's enthusiasm for the young stock.

What should you do if you learn that a stock you own is spinning off a subsidiary? If you think it's a promising new entity, you would hope that the company spins some shares off to its current shareholders, or at the very least that the parent keeps some of the stock for itself (thereby enriching the parent's stock). If you don't think the entity is too attractive, be glad the company is shedding the burden.

If the market feels optimistic about the spinoff, the parent stock may get a boost ahead of the distribution. Speculation over its plans to spin off Hughes Electronics (GMH:NYSE) has sent GM soaring on more than one occasion. Of course, things aren't equal if the spinoff doesn't make sense. Spinoffs in which massive companies are seeking to cut unmanageable operations loose will likely enjoy little interest.

Tracking Stocks

One peculiar sister to spinoffs that has been getting more common in recent years is the tracking stock. Tracking stocks seem like spinoffs. You can trade them just as you would any other stock. But tracking stocks have an immeasurably important benefit for the parent that true spinoffs don't: They leave control of the subsidiary completely in the parent company's hands.

With a tracking stock, the parent company issues the stock. The subsidiary that the stock tracks is really just a division of the parent. Holders of tracking stocks have no voting rights in the business whose performance their shares track. Nor do these shareholders generally have full voting rights in the parent corporation, which can do things like reorganize or even liquidate the assets of the subsidiary without any consent from that subsidiary.

Because of this ownership structure, tracking-stock holders can't go after the parent company in the event that the "tracking company" falters—just as Ford (F:NYSE) shareholders can't demand recompense from Ford if its Mercury division goes under. The tracking-stock holder just has general rights vis-à-vis the parent, similar to the rest of the company's shareholders. But get in line—bondholders have precedence over equity holders. In fact, if the parent company in this scenario ever got into financial trouble, creditors (bondholders) could go after the tracking firm's assets.

Retaining this kind of control is very attractive for the issuer of a tracking stock. And this lack of control is the major drawback of a company that is trading as a tracking stock. In fact, dissatisfaction with its lack of control over its own operations was one reason that eventually led EDS to break off from GM.

Does it make sense to own a tracking stock?

Standard Spinoffs vs. Tracking Stocks	
Spinoffs	Tracking Stocks
Shareholders have full voting rights New company is separate and independent from the parent, though the parent may retain a controlling stake	Shareholders have no voting rights Subsidiary is essentially a division fully controlled by the parent

First, the fact that a company is a subsidiary isn't all bad. Subsidiaries have access to the parent's war chest, nothing to sneeze at in the case of a company like General Motors or AT&T (T:NYSE). Also, regardless of how well hidden a subsidiary's value may be, it can rely on the parent's good credit rating when it comes to raising cash.

There's also the possibility of making money. It's hard to say how tracking stocks perform via their parents, because there isn't much data. One recent study by professors at the Tippie College of Business at the University of Iowa found that tracking stocks generally underperformed market benchmarks long-term, according to *The Wall Street Journal*. But some tracking stocks have done very well. For example, GM's Hughes Electronics, by the end of 1999, had gained about 400% over its 14-year tracking-stock existence, and almost 500% since its nadir in the early 1990s. During both periods, GM rose a more modest 105% and 110% respectively.

From the point of view of an individual investor, the market thus far has shown little downside to buying a tracking stock per se, as long as you like the parent company. Just remember that if a tracking stock one day finds itself faltering, it'll be the shareholders of the parent corporation, not the tracking stock, who'll determine the fate of the tracked operations.

Do shareholders of parent corporations automatically get whatever tracking stock that company creates? Only if the parent decides to spin off a portion of the tracking stocks' outstanding shares to its existing shareholders. An example is Quantum, the computer data storage company. In 1999, it split its shares into two tracking stocks, Quantum-DLT & Storage (DSS:NYSE) and Quantum-Hard Disk Drive (HDD:NYSE). Quantum shareholders received half a share of stock based on the hard-disk biz and one share based on the storage systems for each share of Quantum's existing stock.

Generally, if a corporation decides to spin off a portion of the tracking stock to existing shareholders, it occurs months after the company offers a smaller portion of the total tracking stock to the public in an IPO.

Buybacks

Luckily for management, there are a number of things a company can do if it wants to pump its stock. It could suggest that it's considering a potential spinoff of some underappreciated business. It could announce a cross-marketing agreement with a high-profile company in a hot sector. It can pepper the wire services with press releases heralding countless new and exciting business developments, regardless of how new or exciting any of them really are.

Of course, if a company isn't feeling especially inventive, there's always the tried-and-true option of announcing a stock repurchase plan, or a "buyback."

The stock market tends to like buybacks for a number of reasons. To begin with, a buyback is seen as evidence of a company's belief that its shares are undervalued. If a firm won't buy its own shares, the thinking goes, how could it ever expect others to do so? However, implicit in a buyback is the notion that there's no more productive way for a company to use its cash flow. Surely it could find no better return on equity anywhere else, right?

Not exactly. A lot of repurchase plans are nothing more than attempts to hype a stock or mask fundamental problems. After all, couldn't the company find a more creative way to deploy its cash?

So, how can you measure the impact of a buyback? Look out for companies whose buybacks coincide with a big jump in the number of stock options they grant to employees. In those cases, companies are buying back stock at market price even as they issue new stock. Kind of a wash. Beware, too, of companies that borrow heavily to finance their repurchase plans, thereby raising their debt-to-equity ratio and increasing their vulnerability to changes in the interest rate environment. And be wary of companies that announce plans that are tiny compared to the overall amount of stock in the market. If Procter & Gamble (PG:NYSE)—a $70 billion company measured by market capitalization, or the value of the shares outstanding—announces a buyback of $10 million, that's not exactly going to shake the world.

But regardless of a company's intentions, all stock buybacks have one immediate benefit to shareholders: They allow a company to improve its stock fundamentals without making structural changes to its business model or creating any new growth from its existing operations. That's because buybacks reduce the amount of outstanding stock in a corporation and thereby automatically boost earnings per share.

In other words, buybacks allow the illusion of additional earnings growth. Imagine that a company with 2 billion outstanding shares earned $10 billion in 1998. Now imagine that the next year its earnings fall to $9.5 billion. That's a 5% decline in earnings. But if that firm had used its cash flow to repurchase 10% of its stock, lowering its shares outstanding to 1.8 billion, it could have cheerfully reported 5% earnings-per-share growth.

In addition to inspiring investors' confidence and increasing earnings per share, there's another way that buybacks can boost a stock: the basic mechanical effect of reducing the float. The float is different from shares outstanding, which describes the total number of shares that exist. The float describes the number of those shares that actually trade in the open market. Because of company insiders and other passive investors like pension funds that often hold large positions that they don't adjust from day to day, a stock's float sometimes can be dramatically smaller than the number of shares outstanding.

Assuming that demand remains constant, share prices should rise along with a reduction in the supply of a given stock. Many new technology issues have been able to shoot to such meteoric heights in the past couple of years because of the extremely small floats those companies have compared with the incredible demand they face.

When investors are being told that a hot new issue is going to be the next America Online (AOL:NYSE), and there are only five million shares available to trade, the sky's the limit on price, at least in the short term.

That's a rather extreme example of how float size can affect stock prices, but in the big picture, it may add up. Between 1994 and October 1999, buybacks and cash takeovers helped reduce the overall float of stocks, according to TrimTabs.com publisher Charles Biderman. And though there's no consensus on how responsible that phenomenon is for the concurrent stock market boom, it's interesting to note that the S&P 500 gained 192% during that period.

Stocks often receive an immediate bounce when a company sets a buyback plan. Tech manufacturer GenRad (GEN:NYSE), for example, rallied during the time of its buyback announcement of May 1997. But there's a big difference between announcing a plan and actually carrying it out. Surprisingly few repurchase plans ever get done. Research from Birinyi Associates has shown that fewer than half the firms that planned buybacks in the ten years between 1985 to 1995 completed them in full.

GenRad was in the majority. About a year after announcing its plan, the company said it had canceled its "share repurchase" program, after having not repurchased any shares. The stock was down after the news.

If a company ever does complete a buyback, they'll announce that.

Thankfully, the practical aspects of a stock repurchase plan never enter the shareholders' lives. You won't be bothered by any telephone or door-to-door solicitations to sell your stock. Companies conduct their buybacks piecemeal in the open market, where there is an abundance of potential sellers, or through private transactions with large institutions. You can find the details on this process in the buyback announcement.

The takeaway: Other things being equal, you should probably be more enthusiastic about a company that plans to buy back its own stock than one that doesn't. Just don't reduce your investment decision to that sole factor, since you generally won't find out for quite a long time whether that buyback actually ever comes to full fruition.

Acquisitions

It's one thing when a company buys its own stock. But it's quite another when another company tries to do the same thing. Unlike buybacks, acquisitions have direct and dramatic effects on both stock and stockholders.

The process by which most acquisitions unfold is pretty formulaic. It begins when a potential acquirer (Company A) approaches a potential target (Company B) with an initial bid. Company B's board of directors reviews the bid, evaluating it on a number of levels. Is the price right? What form would the payment take: cash, stock, debt assumption, or some combination of the three? And perhaps most important, exactly what does Company A plan to do with B if the deal goes through? You can't blame Company B management if it recoils from the prospect of losing its power, salaries, and considerable perks.

If B accepts A's offer, the companies will negotiate a merger agreement, and B will recommend that its shareholders approve that agreement through a proxy vote. Shareholders generally follow the recommendations of the board, though they don't need to. While the equity market's workings often seem rather abstract, owning stock is fundamentally about owning a piece of a business. And as a partial owner of a company, you have the right to vote any way you see fit.

B is under no obligation to accept A's bid, of course. In particular, uninvited bids are almost always rejected by boards of directors, which usually claim that the price of the offer is "inadequate" and "not in the best interest of shareholders." Should B reject A's offer, A has the option of revising and resubmitting its bid, taking into account B's original objections.

Company A has another option: circumventing the board by taking the matter directly to B's shareholders through a tender offer, so named because it's an invitation to tender one's stock to an acquirer in exchange for cash or stock. This plan of attack gives rise to a "proxy fight"—that is, a struggle for a controlling share of the proxies (or votes) of B's stockholders. If Company A controls B's proxies, that makes the wishes of B's board of directors irrelevant.

Some companies wary of unwelcome takeover attempts adopt shareholder "rights" plans, which are usually triggered when a suitor assumes something like 15% of the company's stock. There are a number of forms that such plans can assume; one common version allows existing shareholders to buy the company's stock at a discount to the market after the trigger is set off, making it easier for insiders to build positions than the suitor.

In 1999, Italian luxury goods manufacturer Gucci Group N.V. (GUC:NYSE) successfully used a rights plan, or "poison-pill" defense, to thwart an attempt by French rival LVMH Moët Hennessy Louis Vuitton (LVMHY:Nasdaq) to take control of the company. Gucci was able to considerably dilute LVMH's stake by granting its employees options to purchase as many as 37 million new shares, and lending them the money for those purchases.

If a tender offer succeeds, or if a proxy vote supports the board's recommendation of a deal, the matter is pretty much out of your hands. You can either sell your stock or sit tight until the deal takes effect. On that day, your broker will automatically either cash out your shares or exchange them for the predetermined amount of the acquirer's stock, depending on whether the acquisition is being made in stock or cash.

Of course, that's not necessarily a bad thing, since most deals end up getting done because acquirers are willing to pay shareholders a premium to what the market would pay for their stock.

Ultimately, whether you buy or sell a stock of a company that's going to combine with another company comes down to some hard decisions. Does the deal make sense to you in terms of the companies' business plans? In the summer of 2000, Saks (SKS:NYSE) essentially unraveled a two-year-old merger in which mainstream retailer Proffitt's had purchased the luxury store Saks. Industry commentators said the merger had been doomed from the outset as a vain attempt to match up entirely different businesses. If that had been your analysis at the time, you could have dropped the stock—and avoided the subsequent price decline—altogether.

What about outsized egos or culture clash? Could that make it difficult for the companies' management to integrate, as happened in the failed 1998 merger attempt of SmithKlineBeecham (SBH:NYSE ADR) and Glaxo Wellcome (GLX:NYSE ADR)? Or does the company have a history of success at integrating acquisitions, as the ravenous Cisco Systems (CSCO:Nasdaq) does?

Usually about the time of a deal announcement, there are a rash of news articles addressing these very kinds of questions. Use them to help you decide whether the newly created company is one you'd want to continue to own.

Follow-on Offerings

The wild success of a number of fledgling technology and Internet firms has brought massive attention to initial public offerings, a subject we tackle in Chapter 12.

Given investors' focus on IPOs, it's not surprising that investors don't know much about follow-on offerings—called "primaries" and "secondaries." Follow-on offerings are a much less exciting though equally important way for companies to raise money in the equity market. Most people use the term "secondaries" to refer to all offerings subsequent to a firm's IPO. But strictly speaking, that's not accurate.

Secondary offerings are just one type of follow-on offering. With secondaries, the proceeds generally go to specific investors, often insiders who are trying to unload stock they've acquired through exercising options or through pre-IPO investment. When proceeds go to the issuing firm itself, as with an IPO, that kind of follow-on is called a "primary offering." Many follow-ons are combinations of primaries and secondaries. For example, a company might set plans for a 6.5 million share offering, with 4.25 million shares sold by the company itself and 2.25 million by officers and directors.

Follow-on Offerings	
Primaries	Secondaries
Proceeds to firm New stock sold	Proceeds to insiders Existing stock/exercised options sold

You'll notice that follow-ons often take place at a discount to a stock's market price. That phenomenon in itself shouldn't bother you. It doesn't indicate anything unsound about the stock but is part of the logic investment banks are forced to follow when pricing all offerings, whether initial or follow-ons.

An investment bank, or underwriter, has two sets of clients that it needs to satisfy. First, there are the sellers, which include the company itself and possibly insiders. Then there are the buyers, which typically include institutional investors and extremely rich people, as well as some small investors whose retail brokers have access to the offering. The problem is that both sides want to make money, the one by selling at the highest possible price, the other by buying as cheaply as it can.

Underwriters try to balance those interests when pricing both IPOs and subsequent offerings. In an IPO, there's a large measure of conjecture involved in determining a suitable price. Valuation models and estimations of market demand can go only so far. But when pricing a follow-on, underwriters have the benefit (or the burden) of already knowing what the market will pay for a stock.

The lead underwriter in a follow-on has to price the deal at a discount big enough to stir up investor interest. No one wants to buy a stock for more than they could buy it in the open market. At the same time, though, you'd think that insiders would be less than thrilled at the notion of selling their shares below market price.

There's certainly no law that says secondaries have to go through an underwriter. But sellers accept the discounted price as a trade-off for the stability an investment bank provides. A 5% discount to the market may seem low, but imagine what could happen if a multimillion-share block of insider stock hit the market pell-mell. The prospect of the uneven execution that could arise from a disorderly market sends insiders to the bankers, who can guarantee a single price for the whole block.

So what does a follow-on mean to the person who already owns a stock? Isn't his or her stake being diluted? Isn't the company essentially creating money at the expense of existing shareholders?

Trade-offs of Follow-ons

Earnings per share decrease,
but the company raises money to grow.

The float increases, but the stock becomes easier
to buy for big investors looking for liquidity.

The basic trade-off with follow-ons is this: More shares get added to the mix, so the earnings per share decrease. There's nothing mysterious about this process. It's just a matter of supply and demand: Follow-on offerings increase supply without directly increasing demand. Earnings per share are diluted as the amount of outstanding stock increases. On the other hand, the company raises more money to grow and increase its earnings.

Further, companies will often do follow-ons when they believe that there's enough demand for them. If that's the case—and in the case of hot stocks that have relatively small floats, it often is—the existing market demand will be able to absorb the additional stock with no problem. Indeed, the larger float enables some bigger investors who can't buy very small stocks to step in and build a position.

If you're concerned about whether management may be using follow-ons to line its pockets, just look at the company's public filings and see how many of the shares are new and how many are existing shares owned by insiders. If it looks like the insider selling will expand the float enough to damage the supply/demand dynamic, or signals a lack of confidence by management about their company, be wary.

You can find this sort of information on sec.gov or freeedgar.com. Companies have to file an S-1 when they do a follow-on offering, just as they do with an IPO. That filing will tell you what portion of the follow-on is coming from the company and what part is coming from insiders. Here's a section of the S-1 eBay (EBAY:Nasdaq) filed when it did a follow-on in the summer of 1999:

> eBay is offering 4,250,000 shares to be sold in the offering. The selling stockholders identified in this prospectus are offering an additional 2,250,000 shares. eBay will not receive any of the proceeds for the sale of shares by the selling stockholders.

Follow-ons, like everything, involve trade-offs. You may not like the prospect of share dilution. But on the other hand, the success of your investment hinges on the company's chances for growth. A company's ability to leverage the cash it raises in a follow-on offering may outweigh any dilution that occurs. But beware of firms that use follow-ons as a way to deal with extreme and undisciplined burn rates—the rate at which companies "burn" through what cash they have. If a company returns to the equity market less than a year after its IPO, it may be time to reconsider owning that stock.

These are just some of the events that can affect your stock. There are many more things to consider when selling a stock, and that's the subject of our next chapter.

10

When to Sell

Most books about investing ignore the concept of selling. You buy, you hold. But sell? Heaven forbid! Yet, in an era when stocks have become a bigger and bigger piece of one's investment portfolio, the concept of buying for the very long haul begs revision. Knowing when to sell is just as important as knowing when and what to buy.

Buying and holding for the long term—5, 10, 20 years—isn't the enticing concept that many of the market gurus have led everyone to believe. In the past, when relatively strong companies came public, buying and holding, and holding, made more sense. Now we have younger, less-tested companies coming to market in vast numbers. The global marketplace has expanded rapidly, and the fast-paced, creative destruction of capitalism has shortened corporate life expectancy. In such a volatile and perilous world, an investor could end up buying and holding not much. That's precisely why knowing when to sell—and when not to—is so crucial.

Take January 1999. This was a winter month like most others, except for a few thousand unfortunate folks. Their memories of January 1999 come back with a vengeance on those long, fitful nights when they are replaying investments that got away like big fish on a frayed line. During the twenty or so trading days of January, 42 million shares of Qualcomm (QCOM:Nasdaq), at the time a little-known wireless outfit, changed hands at about 8.

Shortly thereafter, Qualcomm began one of the storied runs in market history, eventually hitting 200 a share. A $10,000 investment in its stock in January grew to $280,000 in less than twelve months. For those who sold back in January 1999, that $10,000 of stock became the fortune that never was. While the sellers in January 1999 might not want to remember the pain of forgone fortunes, their move provides us with a fundamental object lesson on the importance of knowing when to sell.

We've spent the better part of this book trying to strengthen your skills as a stock selector. From finding stock ideas to studying financials to pinpointing good entry points with charts, our goal has been to help you succeed in the stock-picking process.

But selling is a very different animal. When is it time to take some dough off the table and move on to the next investment idea? For most folks, selling is more exasperating than buying. The sell point is where an investor's greed and fear do battle. If the stock is up, part of you wants to hang on for even greater gains while another part fears losing what you've already got. If the stock is suffering, part of you yearns for a rebound while another part wants to cut your losses and move on.

Many of the factors that precipitate selling a stock are personal. You may need money to pay for school, for a home, or simply to maintain a desired asset allocation. There are, however, general circumstances that we can address, factors that can help you decide to sell even if you don't "need" the money, or that can help you time your decision when you do. While we don't recommend any set formula for selling (as some, often more technically oriented books do), we advise you to keep aware of these several factors. When one too many of them starts pointing in the same direction, you'll know it might be time to sell.

At the end of the chapter, we offer a checklist of the various "sell" factors, which fall into three main categories: general market conditions, the viability of an individual stock, and tax issues.

I've turned to *TheStreet.com* columnist John Rubino for assistance on the first two sections—so-called economic reasons to sell, and *TheStreet.com*'s resident tax expert, Tracy Byrnes, to address the issue of taxes.

Spotting the Market Bear Before He Bites

As I've mentioned above, conventional wisdom has an easy answer to the when-to-sell dilemma: Don't do it. Legendary investor Warren Buffett, for instance, describes his preferred holding period as "forever." He just picks great companies, settles in, and rides along on the twin axles of great management and superb products. He's got a point—and there's even tax benefits to that ultra-long strategy that we address later. (Though even the great Buffett has struggled in the past several years, partly because of his relatively stubborn adherence to his buy-and-hold strategy.)

Look at the chart of any great stock—we've used America Online (AOL:NYSE), General Electric (GE:NYSE), and Microsoft (MSFT:Nasdaq) as examples here, but there are dozens more—and you'll see plenty of short-term tops where impatient investors found perfectly good reasons for bailing. Yet, after almost each brief dip, the upward march resumed, rewarding the folks who hung on for the long haul with the kinds of returns that the rest of us only dream about. A $10,000 bet on AOL in early 1992, for instance, would have grown to $460,000 by the end of 1997. But it paid ten times that for those who held on for two more years.

Compelling though they are, these charts are deceptive in a crucial way: They cover only the 1990s, one of the great bull markets in human history, a decade without a major bear market. Go back further into American market history and you'll see that in real bear markets, where stocks fall until most people give up hope, even great companies get whacked.

Take the market downturn of the early '70s. IBM (IBM:NYSE), for example, hit a high of 21 (adjusted for subsequent splits) in January 1973 and didn't see that price again until Christmastime 1982. In 1973 Xerox (XRX:NYSE) dropped from near 30 to below 10 and didn't

Unstoppable Stocks

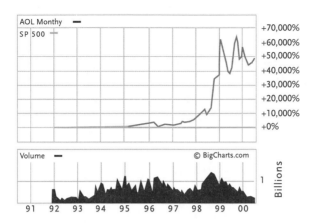

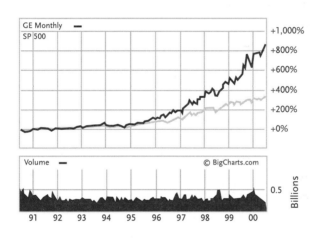

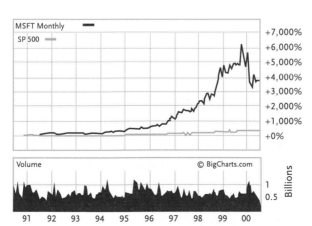

return until 1996. These periods of overall market malaise really test the notion of buy-and-hold as a great long-term strategy. Bailing at the top and buying at the subsequent bottom would have been vastly better—if the top were visible at the time.

So how do you tell when the bear is about to bite? Unfortunately, there is no foolproof way. (That would be too easy, wouldn't it?) But there are some indicators that in the past have had a certain amount of predictive value.

P/E Ratios and Interest Rates

In Chapter 8, "When to Buy," we discussed what the price-to-earnings ratio means for an individual stock. But the P/E ratio also works for the market as a whole, giving a general idea of what investors are willing to pay for a dollar of the economy's earnings. When they're willing to pay a lot (i.e., when the market's P/E is high), they're implicitly predicting that earnings are going to increase dramatically in coming years. Likewise, a low P/E indicates pessimism about future corporate profits and economic growth in general.

Extreme valuations, both high and low, have in the past been a sign that emotion had pushed rationality off the field and that a reversal in fortune was coming. Benjamin Graham, the father of security analysis, used to speak of "Mr. Market," a manic-depressive fellow (remember, this was before Prozac) who, when up, was willing to pay exorbitant prices for stocks, and when down, was practically willing to give the things away.

In the six decades prior to start of the 1990s, when the S&P 500's P/E fell below 8, the market usually did well in subsequent years. But when it exceeded 18, trouble usually followed in the market.

But then Mr. Market threw us a curve. In the latter years of the 1990s, the S&P 500 P/E spiked above 20—and kept going. By decade's end it was 30, higher by far than ever before, and the market was still rising. What does this mean?

It comes back to the concepts we discussed earlier in the book. In many important ways, our economy has changed, proving to be able to grow fairly steadily without bringing on inflation-generating spikes in wages or prices. The stocks of the companies fueling these increased efficiencies—the network infrastructure companies, the chip companies, the telecommunications companies, and others—as well as those

S&P P/E Soars in the 1990s

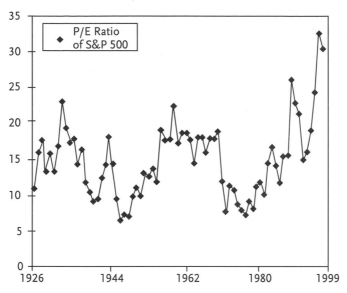

Source: Standard & Poor's

nontech companies that have embraced technology to their advantage, like Charles Schwab (SCH:NYSE)—have been heartily rewarded in the process.

With this kind of fundamental shift in our economic dynamics, you can't necessarily rely on the formulas and P/E benchmarks that were effective just a decade ago. Investors who did rely on them missed out on much of the '90s rise, while those who recognized the sea change profited. As you will recall from Chapter 2, the economy is a dynamic, changing beast that is difficult to measure with static, historical models. The market's dynamism reflects that.

Indeed, throughout much of the '90s, the market truly seemed invincible. An Asian financial crisis in '97 couldn't bring it down. Russian and Brazilian crises of '98 couldn't bring it down. Mexican peso problems were shrugged off. The Department of Justice's landmark case against the flagship stock of the decade, Microsoft, created some rumbles at most.

But there is one contender that's consistently proven to be a match for the stock market. And that's interest rates.

Stocks don't exist in a vacuum. They're in constant competition with other investments, like bonds (which primarily earn interest rather than capital gains), real estate, precious metals, and—let's be realistic—big-screen TVs and sports cars.

But bonds are the main competition. One way to measure the state of the market is to compare it to what you can earn on a high-quality fixed-income instrument like the 10-year Treasury note. If the interest rate is 6%, then that's what you earn from that bond.

With stocks, you earn the earnings. To compare that to bonds, you want to figure out the "earnings yield" of stocks. That's the return you can expect in the year ahead on a dollar invested in the market. The earnings yield is the reciprocal of the P/E ratio, so if the latter is 20, the yield is $\frac{1}{20}$, or 5%. That means that each dollar you invest gives you a claim on 5 cents of current earnings. (A high P/E means a low earnings yield.)

You can compare the earnings yield to what you can get, "risk-free," in 10-year Treasuries. (Treasuries aren't entirely risk free, as we discussed in Chapter 3, because if you sell before maturity, you could face interest rate fluctuation.) The lower the earnings yield compared to the Treasury yield, the more "overvalued" stocks are.

To make the comparison, go to Standard & Poor's site, www.personalwealth.com, and click on "S&P Indexes" and then "vital stats" for the S&P 500. You'll see the P/E ratio there. Reverse that (if the P/E is 30, then the earnings yield is $\frac{1}{30}$, or 3.3%). Bond yields are available at *TheStreet.com* home page "ticker" and most other financial sites that have tickers. In mid-August of 2000 the bond yield was about 6%, which made it almost double that of the S&P's earnings yield.

This is said to be how the Federal Reserve tracks the fairness of stock valuations—and one cause of Fed chairman Alan Greenspan's frequent "irrational exuberance" hand-wringing. According to the somewhat more sophisticated variation on this measure compiled by Deutsche Banc economist Ed Yardeni in the chart on page 231, the method has done a pretty good job of tracking stock prices. Note the 1987 spike in the S&P 500, when its earnings yield was low (meaning P/Es were quite high) compared to the bond. It was quickly followed by a return to its normal relationship via a 30% price decline in stocks overall.

For the '90s, the relationship was fairly close, with the bond staying below the earnings yield for a good part of the decade. If you looked at P/Es alone, they might have seemed high, but compared to the bond yield, valuations didn't look quite as "exuberant" as some contended.

Still, P/Es couldn't go up forever without hitting some ceiling, and that's what you started to see happening in the end of 1999, with an ominously low earnings yield compared to a rising Treasury yield.

Sure enough, in the wake of that low earnings yield and the big gap between the yields on bonds and stocks, Greenspan became restless. A series of ¼-point interest rate hikes initiated by the Fed were simply not putting a dent into the market. It was as if the market were taunting Greenspan, saying "your measly rate hikes can't stop our fun." But Greenspan wasn't taunted away. As he put it in a January 13, 2000, speech:

> When we look back at the 1990s, from the perspective of, say, 2010, the nature of the forces currently in train will have presumably become clearer. We may conceivably conclude from that vantage point that, at the turn of the millennium, the American economy was experiencing a once-in-a-century acceleration of innovation, which propelled forward productivity, output, corporate profits, and stock prices at a pace not seen in generations, if ever. Alternatively, that 2010 retrospective might well conclude that a good deal of what we are currently experiencing was just one of the many euphoric speculative bubbles that have dotted human history.

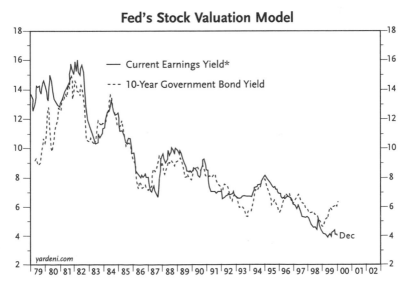

Fed's Stock Valuation Model

* I/B/E/S consensus estimates of earnings over the coming 12 months divided by S&P 500 Index
Source: Deutsche Banc Alex. Brown Topical Study #49 *January 31, 2000,* Dr. Edward Yardeni

Things started to become clearer soon enough—in the spring of 2000—when Greenspan showed that he wasn't going to sit on the sidelines and watch events unfold. Rather, on the heels of various inflationary signals and the lowest unemployment figures in history, Greenspan picked up the pace of his rate-hiking activity. In May 2000, the Fed raised interest rates by a half point, the first rate action of that size since February 1995. That move brought the federal funds rate—the rate at which banks lend to each other overnight—to 6.5%, its highest level since 1991.

Finally getting its comeuppance, the stock market reacted in turn, sinking lower. Nor was there even a "relief rally" after the big hike. As fears of continued rising rates persisted, the market could not get its legs.

By that Memorial Day weekend, the Dow Jones Industrial Average was down 10%, the S&P was off 6%, and the Nasdaq dragged down the bunch at 21%. This, compared to years of double-digit returns on the indices. Though the markets rebounded somewhat in the summer months, they remained unable to sustain any real strength into the fall.

Are interest rate woes a permanent condition? Certainly not. And Fed rate squeezes have become briefer and less intense, mimicking an economic cycle that has produced longer and longer expansions and briefer recessions over the past twenty-five years.

Still, while the events of the '90s show that the economy can stand a lot more heat than it used to, ultimately even this "new" market is not made of Teflon. The market is entwined with, not separate from, macroeconomic forces. And when those get too powerful, even the seemingly strongest stocks will wither.

The upshot—if you follow nothing else macroeconomic in deciding when to sell, pay attention to bonds, interest rates, and the Fed. When those players swing into high gear, even your favorite stocks will likely feel it, relentlessly, until the rate pressure lets up.

How high an interest rate is too high? The most objective way to measure is by looking at the earnings yield on stocks compared with the yield on Treasuries. If interest rates are going up, widening the gap between those figures, that's an indication that stocks are overvalued. The psychological element to that metric is that if the market senses that the Fed's *direction* is to raise rates, it will start pricing in that potential downside by lowering stock prices.

Interest rate trends alone are probably not reason enough to sell individual stocks. Indeed, if you like a stock's fundamentals and see that the price is being hit by macroeconomic trends like interest rates—trends that eventually work themselves through—the down-turn can be a time to buy. Either way, it's important to recognize that macro interest rate shifts can take a toll on an individual stock's price. Consider selling—or buying—accordingly.

When to Sell an Individual Stock

Talk to ten successful money managers about selling, and you'll get ten variations on the theme: The better you understand a company—i.e., the more clear you are about why you own it—the easier it is to know when to sell. As an analyst at a top-performing mutual fund puts it:

> Knowing what a company is worth changes your whole attitude about stock price movements. If you don't know what it's worth, you get excited when it's going up and worried when it's going down. Your psychology moves in line with the stock price. But if you have an idea of what it's worth, as it comes down you get excited and when it goes up you become more worried. . . . It's only through knowing what a stock is worth that you can counteract the tendency to buy high and sell low.

How do you reach this point? First, by understanding our earlier lessons in fundamental analysis in Chapter 6. The more you under-stand a company, the better your chances of finding the things that really make it tick—and that, should they change, will make it a sale candidate. In his classic *One Up on Wall Street*, Peter Lynch calls this "the story," and tells readers to cook a stock down to a few defining sentences that they can use as a touchstone. As long as the story is intact, there's no need to sell. When it changes in an unfavorable way, it's time to reevaluate the position.

We'll talk about signs of a changing story as well as some technical factors that can also tip the balance in the sell decision. Finally, we'll discuss selling for asset allocation purposes.

Fundamental Reasons to Sell: The Changing Story

Business Slowdown By any measure, Coca-Cola (KO:NYSE) by 1997 had had an astounding run. Decades of marketing (and chemistry) genius had turned the sweet drink in the red-and-white can into what many were calling the best brand in the world. Profit margins were huge (because the stuff cost literally pennies to make), and the legendary Warren Buffett loved the stock enough to own millions of shares.

Now it was being touted as the ultimate early-stage "China play." That is, as the developing world got richer, people in China—the most populous nation on earth—would want the same things (and be seduced by the same marketing pitches) as Americans and Europeans. Early on, they wouldn't be able to buy big-screen TVs, but they would be able to scrape up 15 cents to buy a soda. And Coke would use its marketing expertise and first-world cachet to dominate the global soft drink market.

Let's say in early 1998 you own Coke based on its ability to 1) maintain its fat profit margins and 2) grow its developing world sales at high double-digit rates. When the 1997 annual report arrives, you dive in and are gratified to read that earnings were up 19% for the year, while the stock's total return (gains plus dividends) was 28% (acceptable enough on a year that the S&P returned 31%).

In the chairman's letter to shareholders, he challenges you to "name another business with a more popular, affordable product, with a stronger foothold in more countries, yet with the opportunity to serve almost all of the world's nearly 6 billion consumers morning, noon, and night," and asserts that "in country after country and town after town, with consumer after consumer, all over this world, this business is only now starting to take off."

But when you dig into the breakdown of sales by country in the report a few pages later, you find that shipments to crucial developing countries grew a good but not spectacular 10 to 12%—far from high double-digit—and that the big jump in earnings was due in part to an asset sale. The story, in short, has started to change. And there's nothing new to give you comfort—no new product line, no new strategy, no new management. All of a sudden a stock trading at 40 times earnings and 9 times sales, up from 34 and 5, respectively, in 1995, begins to look a little pricey.

Coke's stock kept climbing for the next few months. Armed with growing concerns about the company's situation, you should have been happy to sell into the strength. When trouble in developing economies caused sales to stall and the stock price to tank in the second half of 1998, you would have long since moved on to other things.

Overvaluation In the 1990s, no one sold PCs like Dell (DELL:Nasdaq). By building computers to order and managing its inventory flow with maniacal precision, this upstart computer company blew away the field in the 1990s to become one of the great investments of all time: $10,000 of its stock in September 1990 became $5 million by decade's end. Let's say you discovered it early in the process and defined the story this way: Expanding market share in a high-growth business, superior cost control, and a reasonable price.

In early 1999, after an initial burst in its stock price, the first two parts of the story were still pretty much intact. Dell had become the second-biggest global PC maker, after Compaq (CPQ:NYSE), and with the whole world waiting to be wired up, the future looked at least as bright as the past. But the stock price—now, that was a question. Dell ended 1997 and 1998 with P/E ratios of 23 and 40 respectively; but in early 1999 the ratio spiked to a vertiginous 70. That was more than twice the level of the S&P 500, and considerably higher than the other leading PC makers.

Just how steeply valued was it? Remember, when you buy a stock, what you're really buying is a claim on a company's future earnings. To compare that claim to other potential investments, you can express it in percentage terms using the "earnings yield." Again, that's the reciprocal of the P/E ratio.

Dell's P/E is 70, which means that you're paying $70 for $1 of its earnings. So Dell's earnings yield is 1 over 70, or 1.4%. That is, each dollar you invest gives you a claim on 1.4 cents of its current earnings.

While Dell was yielding 1.4%, bonds were yielding about 6.5%. Now you have an apples-to-apples comparison: 1.4% to 6.5%. The bond's looking a lot better, right? Many investors would say so. Indeed, traditional value investors often argue that stocks with low earnings yields are overpriced and instead purchase stocks with yields at or above the bond yield. That excludes many pricey New Economy stocks where investors are banking on enormous future success.

So what could justify buying Dell at this price? You basically would have had to believe that Dell's earnings would grow at very high rates for a very long time and that investors would pay up for them. Let's figure out how long.

Start by assuming an earnings growth rate of 30%, which is aggressive but in line with Dell's recent past. Then increase the current 1.4% earnings yield by this rate each year (essentially multiplying the earnings yield by 1.3, representing the 30% growth rate). You'd see that if the price of the stock stays the same, it would take about six years for the return on your initial investment to approach the 6.5% you can get in bonds in the present.

The Earnings Yield Calculation

Year/Earnings Yield/Earnings Growth Rate

Year 1: (1.4) (1.3) = 1.8
Year 2: (1.8) (1.3) = 2.3
Year 3: (2.3) (1.3) = 3.0
Year 4: (3.0) (1.3) = 4.0
Year 5: (4.0) (1.3) = 5.2
Year 6: (5.2) (1.3) = 6.8
Year 7: (6.8) (1.3) = 8.8
Year 8: (8.8) (1.3) = 11.4

Now, if you are willing to pay a P/E of 70, it's likely because you believe Dell's earnings growth will match that 30% figure or even ramp up, so that over time—sooner than eight years from now—other investors would be willing to come in behind you and buy the stock at even higher prices. But if Dell doesn't deliver on those demanding expectations, you may end up with a declining stock price. And you would have forgone the extra interest you would have earned in those safer bonds. If you're going to take that risk, you ought to be highly confident that Dell has a robust future.

Is Dell still a great company? Sure. Will it keep growing? Probably. But the valuation part of the story has changed, which is your signal to take a closer look. When you do, you notice that sub-$1,000 PCs are taking a growing share of the market, which is squeezing profit margins industrywide. PCs, in other words, are becoming a "commodity" business, where price is arguably more important than the service and quality by which Dell defines itself. If you were able to read the changing story at Dell, you would have started selling your stock, and you would have been right. Dell trod water for the rest of the year while the Nasdaq nearly doubled.

Deteriorating Earnings Quality   Public companies always face pressure from investors to grow their earnings. But in bull markets, the expectations game takes on added urgency. "Beating the numbers" can mean a big pop in a stock's price (and the value of executive stock options), while missing the number can cause the price to crash. Yet delivering fast, consistent growth isn't easy, since no business moves in a steady, predictable fashion quarter after quarter.

As we discussed in Chapter 6, companies often resort to massaging earnings to fit Wall Street's expectations. As a result, the "quality," i.e., the relationship of reported earnings to actual operations, starts to suffer. This is bad, because if a company has to resort to tricks, its operations may be encountering troubles in unseen ways. And because accounting is complex and accountants infinitely creative, this kind of fancy footwork comes in lots of different flavors. Essentially, to track your holdings, you need to do financial analysis maintenance checks on your stocks—with the methods we discussed in Chapter 6—just as you did when you purchased them.

To illustrate the point, let's consider telecom giant Lucent (LU: NYSE), which was a Wall Street favorite for years after being spun off from AT&T (T:NYSE), consistently beating analyst earnings expectations and making its early investors rich. In 1998 alone, its net income (earnings) grew by 79% and its stock nearly tripled. But a cursory reading of that year's income statement showed that a big part of the jump was achieved by slicing the bloated expenses it had inherited from its former parent: Revenues were growing by 14% a year, while selling, general, and administrative expenses were up less than 10%.

Mathematically speaking, earnings can't rise at five times the rate of sales for very long (79% vs. 14%), especially when no one else in the industry is putting up similar numbers. So a cautious observer would have to view the quality of Lucent's earnings—or at least their rate of growth—as suspect. And by the end of 1999, that view would be proven right. Expenses stopped shrinking, earnings growth fell into line with revenues, and the stock tanked.

Finding and interpreting a decline in earnings quality isn't easy, since your opponents are the highly paid accountants and lawyers whose livelihoods depend on being able to camouflage unfavorable financial news. So by all means read company reports with an eye for unusual events or dramatic disparities between sales and earnings growth rates. Follow the footnotes as we outlined in Chapter 6. But don't expect to see past all the tricks on your own.

Instead, monitor the financial press for stories on "aggressive accounting" and "earnings quality," and become regular followers of the people who make this their beat, like *TheStreet.com*'s Herb Greenberg, Prudent Bear's fund manager David Tice, and Robert Olstein of the Olstein Financial Alert fund.

Heightened Competition   Barnes & Noble (BKS:NYSE) was an icon of the Old Economy, building book superstores and squeezing out mom-and-pop retailers around the country. With 1,500 or so outlets up and running at the beginning of 1998, this company looked invincible. Or at least that's the impression you might have had from watching its stock surge to an all-time high in June of that year.

Let's say you own it, and want to make sure that its leadership position is safe. You dial up your AOL account on your 14.4 modem and do a quick search for news on bookstores and related subjects. You see story after story on something called Amazon.com (AMZN:Nasdaq). You check it out and see that a new technology (the Web) had spawned a new business model (the online superstore), which presents a direct threat to the old bricks-and-mortar way of life.

If you took this as your cue to sell, good move, because three years later, bricks-and-mortar bookstores are seen as dinosaurs, and Barnes & Noble's market cap is about one-tenth of Amazon's.

The lesson? Few companies stay on top forever. Not IBM, not General Motors (GM:NYSE), not even Microsoft. So if you hold stock in an industry leader (which you should try to do), be on the lookout for competitive threats, whether from new technologies, business models, or a changing environment. Fight the tendency to see today's pecking order as permanent.

A Major Change in Strategy   For most of its existence, AOL has been the quintessential new media company, with a valuation to match. At the end of 1999 its stock traded at 183 times earnings and 25 times sales. Then it announced a blockbuster deal to acquire old media giant Time Warner (TWX:NYSE), which carried a traditional—i.e., much lower—stock valuation. At first, Wall Street loved the idea of combining Time Warner's "content" with AOL's Internet delivery channels, and both stocks rose.

But then people started wondering: If you take a company with a New Economy valuation and combine it with a company that the market has decided is worth only 45 times earnings and three times sales, should the new entity trade at an old or new media valuation, or somewhere in between? In the three months following the deal, "in between" seemed to win out, with AOL's stock price falling from the 90s to the 50s.

These kinds of strategy changes happen constantly as companies try to position themselves for the future. Amazon.com expands from books into consumer electronics and toys, Wal-Mart (WMT:NYSE) opens a massive Internet store, Boeing (BA:NYSE) buys space-related assets. Again, your job is to decide whether these new chapters change the story in a negative way or enhance the company's prospects.

Heavy Insider Selling The people running public companies make their decisions behind closed doors. But they do send signals to the marketplace that if interpreted correctly can give you insight into their confidence or fears of the future. One signal is insider stock trading— when a company's officers, directors, and major investors buy or sell their stock. Luckily for investors, the Securities and Exchange Commission requires insiders to tell the world about their trading activity, and a growing number of Web sites, including Yahoo! (www.yahoo.com) and MSN MoneyCentral (www.moneycentral.com), offer that data free. Just type in a ticker symbol, then click on "Insiders," and up comes a chronology of who sold at what price.

Analyzing this data can be tricky. Selling doesn't by itself tell you much, since many insiders often have most of their net worth tied up in their company's stock. They understandably want to diversify. Bill Gates has been selling Microsoft stock for years without a noticeable effect on its price. And even when it seems like an executive is selling a sizable block of his stock, it may be a false alarm if his option package dwarfs his actual stock holdings. But broad-based, massive selling by insiders is often a red flag.

In early 1999, for example, Waste Management's (WMI:NYSE) top people all seemed to bail at once—not long before some negative earnings news sent the stock into the dumpster. This selling was legal because it was apparently based on deteriorating business conditions rather than on foreknowledge of a specific event. But whatever the insiders' motivation, they sent a clear sell signal to anyone wise enough to be paying attention.

For more on insider buying and selling, check out the SEC EDGAR sites we mentioned in Chapter 5. Forms 3, 4, and 5 reflect the ownership of directors, officers, or owners of more than 10% of the company's stock, and changes in that ownership. Form 144 is a notice of sale by anyone with "restricted" securities, which often includes people who had stock before the company went public. (NOTE: Forms 3, 4, 5, and 144 can be filed electronically but are not required to be.) Again, Yahoo! and moneycentral.com are also good sources.

Technical Reasons to Sell

Now, admittedly, most of the above analysis depends on some serious digging into a company's business model and financial statements. If you don't have the time, know-how, or inclination, don't despair. As you know from Chapter 7, proponents of technical analysis say it's mostly wasted effort anyhow, because a stock's price action already reflects the consensus of the accountants, analysts, and money managers who spend their days running the numbers and grilling managements. When a stock trades in an unfavorable way, they claim, the smart money may be sensing trouble. Here are some technical sell signals you should watch:

Moving Averages Online stock charting services (Yahoo!, for instance) will let you compare a stock's price action to 50- and 200-day moving averages, which give a good picture of the short- and longer-term trends. (Moving average is the stock's average closing price over the given time period.) When the 50-day moving average crosses the 200-day average on the way down, this is a sign that momentum has turned negative, possibly implying long-term trouble.

Pure technicians don't need to know why it's happening other than that the people who are really digging into the company's finances and prospects seem to think that's the direction the stock should be heading. But even if you're not a technician, use the marker as a signal for more research. Deciding in advance to consider selling when these lines cross can help get you out of a stock before a downtrend picks up steam.

In the case of Avon (AVP:NYSE), for instance, the 50-day average crossing the 200 was followed by a sharp decline in September 1999, and that point marked a several-month downturn for the stock.

Performance Versus the Rest of the Market Here is another sign that may indicate that it's time to sell. Instead of comparing a stock to its own past, graph it against the action of the S&P 500 or Nasdaq Composite. Consider selling if it underperforms by some pre-set amount,

Moving Averages Cross Paths

Avon Products Inc.
as of 18–Aug–2000   Splits : ▼   Mov Avg: 200 day   50 day

Copyright 2000 Yahoo! Inc.   Volume (1000s)   http://finance.yahoo.com/

Data Source: Commodity Systems, Inc. (CSI) www.csidata.com

like 20%. The idea is that if a stock is doing substantially worse than the market while no overt problems are apparent, then real trouble might be brewing under the surface. Or perhaps the problems are apparent and the stock has just run out of steam. Both Avon and Dell, once they started underperforming, trailed for a long time.

Asset Allocation Issues—An Unbalanced Portfolio

An unbalanced portfolio may be another reason to sell stock. Let's say that back in 1996 you divided your capital equally among five stocks: AOL, Boeing, Cisco, Exxon (XOM:NYSE), and General Motors. Congratulations! By decade's end, depending upon how much you initially invested, you were probably a millionaire. But several years later, your portfolio had a very different profile.

Where at first your risks were spread evenly among the five stocks, by January 1, 2000, 87% of your money would have been in Cisco and AOL, exposing you to big losses should one or both of them blow up. It might be time to "rebalance" by selling some of the winners and shifting the proceeds into other stocks.

Now, say that two weeks after you rebalance you find something with all the makings of a winner: great fundamentals, fast growth, a business model that you can understand and appreciate, low price—

Company	Value 1/1/96	% of Portfolio	Value 12/31/99	% of Portfolio
AOL	$10,000	20%	$250,000	59%
Boeing	$10,000	20%	$11,100	2.6%
Cisco	$10,000	20%	$120,000	28%
Exxon Mobil	$10,000	20%	$20,000	4.7%
GM	$10,000	20%	$22,000	5.2%
Total	$50,000	100%	$423,100	100%

the whole package. Yet here you sit, fully invested, with very little cash to throw around. At this point, to buy the stock, you've got to make one of two decisions. One is to dump the stock that adds the least to your portfolio in terms of diversification or growth prospects. The other is to prorate the pain by selling a little of each.

For a review of all of these "when to sell" factors, please see our "checklist" at the end of this chapter.

Tax Factors in Selling Stock

If you are intent on selling holdings for some of the economic reasons we've just reviewed, then that's what you should do. But precisely *when* do you sell? It's at this point that you should think about taxes.

Calculating Capital Gains Tax

You will owe Uncle Sam tax on any gains you make on the sale of your stocks. You will not owe tax on your losses. How much you owe on your gains depends on what you paid for your stock, what your tax bracket is, and how long you've held the stock.

What You Paid: Your Cost Basis To establish whether you have a gain or loss on the sale of your stock, you first need to determine its cost basis, the original price you paid for a stock, plus commissions and any other expenses incurred at the time of purchase. So if you buy 100 shares of Skechers (SKX:NYSE) for $15 a share, and pay a commission of $20 on the trade, the basis in the position is about $1,520.

Once you know the cost basis of your stock, it is easy to determine your gain or loss upon sale.

In general, the gain or loss on a stock is the difference between your stock's cost basis and its trading price on the day of the sale. If you sell the stock for more than you paid for it, you've got a capital gain. If you sell it for less than you paid for it, you've got a capital loss. In the Skechers case, if you sold for $20 a share, again at a $20 commission, your gain would be $460.

Sale   Minus commission   Minus basis   Gain

($20)(100) = $2000 − $20 = $1980 − $1520 = $460

It's helpful to keep a record of your stock's cost basis so that you can determine your gain or loss in the position. Use an Excel spreadsheet or a personal finance software like Intuit's Quicken or Microsoft's Money, and each time you buy a security, be diligent about entering the purchase price of your holding.

Tracking is especially important if you have your stock's dividends automatically reinvested. It's also important if you participate in an automatic monthly purchase plan of stocks or mutual funds. Same goes if you automatically reinvest your capital gains distributions and dividends from a mutual fund.

In any of those cases, you are buying shares throughout the year. And each time you make a purchase, you have a new cost basis in those shares. Your broker or mutual fund company typically will keep track of these purchases for you, but it doesn't hurt for you to have backup.

Web Sites That Help You Track Your Trades	
Product	Web Address
Money	www.microsoft.com/money
Quicken	www.quicken.com
Gainskeeper	www.gainskeeper.com
TradeLog	www.armencomp.com/tradelog
Captool	www.captools.com
LiveWire	www.livewire-cablesoft.com
Trade Tracker99	www.pcstartups.com
CyBerTrader	www.cybercorp.com

Tracking Cost Basis in Shares					
John Q. Taxpayer's AT&T Cost Basis Detail					
Year	Date of Purchase or Dividend Reinvestment	Dividend Distribution	Stock Price at Purchase	Number of Shares Purchased	Total Purchase (Cost Basis)
1999	1/3/99		51.9166	150.0000*	$7,787.49
	5/3/99	$0.33	51.0325	0.0065	$16.84
	8/2/99	$0.22	51.5000	0.0043	$11.33
	11/1/99	$0.22	47.3125	0.0046	$10.41
	2/1/00	$0.22	52.5000	0.0042	$11.55
2000	5/1/00	$0.22	49.0000	0.0045	$10.78
	8/1/00	$0.22	31.8125	0.0069	$7.00
				150.0310	$7,855.40

* Note that taxpayer originally purchased 100 shares at $77.875 each but there was a 3-for-2 split on April 15.

The Holding Period and Tax Bracket: How Your Gains Are Taxed Now that you know what your gain is, you need to determine your "holding period" to determine how those gains are taxed. The holding period is the length of time you've held your stock.

Your holding period is short term if you've held the shares for one year or less. Any gains generated from those securities will be taxed at your ordinary income tax rate. That could be 15%, 28%, 31%, 36%, or 39.6%, depending on your income, and it can change with changes in the tax laws.

For stocks held at least twelve months and a day, you have a long-term holding period. Any gains at the time of sale will be taxed at the long-term preferential rate of 20% (or 10% if you are in the 15% ordi-

Capital Gains	
Long Term	Short Term
• 12 months and one day or longer • preferential tax rate	• 12 months or less • ordinary income tax rate

nary income tax bracket). (There are new, better rates if you hold more than five years.)

Essentially, you get much better tax treatment if you hold a stock longer than one year. That's a big incentive for holding. Say, for example, you're in the 36% tax bracket and you bought 100 shares of JDS Uniphase (JDSU:Nasdaq) at 20 in July 1999, for a total of $2,000 (not counting commissions). In May 2000, with the stock at 80, that position is now worth about $8,000, representing a $6,000 gain.

It's been ten months. You can take that gain and pay your 36%, shaving off $2,160 in taxes. Or you could hold two more months and then sell for a tax of 20%, or $1,200, if the stock price stays the same.

But that's the big if. You need to decide: Is the $960 you can save worth the risk of losing even more than that? If the stock falls more than 13 points in those two months, to 67, you lose the benefit of holding.

The Taxpayer's JDSU Dilemma: To Sell or to Hold				
July 1999 Value	May 2000 Value	Tax at 36%	Tax at 20%	Difference
$2,000	$8,000	$2,160	$1,200	$960

What to do with your JDSU depends on what your gut says about the state of the stock. If you think the stock will continue to hold at about its current price or go higher, then waiting out the twelve months is the right strategy. That's what happened with JDSU, which vaulted over 100 by July 2000. But if your gut tells you that a stock's seen its day, it's better to sell while you still have gains to take.

Sure, you could be talking about a nearly 20% differential between the capital gains rate and your regular ordinary tax rate if you're in the 39.6% federal tax bracket, but that's a moot point if you lose your gains waiting for the twelve months to expire.

Let's take another example. Say you bought 100 shares of Red Hat (RHAT:Nasdaq) on September 1, 1999, for 43 a share. At December

The Taxpayer's RHAT Dilemma: To Sell or to Hold				
Sept. 1999 Value	Dec. 31 Value	Tax at 39.6%	Tax at 20%	Difference
$4,300	$11,500	$2,850	$1,440	$1,410

31, 1999, the stock was trading at 115. That's around a 168% gain for you. If you're in the highest tax bracket and you sold at that point, you'd owe 39.6% on your $7,200 gain. So $2,850 goes to Uncle Sam. You walk away with $4,350.

"That's too much for Uncle Sam," you say. "I'm waiting for twelve months to get the preferential long-term 20% rate!" Sounds like a great idea, because if you apply 20% to that $7,200 gain, only $1,440 disappears with the taxman. You'd get to keep $5,760, a difference of $1,410, assuming the stock stays at that price.

Bad assumption. By summer 2000, Red Hat was trading below its IPO price of 26. If you waited for the twelve months to pass, you'd be reporting a big loss. Sometimes it is better to be less stingy about sharing gains with Uncle Sam.

That's the basic analysis you need to conduct in deciding whether to hold out for long-term capital gains treatment. Quicken.com has a great calculator to help you calculate your break-even point on the tax question. Check it out at www.quicken.com/taxes/investing/12month/.

One wrinkle: Generally, states assess tax on gains as well. So you need to include those costs in your equation.

Stepped-Up Basis

If you keep your stock until you die, the tax benefits are nearly worth it! Your heirs get what's called a "stepped up" basis, meaning your cost basis gets upped to the value of the stock on the day you die. But before you start hoarding, know that Congress has been reconsidering this pro-hold provision.

Pecking Order of Gains There's a pecking order of short- and long-term gains and losses that bears on your ability to take losses in any given year. Short-term gains and losses are reported separately from your long-term gains and losses on Schedule D, *Capital Gains and Losses,* of your Form 1040, *U.S. Individual Income Tax Return*. (Visit the Internal Revenue Service's site at www.irs.gov for copies of these forms.)

Short-term gains are netted against short-term losses. Long-term gains are netted against long-term losses. The net short-term gain/loss, then, is combined with the net long-term gain/loss to create your final capital gain/loss number.

If the final number is a gain, then the portion of that gain that is short-term will be taxed at your regular income tax rate and the amount that is a long-term gain will be taxed at the preferential rate.

If the final number is a loss, you can take up to $3,000 only of losses on your current year's income tax return. The balance can be carried forward for an unlimited number of years until the loss is exhausted.

Here's an example:

The Pecking Order

Total Short-term Gains:	$6,700
Total Short-term Losses:	($5,400)
Net Short-term Gain/Loss:	$1,300
Total Long-term Gains:	$11,650
Total Long-term Losses:	($22,500)
Net Long-term Gain/Loss:	($10,850)
Net Short-term Gain/Loss:	$1,300
Net Long-term Gain/Loss:	($10,850)
Total Capital Gain/Loss:	($9,550)
Maximum Loss Allowed:	($3,000)
Loss Carried to Next Year:	($6,550)

Schedule D walks you through the process, as will many tax books that are published annually at the beginning of each year.

When Do You Trigger a Capital Gain? There are two dates you need to be aware of when you sell a stock—the trade date and the settlement date. The trade date is the day when the sale transaction occurs. The settlement date is the day either money or securities are exchanged. The settlement date usually is around three days after the trade date.

The trade date is the day that counts for capital gains purposes on your long positions. If you sold, say, 100 shares of Cisco on December 31, 1999, any gain or loss would count for 1999. It doesn't matter that the settlement date—the day money or securities change hands—isn't until early January.

If you make a short sale, however, the settlement date is used for capital gains recording purposes. Why the difference? The idea behind a short position is that you're hoping the position is going to fall. So you borrow the stock from a broker-dealer and sell the certificate on the open market. A few days later, you buy back the stock—hopefully at a lower price. That's the trade date. But you can't really determine

---

Stock Splits and Mergers

What happens to your cost basis if your stock splits or the company merges with another company? Nothing. The dollar value of your initial investment does not change.

Let's say your stock splits 2 for 1 (see our discussion of stock splits in Chapter 9). That means you'll get two new shares for every one you currently hold. Assuming your original cost basis in one share was $100, after the stock split you will have two shares each with a cost basis of $50. Your total basis in this position is still $100.

If your company merges in a tax-free stock swap, the acquiring company will swap your shares for shares in its company. This generally is not a taxable event, so your original basis will be your basis in your newly swapped shares. If you bought your original shares at $100, your basis in the shares of the acquiring company after the swap would still be $100, and your holding period stays the same. You will not have to worry about capital gains tax until you decide to sell those new shares.

how much you've gained (or lost) until you return the stock to your broker. It's at this point that the short position is closed and there is a taxable event. That's why the settlement date is used to record capital gains in a short sale.

As for options, the trade date is the day that counts for tax purposes.

Should You Time Your Sales? If it's the end of the year and you're thinking of making a sale, consider your current tax situation. Have you already done some selling that has racked up your capital gains tax bill? If so, you may want to consider dumping a loser before the calendar year is out to generate a capital loss. Assuming you were looking to get rid of the deadweight in your portfolio anyway, making the sale before the end of the year will help soften the blow of your capital gains tax come April 15.

But if you're considering selling a stock at a gain, think about waiting until the beginning of the next year. If you believe the stock will hold at its current price, waiting until January pushes off your capital gain tax bill for another year. That gives you plenty of time to create some losses to offset that gain.

The Wash Sale Rule and How It Can Whack You

Say you're in Las Vegas and feeling good. You mosey over to the blackjack table with $100 and win $1,000. Beating the dealer seems easy, so you get cocky and keep playing. Sure enough, three hands later, your winnings are gone. You get up and walk away, humbled, with only the $100 you started with. Financially, the whole experience was a wash.

This is the exact scenario animating the IRS's notorious wash sale rule. It's a rule both long- and short-term investors need to pay close attention to, because it can wipe out apparent tax advantages.

Let's suppose you buy a stock, sell it at a loss, then buy it right back. After those few transactions, you're still holding the same number of shares. For tax purposes, though, you now have a loss. But since your economic position has not changed—you still have the same number of shares—Uncle Sam sees no reason why you should be able to take that loss on your tax return.

Here's an example:

Yahoo! Disallowed Loss

Buy on Dec 7, 1999 at $174
Sell on Dec 14, 1999 at $167
Buy on Dec. 17, 1999 at $176

$7 loss from Dec 14 sale is disallowed

This rule sounds like a short-term trader's concern, but it actually can affect both long-term stock investors and mutual fund investors. If you elect to have your dividends reinvested in the form of purchase of additional shares, you end up purchasing stock at several times a year that you might not even be thinking about.

These purchases will disallow your losses on other shares you decide to sell in the 30-day time period that governs the rule. For instance, if you sell 100 shares today at a loss but your dividends are reinvested next week, the amount of loss equal to the reinvestment will be disallowed by the wash sale rule.

Same goes for the mutual fund investor who has automatic investments made periodically out of the checking account or, again, who reinvests capital gains distributions and dividends. So pay attention.

Here's the rule: If you sell a security at a loss, you can't deduct the loss on your tax return if you buy a substantially identical security or enter into an option to buy a substantially identical security 30 days before or after the sale, according to Section 1091 of the tax code.

What's "substantially identical"?

- Shares of the same stock in the same company are substantially identical (though preferred stock is not substantially identical to common stock).
- Options with varying expiration dates are not substantially identical. To be even safer, buy options with different strike prices and expiration dates.
- Stocks/Options: If you sell a stock at a loss and then buy an option on that stock, that will trigger the wash sale rule even if the option is out of the money. (An out-of-the-money call has a strike price that exceeds the share price of the underlying equity. An out-of-the-money put has a strike price that is less than the share price of the underlying equity. If you

exercised either, you would lose money on the trade.) You can't enter into an option to buy a substantially identical security.

On the flip side, if you're long an option, and you're losing your shirt on it, you can sell the option and buy back the underlying stock without triggering a wash sale. Why? The option and the stock are not substantially identical, according to an arcane 1958 IRS ruling.

- Short sales are not excused from the wash sale. If you buy a substantially similar security 30 days before or after the close of that short, or if you reenter the short position during that same window—your loss will be disallowed.

If you're looking for a Web site that keeps track of wash sales, check out Gainskeeper.com.

All Is Not Lost If you do buy back a security before the 30-day period is up, any loss will be disallowed on your tax return, but it's not gone forever. You can add that loss to the "cost basis" of the repurchased stock. (Remember, cost basis is essentially what you pay for a stock; it's the amount used to calculate how much tax you owe when you sell.)

Let's say you first bought Yahoo! at 174 but you sold it at 167. At this point your basis is 174, making for a $7 loss. Before the 30-day waiting period is up, however, you buy the share back at 176. Your basis in that stock is now equal to the old basis (174) *plus* the difference between the repurchase price (176) and the sales price of the original shares (167), or $9. In this scenario, 183 is your new basis.

If, however, your repurchase price is lower than what you sold the stock for, the basis of the new stock equals the original price of the security *less* the difference between the sale price and the repurchase price. So the original shares were 174, and you sold the shares at 167. Before the 30-day waiting period was up you bought the shares back at 158. The basis in the new shares is now the original basis (174) *less* the difference between the sale price (167) and the repurchase price (158). Your new basis is only 165 in this situation.

Finally, there's no wash sale rule on your gains. If you sell a stock at a gain and buy the same stock back within 30 days, you'll owe tax on the gain. Uncle Sam will turn away losses, but not gains.

Minimize That Capital Gains Tax

No matter when you decide to sell, there are tips to keep in mind to lower your tax bill. Here are some:

Identify Specific Lots   Rather than selling your newest or oldest shares first, you can designate specific "lots" of stock to sell, as defined by the price at which you purchased the stock. That way you can unload your highest-cost lots first and minimize your taxable gains. Of course, you should take care to determine which lots would get capital gains treatment and which would still be subject to ordinary income tax.

For instance, let's assume you made the following Microsoft purchases:

Purchase Date	Number of Shares	Cost Basis	Value
July 1, 1999	50	88	4,400
Sept. 2, 1999	50	85	4,250
Oct. 1, 1999	50	90	4,500

It's April 2000 and the stock is at 90 and you want to unload 50 shares. Which lot do you sell? If you sell the July lot, the $100 gain (50 x 2) will be short-term and taxed at your ordinary income tax rate, which we'll assume for this example is 36%. That's a tax of $36.

If, instead, you sell the September lot, you'll rake in a $250 gain, again subject to ordinary income rates. Uncle Sam will take $90.

If you sell the October lot, you won't owe a dime.

To limit the amount of gains you'll owe taxes on, you may elect to sell your highest-cost lot first.

Specific Lot	April 2000 Value	Original Value	Taxable Amount	Tax Due
July 1, 1999	4,500	4,400	100	36
Sept. 2, 1999	4,500	4,250	250	90
Oct. 1, 1999	4,500	4,500	0	0

So it depends on your current situation. Regardless of which lot you elect to sell, it's important to inform your broker, in writing, when you're identifying specific lots.

If you have previously sold shares by some other method (first-in, first-out, for example, meaning you sell first the shares you bought first), it's okay to switch to specific-lot identification. You don't have to file anything with the IRS. Just make sure you receive a written confirmation of this sale from your broker or other agent and keep it with your records.

The rules are different for mutual funds. If you've been selling shares on a first-in, first-out basis, or some other basis, you can't switch to specific-lot identification for your next sale. You can, however, use different selling methods for different funds.

Double Up If you have a stock that has tanked but you still believe in its future, go out and buy more of it. That's right. Buy more. Wait. Then sell. This technique is called doubling up, and it can ease your pain in two ways. It creates a tax loss that you can use to offset some of your gains, and it lowers the cost basis in your tumbling stock.

Let's say you bought 100 shares of Microsoft at 100, and today it's at 70. You think it'll bounce back. Buy another 100 shares at its current price, 70. Wait until the *thirty-first day* and sell your original shares of Microsoft that you bought for 100.

Why wait? You've got to abide by the wash sale rule or the tax loss will be disallowed. If, however, you sell your original shares on the thirty-first day, assuming the stock hasn't rocketed, you will have generated a tax loss that you can use to offset future capital gains. The best part: You're still holding the same number of shares, but now at a lower cost basis.

Be sure to notify your broker that you've chosen to sell the first lot of shares. Make sure there's some notation to that effect on your brokerage statement. Otherwise, the sale might be seen as a last-in, first-out sale, meaning your broker would just assume that the shares acquired last are the ones sold first. Keep this documentation in case Uncle Sam asks for proof one day.

Remember to stay cognizant of commissions and broker fees. Make sure that the costs of these trades don't outweigh the benefits.

Swap Out Another way to avoid the wash sale rule is to sell a losing stock and buy another stock in the same industry. You get the loss without necessarily changing your portfolio's allocation substantially. Wait the requisite 30 days and swap back to your original position if you want.

A Quick Word on Options

The sale and purchase of calls and puts create capital gains and losses, just like stocks. The basis and gains depend on whether the option is exercised, expired, or sold. The easiest way to figure this out is to use the IRS charts (believe it or not). We've included them for you below.

How to Get All This on Your Tax Return

Sale of Stocks Reporting your gains and losses on the sale of your stocks on Schedule D is pretty straightforward. Always include the number of shares sold and an explanation of the property in the description column (a). In addition, make sure the cost basis in column (e) matches the shares you sold in column (d). This is particularly important if you've specifically identified certain lots to sell. This

Taxes on Puts		
When a put:	If you are the holder (buyer):	If you are the writer (seller):
Is exercised	Reduce your amount realized from the sale of the underlying stock by the cost of the put.	Reduce your basis in the stock you buy by the amount you received for the put.
Expires	Report the cost of the put as a capital loss.	Report the amount you received for the put as a short-term capital gain.
Is sold by the holder	Report the difference between the cost of the put and the amount you receive for it as a capital gain or loss.	No effect to you. (But if you buy back the put, report the difference between the amount you pay and the amount you received for the put as a short-term capital gain or loss.)

Source: Internal Revenue Service, Publication 550—Investment Income and Expenses

is the only real way the IRS can keep track of your stock selling. Check out the Microsoft entry on our sample Schedule D on page 256.

Wash Sale Rule If a loss on the sale of a stock or option is disallowed as a result of the wash sale rule, you have a two-line reporting process ahead of you.

First, report the loss as you would any other loss on Schedule D. Show the full amount of the loss as a negative in column (f).

On the next line, just enter "wash sale" in the description column (a), and enter the loss as positive number in the gain column (f). That's all you need for that line item. Our purchase of Ann Taylor (ANN: NYSE) shares on May 14, 1999, created a wash sale on our sample Schedule D.

Taxes on Calls		
When a call:	If you are the holder (buyer):	If you are the writer (seller):
Is exercised	Add the cost of the call to your basis in the stock purchased.	Increase your amount realized on sale of stock by the amount you received for the call.
Expires	Report the cost of the call as a capital loss on the date it expires.	Report the amount you received for the call as a short-term capital gain.
Is sold by the holder	Report the difference between the cost of the call and the amount you receive for it as a capital gain or loss.	This does not affect you. (But if you buy back the call, report the difference between the amount you pay and the amount you received for the call as a short-term capital gain or loss.)

Source: Internal Revenue Service, Publication 550—Investment Income and Expenses

Short Positions Only when a short position is closed is there a taxable event. You report short sales only in the year you cover them. But if you sell short, the sale date is going to come before the purchase date. Don't fret. This is the correct way to record the transaction on Schedule D. See how we reported our AOL short.

Sample Schedule D

SCHEDULE D (Form 1040)	Capital Gains and Losses		OMB No. 1545-0074
Department of the Treasury Internal Revenue Service (99)	Attach to Form 1040. See Instructions for Schedule D (Form 1040). Use Schedule D-1 for more space to list transactions for lines 1 and 8.		1999 Attachment Sequence No. 12
Name(s) shown on Form 1040			Your social security number

Part I   Short-Term Capital Gains and Losses—Assets Held One Year or Less

(a) Description of property (Example: 100 sh. XYZ Co.)	(b) Date acquired (Mo., day, yr.)	(c) Date sold (Mo., day, yr.)	(d) Sales price (see page D-5)	(e) Cost or other basis (see page D-5)	(f) GAIN or (LOSS) Subtract (e) from (d)	
1 10 PUTS IP OCT 35	5.31.99	10.16.99	EXPIRED	3500	<3500>	
30 SHS ANN	5.14.99	12.24.99	990	1515	<525>	
WASH SALE					525	
SHORT 100 AOL SHS	1.6.99	12.24.98	8598	9253	<655>	

2   Enter your short-term totals, if any, from Schedule D-1, line 2 . . . .   **2**

3   **Total short-term sales price amounts.** Add column (d) of lines 1 and 2 . . . .   **3**

4   Short-term gain from Form 6252 and short-term gain or (loss) from Forms 4684, 6781, and 8824 . . . .   **4**

5   Net short-term gain or (loss) from partnerships, S corporations, estates, and trusts from Schedule(s) K-1 . . . .   **5**

6   Short-term capital loss carryover. Enter the amount, if any, from line 8 of your 1998 Capital Loss Carryover Worksheet . . . .   **6** (   )

7   **Net short-term capital gain or (loss).** Combine lines 1 through 6 in column (f)   **7**   <4155>

Part II   Long-Term Capital Gains and Losses—Assets Held More Than One Year

(a) Description of property (Example: 100 sh. XYZ Co.)	(b) Date acquired (Mo., day, yr.)	(c) Date sold (Mo., day, yr.)	(d) Sales price (see page D-5)	(e) Cost or other basis (see page D-5)	(f) GAIN or (LOSS) Subtract (e) from (d)	(g) 28% RATE GAIN or (LOSS) (see instr. below)
8 10 SHS MSFT	1.24.98	10.8.99	950	240	710	
50 SHS ANN	4.13.98	8.20.99	1850	825	1025	

9   Enter your long-term totals, if any, from Schedule D-1, line 9 . . . .   **9**

10   **Total long-term sales price amounts.** Add column (d) of lines 8 and 9 . . . . .   **10**   2800

11   Gain from Form 4797, Part I; long-term gain from Forms 2439 and 6252; and long-term gain or (loss) from Forms 4684, 6781, and 8824 . . . .   **11**

12   Net long-term gain or (loss) from partnerships, S corporations, estates, and trusts from Schedule(s) K-1. . . . .   **12**

13   Capital gain distributions. See page D-1 . . . .   **13**

14   Long-term capital loss carryover. Enter in both columns (f) and (g) the amount, if any, from line 13 of your 1998 Capital Loss Carryover Worksheet . . . . . .   **14** (   ) (   )

15   Combine lines 8 through 14 in column (g) **15**

16   **Net long-term capital gain or (loss).** Combine lines 8 through 14 in column (f)   **16**   1735
      Next: Go to Part III on the back.

*28% Rate Gain or Loss includes **all** "collectibles gains and losses" (as defined on page D-5) and up to 50% of the eligible gain on qualified small business stock (see page D-4).

For Paperwork Reduction Act Notice, see Form 1040 instructions.	Cat. No. 11338H	Schedule D (Form 1040) 1999

If you do have open positions on December 31, the gross proceeds reported on your Form 1099B—*Proceeds from Broker and Barter Exchange Transactions*, will be greater than the amount you report on your tax return.

You'll need to attach a reconciliation schedule. It can be a plain sheet of paper with your name and social security number on it. Write "see attached schedule" in column (a), then attach a form that should look something like this:

> Gross proceeds from broker xxxx
>
> Less short sales to be reported next year .... yyyy
>
> Total reported on Schedule D.............................. zzzz

Options Your option trades are reported on Schedule D just like your stock trades. For some reason, though, your option trades are not reported on Form 1099B. They still must be reported on your tax return, so you should do a simple reconciliation for the IRS.

If the total sales price you're reporting on your tax return is larger than the amount reported on your 1099B, you're probably not going to have a problem. If that's the case, you're paying more tax than the IRS thinks you should, and it's not going to argue.

But if the amount you report is less (i.e., you're a really bad options trader), attach a simple schedule explaining the difference. Be sure to put your name and Social Security number on it. Then show the difference as a lump sum. Say you're down $2,000. Just show that $2,000 as "difference due to option trading losses." There's no need to show every transaction. You'll just confuse the IRS.

If all you do is trade options, you won't get a Form 1099B at all. Again, just attach a quick explanation of your total sales proceeds (i.e., "sales from options trading").

If your options expire worthless or the underlying stock is called away, you need to make that clear. If a purchased option has expired, enter the expiration date in column (c) and write "expired" in column (d). If an option that you sold has expired, enter the expiration date in column (b) and write "expired" in column (e). Our International Paper (IP:NYSE) October 35 puts expired worthless. Check out how we reported them.

Miscellany   As a general rule, keep all your trading records, including your purchase and sales slips, for a minimum of three years after the due date of your tax return. If something has an effect on future years, then hang on to everything as long it is material to your tax return.

You can always attach your own trading schedule. Make sure it contains all the same info as Schedule D. Then just transfer the grand totals to Schedule D and write "see attached schedule" in the description column. Just write "various" in the date columns.

When to Sell: A Checklist

Macroeconomic Factors

Watch interest rates and the broader market's P/E ratio and earnings yield. When the earnings yield of the broader market is much lower than the yield on Treasuries, that's a signal of market overvaluation.

Individual Stocks: Fundamental Factors

✓ Look for a business slowdown facing the company, or its industry.

✓ Watch for overvaluation as measured by the stock's earnings yield compared to interest rates and the stock's P/E ratio compared to other stocks in the same industry.

✓ Look for deteriorating earnings quality as a sign that the company is using tricks to mask broader-based problems.

✓ Seek out information on new competitors and try to evaluate the threat they pose.

✓ Pay attention to any major change in strategy. It could be a reason to buy—or sell.

✓ Study signs of heavy selling by insiders. While much insider selling is normal, hefty bouts are not always a coincidence.

Technical Factors

✓ Consider selling when the 50-day moving average crosses the 200-day moving average on the way down.

✓ Graph your stock against the performance of the Nasdaq Composite or S&P 500, and consider bailing if it underperforms by a preset amount.

Asset Allocation Issues

✓ A portfolio out of whack compared to your goals is a reason to trim or replace a position.

Tax Issues

✓ Size up whether you're eligible for long-term capital gains treatment based on when you purchased shares.

✓ Consider timing your sale before or after the calendar-year end, to delay payment of taxes or have losses to offset your gains.

✓ Figure out whether you'll run up against the wash sale rule and end up unable to take all of your losses.

11

When Options
Are an Option

So far, we've talked almost entirely about stocks and mutual funds. These investments are the staples of most individuals' portfolios. As well they should be. But there's another financial instrument that individual investors are increasingly turning to as an enhancement to their core holdings: options.

Options are essentially a way to make money on the rise or fall of a stock without actually buying the stock. If used wisely, options can be a tremendous tool. They enable an investor with a hunch about a stock's direction to try to profit from that point of view without having to lay out the full amount it would cost to purchase the stock. That's the best way to use options, and it's the way we'll discuss in this chapter.

But as with all good things, if taken to extremes, options can actually be quite dangerous. When you buy (or sell) options, you stand to lose your entire investment in a flash. So if you trade options too often, for too much money, you can end up much worse off than you'd be with individual stocks.

Before I proceed further with this material, I want to give you the requisite, and appropriate, warning: If you are just getting started with options, limit your foray to 2 to 3% of your investing portfolio. If you gain confidence and have some regular successes, venture to up to 5%. But try to limit it there. Using options can be addictive. Even professional floor traders have been known to seek the help of Gamblers Anonymous to kick the options habit. You don't want that to be you.

In some respects, the obsession with options is understandable. When most investors think about options and other more exotic investments, their imaginations run to spectacular gains and crushing losses. Self-styled options gurus sell as many books as Danielle Steel does on love affairs. Investors desperately want to mimic this apparent alchemy.

Maybe what makes options so appealing is the whiff of danger. Since the 1987 crash, options have been associated with high risk for even the most sophisticated investors. In the wake of the Dow's more than 500-point fall on October 27, 1997, a "put option" play on the S&P 500 index cost chess-playing, super-genius hedge fund manager Victor Neiderhoffer more than $50 million, and temporarily put him out of business.

Still, options don't have to take investors to these kinds of hair-raising extremes. The concept is actually relatively simple: pay a small amount—much like a security deposit—for the right to buy or sell a specific stock to someone else by a certain time and for a certain price. You can either exercise the option (that is, buy or sell the stock in question), sell the option contract to someone else at a profit, or let it expire worthless. In short, options provide, well, options.

The odds are if someone told you that there was an investment that could produce returns whether a stock was rising or falling (or even just sitting around doing nothing), you'd probably dismiss him as a lunatic. Yet, you can do just that with options. You get the chance to buy Cisco Systems (CSCO:Nasdaq) for 65 even as it rises to 75; or you can sell Amazon.com (AMZN:Nasdaq) for 70 as it falls to 65. It's not snake oil or voodoo. Options can actually be a low-risk way to apply any idea an investor would use in buying a stock outright.

Sure, you can make the big score in options, and you can lose as well. But for most individual investors, options can and should be safer than buying the actual equities they represent. As I'll explain shortly, risk is frequently finite and the leverage of options allows for other capital to be used in more conservative investments. In fact, the options market is a good place to consider a few different offbeat investments because their alleged complexity frightens off most and hamstrings others, leaving opportunity for the enlightened.

Dan Colarusso, *TheStreet.com's* veteran Wall Street writer and creator of our daily "Options Buzz" column, will take us behind the scenes of the options market. This chapter should serve as a valuable introduction on options for all investors, and a valuable refresher and reference for the more advanced among you.

Why Options?

The first question most investors almost always have is: Why bother with options when I can just buy or sell a stock?

In many cases, simply buying or selling a stock is the most appropriate strategy. But every investor has been bedeviled by those what-if stocks, the kind of investments for which you have neither the courage nor the capital. Let's take an example. In January you spot a $30 stock you think will rise after the introduction of a hot new product.

You decide buying 1,000 shares would be the thing to do, but one, you might have to sell other lucrative long-term investments to come up with the money, and two, if that product flops, your 30 grand could be 15 in a hurry. You decide it's a risk you can't take right now; the kids need braces, the house needs a new roof, or maybe you've tried the company's new product and now realize it doesn't work. You suspect the stock may even fall. But the last thing you want to do is "short" the stock, that is, borrow shares with the hope they'll fall in value. Shorting involves margin—borrowing—and if the rest of America loves this product and the stock rallies, your losses can be limitless.

With options, you can play both scenarios. Sometimes, however, it will seem like asking for directions in a foreign country—the basics are the same but the language is indecipherable. So let's get some help on the jargon, first.

A Quick Vocabulary Lesson

Assignment: When an option seller is called upon to fulfill the obligations of the contract.

At-the-Money: An option with the strike price equal to the current stock price.

Call Option: An option that gives the holder the right but not the obligation to buy a stock or an index at a pre-set price by a certain date. These are purchased to express a positive sentiment about a stock's future, typically in the short term, e.g., the right to purchase 100 shares of XYZ at $10 a share by January 21.

Exchanges: Options are traded on five exchanges: the Chicago Board Options Exchange, the American Stock Exchange, the Philadelphia Stock Exchange, the Pacific Exchange, and the International Securities Exchange, a New York–based electronic market.

Exercise: The act of closing out an options contract by choosing to buy (in the case of a call) or sell (in the case of a put) the commensurate amount of shares. A client must simply notify his broker that he wants to exercise the option. In the case of a call, which involves purchasing shares, the investor must be ready to pay for the shares at exercise.

Expiration: The third Friday of every month, at which time the option contract will cease to exist. There are two types of options: American exercise, which can be exercised anytime before or at expiration, and European-style options, which can be exercised only on expiration Friday.

Most single equity options are American exercise. Index options on the S&P 500, the Nasdaq 100, and many other sectors are generally European-style expiration. Either type can be traded until the expiration day. Options officially expire on the Saturday following the third Friday but are based on Friday's closing prices.

In-the-money: The status of an option that possesses "intrinsic value," or the capacity to be exercised at a profit. A call option is in-the-money when its strike price is lower than the stock price (e.g., a call option with a strike price of 20 with the stock having risen to 25). A put option is in-the-money when the strike price is higher than the stock price (e.g., a put option with a strike price of 20 a share with the stock having fallen to 15).

LEAPS: The acronym for long-term options. Standard options typically expire within a three- to six-month time period. LEAPS have life spans of up to two years and are often used as proxy investments for common stock. LEAPS is short for Long-term Equity AnticiPation Securities.

Open Interest: The number of contracts that have been opened—either by buying or selling—in an individual option. Open interest is calculated at the end of each trading day.

Out-of-the-money: The status of an option that has no intrinsic value or can't immediately be exercised at a profit. A call option is out-of-the-money when its strike price is higher than the stock price (e.g., a call option with a strike price of 25 when the stock is at 20). A put option is out-of-the-money when the strike price is lower than the stock price (e.g., a put option with a strike price of 15 when the stock is at 20).

Premium: The cost of the options contract. Don't confuse premium with commissions. The premium is the cost of the instrument; the commission is the cost of the transaction. You must pay both.

Put Option: An option that gives the holder the right but not the obligation to sell a stock or an index at a pre-set price by a certain date. These are purchased to express a negative sentiment about a stock's short-term prospects, e.g., the right to sell 100 shares of XYZ at 10 a share by January 21.

Strike Price: The price at which the options contract stipulates the stock or index will be bought or sold.

Putting Words into Action

Here's a quick practical application of some of these definitions.

It's January and the stock you love is trading for $30 a share. In order to act on your bullish intentions, you decide it's in your best interest to buy the March 30 call for 3¼. What does this mean?

The March date means that the option ceases to exist the third Friday in March; that's called the expiration day. It is by that day that you must decide whether to exercise the option by buying the stock, close out the option at a profit by selling it back, or let it expire worthless.

Whoaaa! How'd this thing become worthless? That's where the 30 comes in. That's called the strike price, the price at which you have decided, in this case, that you will buy the stock. Now, because the stock is at 30, that classifies the option you've bought as at-the-money, because the option's strike price and the underlying stock price are the same. In the case of a call, if the strike price were higher than the stock price, it would be considered out of the money. If the strike price were lower, it would be considered in the money. As with every other situation in life, in-the-money is where you want to be.

Now, about that 3¼ tacked on to the end. That's your premium, or the amount you'll pay per share for the right to buy 100 shares of this stock for 30 a share by the third Friday in March. Because most options contracts account for 100 shares of common stock, you must multiply that number by 100 to get the cost of the contract. In this case, 3¼ equals $325.

How is that premium determined? Since the mid-1970s it has been calculated by a complex formula called Black-Scholes. For the layman, it's enough to remember that there are three important factors built into this premium: intrinsic value, implied volatility, and time.

Intrinsic Value First and foremost is the option's intrinsic value, the amount by which the strike price is lower than the stock price. If the stock was trading at 30, and you opted to buy the March 25 call, there would be $5 of intrinsic value in that option. Not all options have intrinsic value. Out-of-the-money options don't, a factor that makes them risky, albeit less expensive, to buy. Generally, the more intrinsic value, the higher the premium.

Implied Volatility The second factor affecting the premium is implied volatility, which reflects how much a stock is expected to move over the life of the option. Riskier stocks carry a higher implied volatility, and the measure will increase on almost every stock during periods of uncertainty, whether it's earnings time, a new product launch, impending management change, or anything else with the potential of moving a stock dramatically in a short period of time. The greater the implied volatility, the higher the premium.

Time The third factor affecting the premium is time. (There are other factors such as *delta* and *theta* that professionals use, and options books have whole sections dedicated to what are called the "Greeks," or esoteric options pricing measures. That is not our concern here, and it shouldn't be yours until after the rest of the family has moved away because you're spending too much time trading stocks.) In the options world, time equals risk. If an option is six weeks from expiration, it has more potential to land in-the-money than if it were six days from expiration.

Options market makers (the folks on exchange floors who take the other side of most investor orders) build that risk into the price. Time value erodes dramatically during the last three weeks of an option's existence. The greater the time period, the higher the premium.

Commissions, a Different Beast

Commissions and premium are two entirely separate things. Again, the premium is the cost of the option contract, the commission the cost of the transaction. Commission charges for options are analogous to commissions for stocks, though options commissions cost more than simple stock transactions. Most brokerage firms such as Schwab or E*Trade will transact options business for you. Online and discount broker commissions range from roughly $25 to $35 per trade, and those firms often tack on a per contract charge of less than $2 on a small trade—just a handful of contracts.

At traditional firms such as Merrill Lynch and PaineWebber, the commission costs are much more variable. A typical options trade on one stock can cost you, say, $250 in commissions, though it depends largely on the price of the options.

Getting Long

The best way individual investors can use options is to make an investment decision, then see if options are the best way to implement that particular strategy. There are two main ways to use options to go "long" or act on a positive hunch on a stock: buying call options and selling put options.

Buying Calls

Amazon.com is a great study in buying calls because the stock is volatile and became legendary just a few years back as a roller-coaster stock. Now, everyone loves a good roller coaster, but motion sickness can make investors less appreciative of its thrill.

For instance, say Amazon is trading at $76\frac{3}{16}$ per share. Perhaps you feel it's a good time to buy the stock. It is down from its highs and you feel the future positives outweigh the negatives, a fact the market may just realize in a few weeks. You would love to buy 500 shares, but that's going to cost about $40,000. Not only is this steep, but Amazon is still a risky play, and if it goes down another 15, you could be out $8,000. What you want is an uncomplicated and less risky way to benefit from the appreciation of the stock.

In-the-Money Call Options Call options may be the logical choice. Remember, the purchaser pays for the right to buy the stock at a certain time for a certain price. If you like Amazon at 76 a share, you'll like it even better if it costs you 70 a share. Let's say it's February, and the price of the calls that expire on the third Friday of the month look like this at any of the option exchange Web sites:

Calls	Last Sale	Net Change	Bid	Ask	Vol	Open Interest
Feb 70	$6^3/_8$	0	$6^3/_8$	$7^1/_8$	639	5440

First, look at the last two columns, headed "Volume" and "Open Interest," in the above chart. Volume is the number of contracts that have traded that day. Open interest refers to the number of contracts already outstanding (unlike shares of stock, an infinite number of options contracts can be created). Both of those numbers should be in the hundreds or thousands, because it illustrates the depth of the market and, as a result, the ability to trade out of this instrument at a later date.

Now move back to the first column. The February 70 call will allow you to buy Amazon shares for 70 anytime before or on the third Friday of February. Now, why would someone sell you a 76-dollar stock for 70? Because you'll have to pay $6^3/_8$ to buy the option. (Remember that option contracts represent 100 shares of the underlying stock, so whatever price is quoted must be multiplied by 100. In this case, an option trading for $6^3/_8$ would cost you $637.50.)

All of a sudden, this isn't looking like a bargain, right? But remember, to buy 500 shares of Amazon stock would cost you $40,000. Buying five February 70 calls will cost you about $3,200, a fraction of the cost.

There are more decisions to make, however. First you have to decide whether you like Amazon for the length of time of the option or for a quick turnaround. If it's the former, you're hoping the stock will rise to at least $76^3/_8$ by the third Friday in February, the point at which you exercise the options to buy the shares. The price covers what you laid out in your options' premium. The sum of the stock price ($70 x 500 = $35,000) plus the premium paid for the option, $3,200, is called the effective selling price, $38,200. That's equal to $76^3/_8$ x 500.

If you're holding the option for a quick turnaround, you don't particularly want to wait long enough to exercise the shares. You're hoping the stock rises and you can sell the option back at a profit. But the value of that option is dependent on the time remaining until expiration. Those options are in-the-money, and as the expiration date gets closer, the components of the options price—the premium—shift. Essentially, the options buyer pays up for a longer time period. As the time period shrinks, that component of the options price shrinks in turn. What follows is that the "intrinsic value"—the difference between the strike and actual price—becomes a greater portion of the premium price.

If the option stays in-the-money, at some point in its last week the option will rise $1 for every $1 move in the stock. We like that the price of the option increases, because it becomes clearer that the call option will be a winning bet. You can sell the option back the day before it expires—after all, why take chances?—at a significantly higher price than you paid.

The option price can double from 6⅜ if the stock rises quickly, turning your $3,500 into $7,000. Trying to get the same percentage appreciation from a $40,000 investment in Amazon shares would have required the stock running to almost double, to 140 a share. That's the joy of options.

The pain of it would be this: Say you're wrong. Dead wrong. Amazon reverses course and lands at 69 on the third Friday of the month. What's your February 70 call worth? Nothing. You can fly to Chicago and, as the CBOE traders say, visit your money.

Out-of-the-Money Call Options If that 6⅜ premium seemed onerous, and you held a stronger opinion on the stock's strength, there are such

---

Where to Find Options Quotes

You can start looking at options quotes on a delayed basis and try different analytical tools at the options exchange Web sites. They also have plenty of educational material to take you thought the essentials of options trading.

You can start with the industry trade group's site, www.Optionscentral.com, from which you can link to the American Stock Exchange (www.amex.com), Chicago Board Options Exchange (www.cboe.com), Philadelphia Stock Exchange (www.phlx.com), and Pacific Exchange (www.pacificex.com).

things as out-of-the-money options, that is, call options with a strike price higher than the current share price. In the Amazon example, that could be an option with a strike price of 80 with the stock currently trading at $70.

If you wanted to buy that strike price with a February expiration, it would cost a scant 1⁵⁄₁₆, or $131.50. Now, that's cheap, but one of the key mistakes rookie options traders make is that they don't pay attention to the time left before it expires. With this kind of speculation in options, you have to be right on two counts: not just the direction of the stock's move, but also the time it will take to get there. A stock itself you can hold forever, pass it down to the kid who needs braces. Options die—quickly.

So, if you want a less expensive way to profit from a stronger move in the stock, then consider buying options that expire at least five or six weeks from the time you buy them so your hunch has a chance to materialize. The downside is that it will cost you more: In the Amazon example, buying March options in early February will cost you about 5⁷⁄₈ (or $587.50 per contract). The higher premium is a result of having more time value—more things can happen to Amazon.com in five weeks than can happen in two. That way, if you're right about the stock, but if the option takes more than a week to unfold, you've bought more time to make a profit.

Selling Puts

Buying calls is one way to act on the theme that a stock will appreciate. There's one other interesting, although more risky, way to play the same idea. You can sell puts. Now, everything you've probably read about puts associates them with bearish sentiment, playing for a stock to fall. But that sentiment applies for put *buying*. Selling puts is the opposite. It's bullish, or, at the very least, neutral.

While options buyers pay for the right to buy or sell stock, options sellers—also called options writers—get paid for taking on the obligation of that option contract. It's a simple concept: Someone must be willing to sell shares to the call holder if she decides to exercise that type of option; someone must be willing to buy shares from a put owner if he decides to exercise and sell.

If being on the other side of such an equation seems risky, well, it is. But like most risks, you may be rewarded well for taking it. In the case of selling puts, you get paid the option's premium. There are two scenarios that follow, and we'll look at them through the time-honored ideal of put selling.

First and foremost, investors should sell puts only on stocks they absolutely love, the kind they would bring home to meet Mom. Here's why:

Say General Electric (GE:NYSE) is trading at 133¾. Now, buying a substantial amount would be a tremendous capital outlay. And besides, you think GE's in for another few weeks of slippage. Still, you like the stock at 133 and would really, really like it about $10 cheaper.

Here is the alternative plan to sitting around and waiting for the stock to fall. Say it's January, and on the day when GE closed at around 133¾, you could sell a March 125 put for 2½ (or $250 per contract). You decide to sell three, equivalent to 300 shares. You take in $750. Someone out there is buying that put from you, betting the stock will fall to 125.

Two things can happen. GE could reverse its decline and run to 140. On the downside, you've lost the opportunity to make about $2,100 if you had taken a commensurate position in GE's underlying shares. You have, however, taken in $750 to sell a put that will likely expire worthless for the buyer of that put. You essentially laid out nothing to make $750 while you could've invested $40,000 for 300 shares to make $2,100.

The second scenario would be that GE continues to fall. During the third week of March, it hits 125 and at expiration the puts you sold get exercised. You have to pony up $37,500 to buy the 300 shares the put holder sells via the exercise. Now, since you decided you loved GE stock but only for 125, this isn't a bad thing. You're happy to pay the money, because you're getting the 300 shares at that price. You've been allowed to call your own bottom on the shares and get paid $750 to wait for it to happen.

When bad things start is when GE keeps falling and declines to 120, then to 115, and doesn't stop until 110. It's bad, because now you're on the hook to buy at 125, no matter how low it goes. By selling the option, you lost control of your buy-in point.

The one piece of control you still do have is that if you change your mind before expiration, you can buy the put option back, liberating yourself from the contract's obligation to buy the shares. As the stock falls, though, the option's premium will become more expensive—maybe double the $750 you took in. But that scenario—a $750 loss—would likely be better than paying 125 for GE when it's trading for 110 and hoping for a quick rebound.

Put selling is a risky, risky strategy. Optimists who fall in love with a stock they can't imagine falling get destroyed doing it. The loss potential is the difference between your stock price and zero. In other words, in the above example, you could be on the hook for buying shares of GE at 125 that have become worth next to nothing or nothing!

But, you're thinking, no stock ever falls to zero, right? Well, some sure come close, and your losses can mount to the point where there's not much of a psychological difference. If you sold a put on an Internet stock before the spring 2000 decline in those stocks with a strike price 20% lower than the stock price, before the dust settled you could have been down 20% because the sector fell about 40%. And remember, *selling* options of any kind brings with it an obligation to buy or sell the stock. It's not like buying options, where your losses are limited to the premium you pay to initiate the trade.

The volatility of stocks is a factor not to be trifled with when selling puts; most stocks eventually go down at some point, and there are times that no premium, however high, is worth the risk. Even professional market makers who have to sell puts take great pains and expense to hedge against the risk by taking big short positions that will counter losses from such long positions.

Getting Short

Almost every investment book focuses on the long side of the business. But what about the so-called short side?

Shorting stocks is essentially a bet that a stock price will fall. There are a number of ways to make this bet from traditional shorting to using options. Shorts often get a bad rap in the financial press. Coverage of "shorts" who point out the foibles of a company frequently drip with disdain. Somehow, it's okay for those who are long in a stock to make bold boasts about a company's prospects. But the pessimists, the shorts, are less revered. Some on Wall Street call the practice of shorting "un-American."

But whether it's un-American or not, the fact is that stocks do also go down. And there's money to be made if you can find stocks that are overvalued. It's the logic of digging for undervalued shares, only in reverse. Those who thrive on short selling tend to be dogmatic, moralistic investors who have incredible discipline and faith in their own judgment. In essence, they are saying that the market is wrong and they know why the market is wrong, and they are going to short that stock until the market figures out it is wrong. It takes a certain kind of personality to pursue this kind of strategy, as it has enormous risk.

Shorting Common Stock

Traditionally, traders played their bets that a stock will go down with what have come to be known as short positions in the common stock. Technically, you borrow shares from a securities firm and sell them in the open market with the hope of buying them back at a lower price to close the transaction.

Say, for example, you are convinced Commerce Onc (CMRE:Nasdaq), in the B2B sector, is going to go down. If the shares are trading for 140, let's say you "borrow" 1 share and sell it at that price of 140. Now you've got $140. If the stock drops to 100, you can buy it back at that price, return the borrowed share, and pocket the $40 difference.

While that sounds simple enough, wrongheaded short plays can be disastrously painful.

If a stock runs up rapidly, the borrower (known as a "short") has to buy the shares back at a substantially higher price than he sold them, thus losing money on the trade. The amount of risk is open-ended, depending on the movement of the stock. The investor can make a quick decision that he chose wrong, "cover" the short—that is, buy back the stock for, say, $150—and exit quietly with minimal losses. Or, more likely, he can get emotionally attached to the position, refuse to admit he's wrong, and ride it all the way up. He can lose an unlimited amount of money as the stock climbs higher and higher.

If a heavily shorted stock starts shooting higher, you can run into what market pros call a "short squeeze." Imagine a crowded room with but one door. Someone yells "fire" and a mad scramble to the door ensues. This is what happens in a short squeeze. The shorts have bet wrong, and they scramble madly to buy the stock and cover their position before it goes any higher, which serves to drive the share price higher and higher. Since shorts live on borrowed shares, meaning they ultimately have to purchase the stock, some investors view heavy short positions as a contrarian positive indicator. That is, they see it as a sign that so much negative sentiment is in the stock, there could be only upside from there. But sometimes the heavy short position means the stock just plain stinks. So be careful with that indicator.

Using Put Options for Short Bets

Buying a put option lets an investor express the same skepticism as in a short play while capping the potential losses. Here's how it works:

Buying a put gives the investor the right, but not the obligation, to sell 100 shares of a stock at a certain price by the third Friday of the month stipulated by the options contract. Again, let's look at some real-world stocks to show how put buying can work to an investor's advantage.

Let's consider Ford (F:NYSE), one of the world's largest automobile companies but one that could be subject to labor problems or other difficulties. Let's say the stock is trading at about 51. But interest rates are rising, and that might make prospective customers a little less enthusiastic about buying or leasing an SUV. The investor decides that Ford may suffer in the short term, even if over time American car buyers come back.

There's a way to make money on this view based on your expectations of how Ford's stock will respond to the increased interest rates. Ford is trading at 51. A 60-day put option has a strike price of 55; it's trading for 3⅞ (or $387.50 per contract). Buying this put gives you the right to sell 100 shares of Ford for 55 anytime before the third Friday of the month, no matter what price the underlying stock is trading at.

This 55 put is an in-the-money option because it has intrinsic value (in other words, the strike price of 55 is higher than the current stock price of 51). Essentially, if you purchased a Ford March 55 put and the stock was at 50, you'd exercise by buying shares for 50, then selling them for 55 based on the right you paid for by opening the contract.

The goal in any put purchase intended to be exercised is that the stock falls below the strike price by at least the amount of the premium. In this case, it would be 51⅛ (55 minus the 3⅞ premium). If the intention is simply to let the put appreciate, then sell it back at expiration, the stock simply needs to decline enough for the value of the contract to increase. You can do either. Some investors choose to trade options because they don't have or don't want to tie up the capital needed to play in the underlying shares. Trading the option back at a higher price—especially with puts—results in fewer commission costs than does exercising the option and selling the stock. But it's a choice that every investor should be clear on before investing. The options market moves so fast that waiting to exercise can result in a missed opportunity.

There is always the chance in our Ford example that the market has already counted in the interest rate troubles; as a result, not only won't the stock fall, it may rise. This is especially true if the market believes Ford's problems may be short-lived. As a result, Ford shares rally.

If you are short the common stock, then your broker is now calling, asking you to ante up more money to make sure you can cover that position. If you had instead bought the puts, you would be out $387.50 for each option if the third Friday of the expiration month brought with it Ford sitting pretty at 65. But that's where your losses would end, whether the stock's move left your option 50 cents out-of-the-money or $50. That's the benefit of puts.

Puts As Protection

Put buyers typically are regarded as having ill will toward the stocks on which they are speculating, and that's often true. But many put buyers are simply using options as insurance, buying a put against a stock they may be holding but are worried about.

Let's use Qualcomm (QCOM:Nasdaq), a recent market darling, as a case study here. Let's say you've owned this stock throughout its strong ride in 1999, when it rose some 2,400%. But now you feel that maybe, just maybe, the competition is catching up. With the stock trading at 139, you take a look at a 60-day 135 put. That's out-of-the-money because the stock has to move toward the strike price—below 135—to gain intrinsic value.

Now, say you're holding 1,000 shares of Qualcomm. You'd like to hold some of it for another two years, but the worries are keeping you up nights. You decide to buy five of the 135 puts for 12¾ (or $1,275 each) for a total cost of $6,375 to cover half of your 1,000-share position. In other words, you're willing to sell half your Qualcomm but you'd like to hold on to the other 500 shares for a while longer.

If that $6,375 seems like a high price to pay to protect about $69,000 of stock (500 shares x 139), it is. But the price is high because it turns out you're not the only one worried—other people are demanding the same put. And since you're buying an option that expires in two months, you'll be paying more than if you bought one that expired sooner. The high implied volatility and the time premium add to your cost.

So now Qualcomm falls to 130 and you decide to exercise. In closing out the five contracts you bought, you sell half your stock position for 135. The options contracts are now closed. So, while you've spent $6,375 for protection, you managed to save $2,500 (the 5-point difference between 130 and 135 x 500 shares) that you would've lost had you hung around in the stock and then sold.

More important, you've given yourself some time to make a decision regarding your stock position. The puts cost you more money than if you had just sold the 500 shares, but don't discount the breather it gave you and the peace of mind to consider what to do over the longer term.

And what if Qualcomm doesn't fall? If you're willing, you can sell the puts back into the market before expiration, though they may be close to worthless by that point. Either way, don't despair. In this case, you were using puts as an insurance policy, a hedge. You wouldn't be upset if your homeowner's policy never was used because your house didn't burn down, would you?

Summing Up

At this point, we've reviewed the basics of options, including long and short positions. I want to take a moment to reiterate the words of caution I offered as we set out. The idea of all the strategies we've discussed is to use options to express your confidence (or lack thereof) in a stock without laying out as much as you'd have to in order to buy the actual shares. Let's take an example as a review.

If you're using call options to act on the belief that Cisco shares will appreciate, you shouldn't invest the same amount in options as you would stock. If Cisco is trading at 63, and you have $10,000, you shouldn't buy $10,000 worth of Cisco options.

At 63 a share, $10,000 would get you 158 shares of Cisco, a little less than two options contracts. But two Cisco 60-day call options (representing 200 shares) with a strike price of 55 would cost 9 ($900) each. You lay out the $1,800 plus commissions for the contracts and put the other $8,200 in Treasuries, a bank account, heck, even put it in a shoebox in your mother's closet.

Come expiration, if you want to buy the shares, you'll have about 80% of the capital needed sitting in the shoebox to do it. If you change your mind about committing to Cisco for the long term, you can sell the contract back at a profit without ever having put the whole 10 grand at risk.

And if those Cisco options end up expiring worthless, you're not out the $10,000. You're out $1,800 and the rest is safe, maybe even earning a little interest. Done this way, options are actually a conservative way to act on a view on stocks.

12

The IPO Game

Initial public offerings—the general public's first chance to buy shares of a young company—have always held out great promise for investors lucky enough to get a piece of one. But in the late 1990s, the craze took on a life of its own. Waves of start-up technology companies, mostly focused on the Internet, rushed to raise money in the public markets. In the process, their shares rose dramatically, sometimes to more than 200% of the initial price on the first day—performance unprecedented in the modern markets.

Someone makes lots of money in these efforts. Unfortunately, it's not usually individual shareholders. The spoils end up in the hands of brokers, company executives, and venture capitalists. Little finds its way back to the individual.

But that doesn't mean that individual investors can't skin the IPO cat. You can. The first step is to understand how IPOs work. Then we show you how to outmaneuver them.

Technology IPOs in the 1990s		
Year	Technology IPOs IPOs (in billions)	Money Raised by Tech
1990	29	$0.63
1991	73	2.6
1992	98	4.4
1993	140	4.8
1994	138	5.2
1995	212	8.8
1996	270	18.0
1997	189	10.0
1998	126	8.3
1999	398	39.2

Source: Thomson Financial Securities Data

The Power Structure

To survive in the brutal IPO market, you need to understand the process from the perspective of the ones in power—the investment bankers, the corporations they take public, and the institutional investors who are the bankers' main customers. And even those parties' goals conflict.

What's in It for Me? Goals in the IPO Game

Pre-IPO company: Raise as much fresh cash as possible to fund its business and to get some publicity in the process.

Investment banks: Keep costs and risk to a minimum while earning hefty fees.

Institutional investors: Buy the shares at a low "insider's" price and "flip" (sell) them when individual investors bid up the prices.

Investment Banks

Pre-IPO companies generally hire a few different banks to underwrite or bring to market their shares in an IPO, with one bank acting as the lead. Lead banks typically make a "firm commitment" to move their client's shares out to willing buyers. This means that the investment bank agrees to assume the cost of any unsold shares sitting in its shop at the end of the day. Lead banks also generally agree to "support" the stock in the secondary market—the term for the standard stock market trading after an IPO—for a certain period by buying up shares if the price falls below the original offer. In return for their services, banks typically charge companies about 7% of the total offering (or $7 million on a $100 million deal).

To mitigate their risk of getting stiffed with a bunch of bad merchandise, banks take certain steps to ensure a deal is popular. Top-tier firms don't need to do much. The mere involvement of investment banks such as Goldman Sachs, Morgan Stanley Dean Witter, Merrill Lynch, Credit Suisse First Boston, and a few others serves almost as a benediction on a deal, giving it instant credibility not only with individuals but with the giant institutions. These banks have this cachet because they can back up deals with a sales push by brokers and with support from research analysts who churn out positive reports on stocks.

Still, to protect themselves, lead banks typically spread their risk by engaging a "syndicate" of other brokerage firms that agree to sell shares through their own distribution channels. The tactic is a kind of insurance policy, ensuring that no single bank will get stuck with a big loss should the deal go sour. The downside is that, like paying an insurance premium, the policy also cuts into the lead bank's profits.

Finally, there are the "co-underwriters." These banks play a kind of deputy role to the lead. Why bother with helpers? The more underwriters you have, the more positive investment banking analyst coverage you're likely to get. It's all part of the unspoken expectations set in motion when a pre-IPO company selects its bankers.

The Valuation

Given that the capital markets are supposed to be efficient, the difference between the offering, or the insider's price, on an IPO and the public market price on the first day of trading seems nothing short of bizarre. Until, that is, you understand the conflicting motivations. Investment banks are known to deliberately price shares well below what they think the market will bear (anywhere from 11% to 50% on average, depending on the study you look at). This kind of intentional underpricing can result in huge one-day profits for those who get in at the offering price. The idea of buying a stock at 10 and then "flipping" it on the open market for 30 a few seconds later at a 200% return is the whole foundation of IPO frenzy.

The difference between the offering price for the institutions and the closing price on the first day of trading represents money "left on the table." In other words, it's the cash that could have gone into the corporate coffers if the stock was priced to market but instead went to the lucky first-round shareholders in the form of windfall profits.

Companies aren't totally innocent in this game. While they have a counterincentive to keep as much of that money for themselves with a higher initial price on their stock, they also want to see their shares fly just like the bankers do. Stocks with big one-day price pops get the most press coverage, so rampant underpricing plays right into a company's hunger for positive PR.

Individual Investors

Where in this game do the individual investors fit? Not in a good spot. The reason is simple. Big investors play mostly for the one-day pop. Smaller investors, who don't have access to the insider's price, chase huge gains and are willing to pay more than they typically would on the chance of a big score. The institutions see smaller investors bidding up the shares in the process, and sell in to that froth.

"Friends and Family" Programs

So-called friends and family programs are essentially a form of legal graft. Basically, the underwriters allot the company a certain number of shares that it can distribute to "friends and family" of the company at the insider price—the same price that institutions get. Of course, if the stock doesn't soar, it's not such a great perk. But if it does, then it's a nice goody to get. Companies give this opportunity to big clients, suppliers, and even relatives of the top execs. If a stock expected to take off actually flops, though, the program might find itself redubbed the "friends and enemies" program.

So if an IPO prices at $20 a share, you probably don't want to buy in much higher than that level on IPO day, because it's likely that after the first day's frenzy fades, you'll have an asset that's stopped appreciating for a while. The frenzy is not your friend.

But that doesn't mean you can't play the game at all. If you can't get an insider price, either through a strong broker relationship or a "friends and family" program (described in the box on page 280), there's always the after-market beyond the first day. And there are ways to use that waiting to your advantage. But you first need to decide whether you like the stock.

Understanding Prospectus-ese

The first step in evaluating an IPO sounds like the disclaimer for some mutual fund ad: Read the prospectus. Well, at least read the parts of it we suggest and you can skip the rest. It may sound trite, but the prospectus is your bible for the stock. Download it from www.sec.gov (it's called the S-1). If the prospectus is not available yet, a preliminary prospectus, also known as a red herring, should be.

Red Herring

In investment terms, this is the "preliminary prospectus." Its name comes from the warning, printed in red, that information in the document is still being reviewed by the Securities and Exchange Commission and is subject to change before the final prospectus is published.

The prospectus is partly a marketing piece to showcase the corporate wares, but it's mostly a liability shield to cover the company's butt if anything ever goes wrong (the idea being that investors were forewarned).

Most investors don't read much of prospectuses beyond the gossip pages—the bios of execs and directors and their cash and stock options. This is a huge rookie mistake. Other parts are essential.

Savvy IPO investors start with the front cover and the list of the investment bankers—the underwriters. The point here is that if you don't recognize the names, use caution. In a strong market, companies with a good story and bright prospects have little trouble attracting big-name firms with lots of muscle to take their companies public. In gen-

---

Key Prospectus Checkpoints

- Underwriters
  Big-name firms are a plus, implying higher confidence in the company's prospects.

- Risk Factors
  Make sure you understand what you're getting into on a worst-case basis.

- Plans for IPO Proceeds
  Funding expansion or paying down debt is one thing; padding the pockets of the insiders is another.

- Reality Check
  Does the concept even make sense as a viable business idea?

---

eral, only the mangiest offerings need to dip into the second- and third-tier regional banks to run their offerings. And the more respected the underwriters are, particularly in the market sector of the given stock, the better the chances for the stock's success.

Next, turn your total attention to the "risk factors" section. Here you'll find the company undressed and fully exposed, eagerly pointing out all potential weaknesses. Every worst-case eventuality is described in detail, in stark contrast to the glowing business summary that precedes the risk section. It's a pretty pessimistic read, and the probability of absolutely everything going wrong with the firm all at once is slim. Still, if some of the risks seem too heavy for your tastes in a long-term hold, let the next guy chance it.

Perhaps most important, the prospectus includes the company's financials. Here's where you get to apply your newfound skills reading the financial statements (see Chapter 6). With IPOs, you need to be extra diligent. While an established private company has a track record, New Economy IPOs often have only a scant history. Remember to read the footnotes and pay close attention to items like market share and industry position.

Finally, take a step back and see if the whole picture makes sense. Should the company even exist on the face of the earth?

When you've got a good picture of the company, compare it with some publicly traded competitors. What are their valuations? Run a few

Top Investment Banks for IPOs			
Rank	Investment Bank	Total Amt. in $ millions	No. of Deals
1	Goldman Sachs	11,948.58	38
2	Morgan Stanley Dean Witter	8,467.47	26
3	Salomon Smith Barney	6,728.84	22
4	Credit Suisse First Boston	6,570.96	40
5	Merrill Lynch	6,363.10	21
6	Donaldson, Lufkin & Jenrette	2,899.63	20
7	Lehman Brothers	1,858.47	22
8	Robertson Stephens	1,713.31	24
9	Deutsche Banc Alex. Brown	1,364.50	20
10	Chase H&Q	1,351.30	23

First three quarters 2000
Source: CommScan EquiDesk

financial ratios. These will help you better compare companies and give you a rough idea of where your company stands among its peers.

If you like the company, the next step is to decide when to buy.

The Virtue of Patience

If you are an important enough client to your broker—or, in the case of most online brokerages, have enough assets—to qualify for a piece of an attractive IPO at the offering price (or are a friend or family), take it. (We list online brokers' current rules/minimums below.) If it runs and you're so inclined, flip it. Be warned: If your broker imposes the arcane double standard of punishing individuals who flip (institutions do it with impunity), you'll deal with the consequences of not being able to play an IPO for a while. Most investors, though, are not in the "insider" league. Which means that patience and discipline are important qualities to have when investing in IPOs.

After you've found an IPO that you want, wait a few weeks, or even months, for the stock to stabilize. Remember, the stock isn't going away (and if it does, you'll be glad you waited!). Use the time to observe the trading patterns and confirm that the company has substance. You want to be able to wait out some milestones that can have a big impact on price.

25-Day Mark

The first milestone is the 25-day mark. Those first 25 days of trading you won't hear much news from the company or the banks' Wall Street analysts, because they're still in an SEC-imposed "quiet period." The minute that 25-day chunk ends, however, the newly public company will get more love than the captain of the football team, as a blitz of news, analyst "buy" ratings, and glowing research reports hit the tape. This "news" can result in a short-lived pop for the stock.

Another key fact about the 25-day mark is that it usually signals the end of the investment banker's price support obligation. Once the price floor is removed, weak stocks could be in for a tumble as normal market forces take over. At this point, patient investors might be able to pick up shares well below the original offer price.

Lockup Period

Further out, the six-month milestone marks the traditional end of the investment-bank-imposed "lockup period." Banks typically require corporate insiders to hold their shares for a minimum of 180 days after the IPO to prevent a destabilizing amount of trading volume on the infant stock and to convince the public that the insiders are in for the long haul—or at least the six-month haul. After this period, locked-up investors are finally free to sell certain shares they bought or acquired before or during the IPO.

The post-lockup insider action can hurt the stock price, as the supply of stock rises without necessarily an increase in demand. The shares potentially becoming available for sale, called the "overhang," can wreak havoc, especially in a weak market. Thankfully, the market is complex, and it doesn't always work out that way. Still, if you haven't yet bought a stock, don't rush to buy ahead of a lockup expiration. It can't hurt to see the effect the expiration has on the stock.

The timing on insiders' lockups can be found in the prospectus. If you're looking online, IPO expert Ben Holmes, a columnist for *TheStreet.com* and founder of www.ipoPros.com, part of *TheStreet.com* network, suggests opening the document and searching for the word "eligible." That will bring you to a section titled "Shares Eligible for Future Sale." Somewhere in that section there will be a description of the lockup provision. It may look something like this:

Sample Lockup Provision

Number of Shares	*Date*
\<S>	\<C>
566,770	After the date of this prospectus
322,974	After 90 days from the date of this prospectus
26,676,955	After 180 days from the date of this prospectus
	(subject, in some cases, to volume limitations)

Beyond the lockup, the stock really joins the masses of regular issues out there.

Summing Up

While gains on IPOs can be tremendous, it's important to remember that for most individuals, playing this market is a game, not an investment, even if you have the best intentions. With relatively less information available on the stock, the valuation is left to the most primal supply-and-demand forces. Those forces can be fickle and leave investors vulnerable to disaster.

It's also akin to going from playing a game of pickup basketball in the playground to opposing Michael Jordan and the champion Chicago Bulls. In the IPO game, individuals play against institutional investors with the capital, the information, and the connections to push the market the way they want. The lucky individuals get in and out, or hold on for the long term as this is happening. The unlucky—and there are many more of those—get caught in between and end up buying in to a new stock at a high price and watching it fall as institutional investors quickly sell their positions.

That's a game you may not want to be in, even though the lure of triple-digit returns is often dangled in front of you. There are plenty of other stocks to buy—the kind of "high-octane" stocks we talked about in Chapter 3—where the rules of play aren't so stacked against you.

Online Brokerages and IPOs

Online brokerages have come a long way in the past few years in terms of leveling the playing field for individual IPO investors, but there's still plenty of room for improvement. The number of shares you get (if any) will depend on what kind of customer you are and whether the issue is hot. Some online brokers have agreements with investment banking houses that entitle the broker to a percentage of IPO shares. But it's generally a small percentage, and that little bit has to be parceled to some subset of a broker's huge customer base.

Here's a quick rundown of some of the online brokers that offer IPO shares and the requirements for customers to participate.

Charles Schwab	
I-banker Deals	Epoch Capital
Eligible Customers Need	$1,000,000 in assets or execute 4 trades per month (on average) and have $50,000 in assets
Flipping Requirement	Must hold for 30 days or risk not being able to participate in IPO program for six months

Fidelity	
I-banker Deals	Lehman Brothers
Eligible Customers Need	$500,000 in retail brokerage account or execute 36 or more trades per year
Flipping Requirement	Must hold for 15 days or risk being excluded from future offerings

DLJdirect	
I-banker Deals	*Credit Suisse First Boston (parent company)
Eligible Customers Need	$100,000 in account assets
Flipping Requirement	None

*Pending CSFB's completed acquisition of Donaldson, Lufkin & Jenrette

E*Trade	
I-banker Deals	Wit Soundview
Eligible Customers Need	Lottery system
Flipping Requirement	Have to hold for 30 days or risk being restricted from participating in future IPOs for 60 days

Morgan Stanley Dean Witter Online	
I-banker Deals	Morgan Stanley Dean Witter
Eligible Customers Need	100,000 in cash or equity assets
Flipping Requirement	Hold for 30 days or may be excluded from future IPO offerings

13

Final Thoughts

As I hope this book has indicated, the investment world has gone through stunning changes during the past five years. Once the purview of cigar-smoking, dark-suited, heavyset old men, the investment arena now includes at-home traders working in shorts, secretaries sneaking trades from their desks, and mutual fund investors from Whitefish, Montana, to Miami, Florida. The business section of most newspapers, once an impregnable array of charts, figures, and dull reports, has become more like the sports page for a public enthusiastically tracking investment winners and losers. And the Internet, perhaps the biggest change of all, has created an entirely new spigot of information for stock addicts and long-term buy-and-hold investors alike.

There's no going back. As much as some Wall Street pros would like to stuff the genie into the bottle, the expanding flow of information, the increasing ease with which investors access knowledge and ideas, has transformed the way we approach the investing part of our life. We can, today, sit on a train and read stories, trade stocks, and manage our portfolio via a wireless modem. Our ability to access, process, and act on information will only become easier in the years ahead.

These changes in investing are, in fact, a paradigm for what's happening throughout the country and increasingly throughout the world. That's because they are largely technology driven. Companies that embrace technology to improve their productivity, product line, and customer experience—companies like Charles Schwab and Wells Fargo—have thrived. Companies unable to modify—companies like AT&T—fall behind.

Technology is lately hailed as the great panacea. But the very promise of technology also poses enormous challenges to companies. Just when you implement a costly and complex system, it becomes outdated. Just when you add a new feature to your Web site, a competitor tacks on an even fancier service. Just when you invest in a tech product line because you think the future is headed one way, it suddenly shifts in the exact opposite direction. Just when you get a new computer on your desk, it crashes!

High technology, and the rapid, destructive change it brings can actually make running a business much tougher than it was in the days of ledgers and cash registers. Having the latest efficiency gizmo, being able to translate technology strength into revenue growth, and above all finding the right people to work in this intense high-tech world are all vital challenges that help set the great companies apart from the good ones.

In the coming years, the speed of technological creative destruction will only increase. Companies will flourish and fail in a whisper of time compared to the lumbering giants of only ten or fifteen years ago. Think about 2000. In just six months, Amazon.com went from boasting about the selection of its chairman, Jeff Bezos, as *Time* magazine's Man of the Year, to fielding questions about whether it would survive.

With so much change swirling about, what big ideas should investors hold on to as they peer out into the future? Below I lay out five themes that I anticipate will emerge in the coming decade. These themes, along with the practical teachings you've received in this book, can help you frame your investment strategy as you build your portfolio in the twenty-first century.

Again, I am eager to hear what you think about these themes, and this book in general. Please send e-mail to smartinvesting@thestreet.com.

1. People Matter

People will matter more than ever before. A great deal of the 1990s bull market revolved around substituting capital investment for labor. This idea worked and will work still. But it is becoming more apparent than ever that good training and management—the ability to harness the skills of people in a fast-changing world—is becoming one of the key differentiating factors when evaluating a company. Someone hired one year will need an entirely new skill set the next year.

The paradox in American business is that it's easier to keep pace with rapid change when you are a smaller company. Yet, in a competitive world, it's nearly impossible to stay both small and successful. If you create a profitable enterprise, some bigger fish will likely either try to buy you, or snuff you out with a similar service. The only way to survive is to become big enough to butt heads with the competition.

But growing from promising idea into big company is a challenge that all too many management teams can't hack. Many great ideas sputter and die for lack of effective leadership and training, as these concepts grow into companies. So look for news reports and surveys that reflect on a company's ability to train and maintain its staff. One company that has stood out in this regard is General Electric. It's not a mistake that this far-flung conglomerate has done so well in the stock market.

2. Mobility

Mobility will become the word of the decade. The ability to do anything no matter where you are is already seeping into the culture. You'll notice a lot of previously distinct devices doing a lot of the same thing. In the mobile world today, people lug around pagers, cell phones, personal digital assistants, and laptop computers. Eventually, all of these things will merge into a single device that will have the horsepower of your own desktop computer. That will mean a few winners and many losers.

Picking the right path to mobility (whether it will be a device such as Palm Pilot computer phones or digital handset Internet pagers) and the companies that will triumph in this space will be a big issue for investors. Will Nokia develop a computer/PDA/phone? Will Toshiba? Will Palm Pilot? Will Microsoft? Many of the best companies of the past decade are racing toward this solution from different directions. The winner will be an important investment choice.

3. The Mass Market

The amazing resilience of the mass market. Today many forecast the death of the mass market. New technologies will provide for incredible customization and remarkable individual service. Mass customization possibilities have futurists arguing that mass media—like network television and national magazines—will become irrelevant. But investors should be wary of such pitches.

The overwhelming trend over the past fifty years has been toward a more collective experience, not less. When a king or a pope would die one hundred years or more ago, it was chatted about in the town square. Today, major human events become a massive global moment instantly. Remember Princess Di? JFK, Jr.? Elian?

Consumers of information want to share their experiences. Customization creates a sense of isolation and lack of context that most folks find disturbing, not gratifying. Sure, elements of customization, like choosing when you want to watch a movie, will emerge. But the predictions of mass customization will not come to pass.

This theme is most important in the media and entertainment arena, where continued consolidation will provide investment opportunities. Well-run smaller operations will be bought up by large information conglomerates. These big companies will pay a premium to expand their stable of offerings and maintain their ability to reach the mass market.

4. Peace

Peace is good for stocks. And we've had peace breaking out all over for a good chunk of time now in the industrialized world. People taking the longer view should be wary of this remarkable run of peace. I'm not saying that war is around the corner or conflict will suddenly emerge. But investors should keep their eye on possible hot spots from China to the Middle East to Eastern Europe.

We have in the past several years seen great prosperity in some areas, great poverty in others. Capitalist democracies thrive when there is a reasonable balance between rich and poor, with a clear path of opportunity for those who want more. With the massive expansion of information, it is easier for the have-nots to see what the haves have. This flood of information has become the main weapon for liberal democracy capitalist evangelists. The path from have-not to have is theoretically through the embrace of the Western system. But that embrace has not always worked very well, especially in Eastern Europe.

What does that mean? Conflict could arise out of the frustration, and investors should always keep one eye on that possibility. Cold-heartedly, conflict is usually good for energy and aerospace/defense stocks. Heavy conflict, coldheartedly, is bad for most stocks.

5. Do It Yourself

The democratization of investing will continue to flourish. In America, the ability to do it yourself has become a powerful theme. It was brought to us by The Home Depot and E-Trade. And now companies in all arenas are coming aboard.

In the investing area, we will see Wall Street become more and more transparent, and more and more individuals will take responsibility for their finances and their investment future. Changes in the Social Security system, including potential privatization, will augment this transformation.

With the changes will come more companies aimed at serving individuals in managing their finances. Not just firms that provide inexpensive trades, but firms that provide service tailored to individuals' preferences. The flow of information will grow and the ability for individuals to do the things pros do—from trading overseas to hedging portfolios—will become increasingly commonplace.

It truly is a brave new world for investors. We hope this book has made you better able to forge ahead with confidence.

L'Etoile du Nord

Dave Kansas
Editor in Chief

Appendix A
Analyst Rankings

TheStreet.com Analyst Rankings is a survey that aims to help investors identify the very best stock analysts on Wall Street. Not just the ones who are telegenic or the one-time lucky stock pickers, but the ones who can really help individual investors make money.

It's the first analyst ranking to combine qualitative and quantitative measures of analyst performance, identifying analysts who have the respect of key institutional investors as well as strong stock-picking skills.

To conduct the ranking, we first polled institutional investors at the 160 money management firms that use analysts the most and know them the best. For the stock-picking portion of the survey, we used data from I/B/E/S International that tracked analysts' success at rating stocks. The final score combined analysts' voting scores and the stock-picking scores, weighted 70%/30%, respectively.

The names of these top-ranked analysts are listed below.

TheStreet.com Analyst Rankings 2000

Note: Analysts are listed at the firm they worked for as of July 2000, to the best of our knowledge. An asterisk indicates a tie; analysts are considered tied when their scores differ by less than one point.

Category	Analyst Name	Firm	Rank
Industry Categories			
Advertising	Bird, William	Salomon Smith Barney	1*
Advertising	Fine, Lauren Rich	Merrill Lynch	1*
Advertising	Russell, Mike	Morgan Stanley Dean Witter	3
Aerospace & Defense	Binder, Steven	Bear Stearns	1
Aerospace & Defense	Callan, Byron	Merrill Lynch	2
Aerospace & Defense	Rubel, Howard	Goldman Sachs	3
Air Freight & Couriers	Wolfe, Edward	Bear Stearns	1
Air Freight & Couriers	Burns, Gregory	Lazard Frères	2
Air Freight & Couriers	Yablon, Gary	Credit Suisse First Boston	3
Airlines	Buttrick, Sam	PaineWebber	1
Airlines	Harris, Brian	Salomon Smith Barney	2
Airlines	Donofrio, Susan	Deutsche Banc Alex. Brown	3
Alternative Carriers	Grubman, Jack	Salomon Smith Barney	1
Alternative Carriers	Henry, James	Bear Stearns	2
Alternative Carriers	Kastan, Mark	Credit Suisse First Boston	3*
Alternative Carriers	Kennedy, Peter	Morgan Stanley Dean Witter	3*
Apparel Retail	Telsey, Dana	Bear Stearns	1
Apparel Retail	Kloppenburg, Janet	Robertson Stephens	2
Apparel Retail	Filandro, Tom	J.P. Morgan	3
Application Software	Phillips, Chuck	Morgan Stanley Dean Witter	1
Application Software	Gilbert, George	Credit Suisse First Boston	2*
Application Software	Sherlund, Rick	Goldman Sachs	2*
Auto Components	Girsky, Steve	Morgan Stanley Dean Witter	1
Auto Components	Bradley, David	J.P. Morgan	2

Category	Analyst Name	Firm	Rank
Industry Categories			
Auto Components	Stover, Matthew	Salomon Smith Barney	3
Automobiles	Girsky, Steve	Morgan Stanley Dean Witter	1
Automobiles	Lapidus, Gary	Goldman Sachs	2
Automobiles	Bradley, David	J.P. Morgan	3
Banks	Dickson, Henry "Chip"	Lehman Brothers	1
Banks	Merdian, Diane	Morgan Stanley Dean Witter	2
Banks	Mayo, Michael	Credit Suisse First Boston	3
Biotechnology	Chovav, Meirav	Salomon Smith Barney	1
Biotechnology	Ho, Maykin	Goldman Sachs	2
Biotechnology	To, Alex	Credit Suisse First Boston	3
Broadcasting & Cable TV	Bilotti, Richard	Morgan Stanley Dean Witter	1
Broadcasting & Cable TV	Reif Cohen, Jessica	Merrill Lynch	2
Broadcasting & Cable TV	Gupta, Niraj	Salomon Smith Barney	3
Building Products	Zelman, Ivy	Credit Suisse First Boston	1
Building Products	Kasprzak, Jack	Scott & Stringfellow	2
Building Products	Susanin, Chris	Lehman Brothers	3
Casinos & Gaming	Ader, Jason	Bear Stearns	1
Casinos & Gaming	Linde, Stuart	Lehman Brothers	2
Casinos & Gaming	Curtis, Harry	Robertson Stephens	3
Computer & Electronics Retail	Caruso, Peter	Merrill Lynch	1
Computer & Electronics Retail	Balter, Gary	DLJ	2
Computer & Electronics Retail	Rubinson, Aram	PaineWebber	3
Computer Hardware	Schutte, Rick	left the sell side	1
Computer Hardware	Milunovich, Steven	Merrill Lynch	2

Category	Analyst Name	Firm	Rank
Industry Categories			
Computer Hardware	Niles, Dan	Lehman Brothers	3
Computer Storage & Peripherals	Alexy, Kimberly	Prudential	1
Computer Storage & Peripherals	Conigliaro, Laura	Goldman Sachs	2
Computer Storage & Peripherals	Schutte, Rick	left the sell side	3
Construction & Farm Machinery	Levkovich, Tobias	Salomon Smith Barney	1
Construction & Farm Machinery	Bleustein, David	PaineWebber	2
Construction & Farm Machinery	Shalett, Lisa	Sanford C. Bernstein	3
Consumer Finance	Gordon, Gary	PaineWebber	1
Consumer Finance	Eisman, Steven	CIBC World Markets	2
Consumer Finance	Orenbuch, Moshe	DLJ	3
Containers & Packaging	Staphos, George	Salomon Smith Barney	1
Containers & Packaging	Khoshaba, Dan	Deutsche Banc Alex. Brown	2
Containers & Packaging	Davis, Scott	Morgan Stanley Dean Witter	3
Department Stores	Exstein, Michael	Credit Suisse First Boston	1
Department Stores	Balter, Gary	DLJ	2
Department Stores	Strachan, George	Goldman Sachs	3
Diversified Chemicals	Carson, Donald	J.P. Morgan	1
Diversified Chemicals	Copley, Graham	Sanford C. Bernstein	2
Diversified Chemicals	Vasnetsov, Sergey	Lehman Brothers	3
Diversified Financial Services	McVey, Henry	Morgan Stanley Dean Witter	1
Diversified Financial Services	Moszkowski, Guy	Salomon Smith Barney	2
Diversified Financial Services	Galbraith, Steve	Morgan Stanley Dean Witter	3
Electric Utilities	Fleishman, Steve	Merrill Lynch	1

Category	Analyst Name	Firm	Rank
Industry Categories			
Electric Utilities	Raleigh, Jonathan	Goldman Sachs	2
Electric Utilities	Ford, Daniel	ABN Amro	3
Electrical Components & Equipment	Cornell, Bob	Lehman Brothers	1
Electrical Components & Equipment	Sprague, Jeffrey	Salomon Smith Barney	2
Electrical Components & Equipment	Heymann, Nicholas	Prudential	3
Electronic Equipment & Instruments	Labowitz, Jerry	Merrill Lynch	1*
Electronic Equipment & Instruments	Dunne, Keith	Robertson Stephens	1*
Electronic Equipment & Instruments	Conigliaro, Laura	Goldman Sachs	3
Energy Equipment & Services	Hall, Gordon	Credit Suisse First Boston	1
Energy Equipment & Services	Darling, Terry	Goldman Sachs	2
Energy Equipment & Services	Simpson, Kevin	Merrill Lynch	3
Environmental Services	Genco, William	Merrill Lynch	1
Environmental Services	Augenthaler, Douglas	CIBC World Markets	2
Environmental Services	Pavese, Alan	Credit Suisse First Boston	3
General Merchandise Stores	Balter, Gary	DLJ	1
General Merchandise Stores	Exstein, Michael	Credit Suisse First Boston	2
General Merchandise Stores	Church, Richard	Salomon Smith Barney	3
Health Care Distributors & Services	Marsh, Larry	Lehman Brothers	1
Health Care Distributors & Services	Risinger, David	Merrill Lynch	2*

Category	Analyst Name	Firm	Rank
Industry Categories			
Health Care Distributors & Services	Rossi, Marie	Morgan Stanley Dean Witter	2*
Health Care Equipment & Supplies	Weinstein, Michael	J.P. Morgan	1
Health Care Equipment & Supplies	Reicin, Glenn	Morgan Stanley Dean Witter	2
Health Care Equipment & Supplies	Malone, Anne	Salomon Smith Barney	3
Health Care Facilities	Lawson, Deborah	Salomon Smith Barney	1
Health Care Facilities	Rice, A.J.	Merrill Lynch	2
Health Care Facilities	Weakley, Kenneth	Bear Stearns	3
Home Improvement Retail	Caruso, Peter	Merrill Lynch	1
Home Improvement Retail	Balter, Gary	DLJ	2
Home Improvement Retail	Quilty, Susan	Morgan Stanley Dean Witter	3
Household Products	Shore, Andrew	Deutsche Banc Alex. Brown	1
Household Products	Chasen, Amy Low	Goldman Sachs	2*
Household Products	Longley, Alice Beebe	DLJ	2*
Industrial Conglomerates	Sprague, Jeffrey	Salomon Smith Barney	1
Industrial Conglomerates	Young, Phua	Merrill Lynch	2
Industrial Conglomerates	Kelly, Jack	Goldman Sachs	3*
Industrial Conglomerates	MacDougall, Don	J.P. Morgan	3*
Industrial Machinery	Levkovich, Tobias	Salomon Smith Barney	1
Industrial Machinery	Inch, John	Bear Stearns	2
Industrial Machinery	Bleustein, David	PaineWebber	3
Integrated Oil & Gas	Mayer, Michael	Prudential	1
Integrated Oil & Gas	Ting, Paul	Salomon Smith Barney	2
Integrated Oil & Gas	Terreson, Doug	Morgan Stanley Dean Witter	3
Integrated Telecommunications Services	Grubman, Jack	Salomon Smith Barney	1

Category	Analyst Name	Firm	Rank
Industry Categories			
Integrated Telecommunications Services	Jacobs, Tod	J.P. Morgan	2
Integrated Telecommunications Services	Flannery, Simon	Morgan Stanley Dean Witter	3*
Integrated Telecommunications Services	Reingold, Daniel	Credit Suisse First Boston	3*
Internet Software & Services	Blodget, Henry	Merrill Lynch	1
Internet Software & Services	Baker, Lanny	Salomon Smith Barney	2
Internet Software & Services	Meeker, Mary	Morgan Stanley Dean Witter	3
IT Consulting & Services	Kissane, James	Bear Stearns	1
IT Consulting & Services	Wolfenberger, Mark	Credit Suisse First Boston	2
IT Consulting & Services	Togut, David	Morgan Stanley Dean Witter	3
Life & Health Insurance	McIntosh, Ronald	Fox-Pitt, Kelton	1
Life & Health Insurance	Devine, Colin	Salomon Smith Barney	2
Life & Health Insurance	Spehar, Ed	Merrill Lynch	3
Managed Health Care	Goodman, Roberta	Merrill Lynch	1
Managed Health Care	Arnold, Christine	Morgan Stanley Dean Witter	2
Managed Health Care	France, Joseph	Credit Suisse First Boston	3
Metals, Mining & Steel	Atwell, R. Wayne	Morgan Stanley Dean Witter	1
Metals, Mining & Steel	Applebaum, Michelle	Salomon Smith Barney	2*
Metals, Mining & Steel	Rizzuto Jr., Anthony	Bear Stearns	2*
Metals, Mining & Steel	McNamara, Thomas	CIBC World Markets	2*
Movies & Entertainment	Bilotti, Richard	Morgan Stanley Dean Witter	1
Movies & Entertainment	Reif Cohen, Jessica	Merrill Lynch	2

Category	Analyst Name	Firm	Rank
Industry Categories			
Movies & Entertainment	Simon, Richard	Goldman Sachs	3
Networking Equipment	Cena, Alex	Salomon Smith Barney	1
Networking Equipment	Geiling, Gregory	J.P. Morgan	2
Networking Equipment	DePuy, Chris	left the sell side	3
Oil & Gas Exploration & Production	Herrlin Jr., John	Merrill Lynch	1
Oil & Gas Exploration & Production	Pace, Phillip	Credit Suisse First Boston	2
Oil & Gas Exploration & Production	Morris, Robert	Salomon Smith Barney	3
Packaged Foods	McMillin, John	Prudential	1
Packaged Foods	Long, Erika Gritman	J.P. Morgan	2
Packaged Foods	Ghez, Nomi	Goldman Sachs	3
Paper & Forest Products	Schneider, Rich	PaineWebber	1
Paper & Forest Products	Dillon, Chip	Salomon Smith Barney	2
Paper & Forest Products	Connelly, Mark	Credit Suisse First Boston	3
Pharmaceuticals	Tighe, Steven	Merrill Lynch	1
Pharmaceuticals	Rubin, Jami	Morgan Stanley Dean Witter	2*
Pharmaceuticals	Scala, Stephen	SG Cowen	2*
Property & Casualty Insurance	Hicks, Weston	J.P. Morgan	1
Property & Casualty Insurance	Dowling, V.J.	Dowling & Partners	2
Property & Casualty Insurance	Schroeder, Alice	Morgan Stanley Dean Witter	3
Publishing & Printing	Drewry, William	DLJ	1
Publishing & Printing	Fine, Lauren Rich	Merrill Lynch	2
Publishing & Printing	Bird, William	Salomon Smith Barney	3
REITs	Litt, Jonathan	Salomon Smith Barney	1
REITs	Raiman, Larry	DLJ	2
REITs	Whyte, Greg	Morgan Stanley Dean Witter	3
Restaurants	Oakes, Peter	Merrill Lynch	1

Category	Analyst Name	Firm	Rank
Industry Categories			
Restaurants	Buckley, Joseph	Bear Stearns	2
Restaurants	Penney, Howard	Morgan Stanley Dean Witter	3*
Restaurants	Meyer, Janice	DLJ	3*
Road & Rail	Valentine, Jim	Morgan Stanley Dean Witter	1
Road & Rail	Yablon, Gary	Credit Suisse First Boston	2
Road & Rail	Flower, Scott	Salomon Smith Barney	3
Semiconductor Equipment	Miller, Gunnar	Goldman Sachs	1
Semiconductor Equipment	Deahna, Jay	Morgan Stanley Dean Witter	2
Semiconductor Equipment	Rogers, Elliot	Credit Suisse First Boston	3
Semiconductors	Edelstone, Mark	Morgan Stanley Dean Witter	1
Semiconductors	Niles, Dan	Lehman Brothers	2
Semiconductors	Glavin, Charles	Credit Suisse First Boston	3*
Semiconductors	Peck, Drew	SG Cowen	
3*Soft Drinks	Conway, Andrew	Morgan Stanley Dean Witter	1
Soft Drinks	Pecoriello, William	Sanford C. Bernstein	2
Soft Drinks	Cohen, Marc I.	Goldman Sachs	3
Specialty Chemicals	Gerdeman, Timothy	Lehman Brothers	1
Specialty Chemicals	Gulley, Mark	Bank of America	2
Specialty Chemicals	Ottenstein, Robert	Morgan Stanley Dean Witter	3
Specialty Stores	Telsey, Dana	Bear Stearns	1
Specialty Stores	Kloppenburg, Janet	Robertson Stephens	2*
Specialty Stores	Balter, Gary	DLJ	2*
Systems Software	Phillips, Chuck	Morgan Stanley Dean Witter	1

Category	Analyst Name	Firm	Rank
Industry Categories			
Systems Software	Kwatinetz, Michael	left the sell side	2*
Systems Software	Sherlund, Rick	Goldman Sachs	2*
Telecommunications Equipment	Geiling, Gregory	J.P. Morgan	1
Telecommunications Equipment	Cena, Alex	Salomon Smith Barney	2
Telecommunications Equipment	Jungjohann, James	CIBC World Markets	3*
Telecommunications Equipment	Theodosopoulos, Nikos	UBS Warburg	3*
Tobacco	Feldman, Martin	Salomon Smith Barney	1
Tobacco	Adelman, David	Morgan Stanley Dean Witter	2
Tobacco	Cohen, Marc I.	Goldman Sachs	3
Wireless Telecommunications Services	Fleming, Colette	Morgan Stanley Dean Witter	1
Wireless Telecommunications Services	Lee, Thomas	Chase H&Q	2
Wireless Telecommunications Services	Freedman, David	Bear Stearns	3

Category	Analyst Name	Firm	Rank
Economics and Strategy Categories			
Economics	Hyman, Ed	ISI Group	1
Economics	Yardeni, Ed	Deutsche Banc Alex. Brown	2
Economics	Roach, Steve	Morgan Stanley Dean Witter	3
Portfolio Strategy	Cohen, Abby Joseph	Goldman Sachs	1
Portfolio Strategy	Goldstein, Michael	Sanford C. Bernstein	2
Portfolio Strategy	Kerschner, Ed	PaineWebber	3
Quantitative Strategy	Bernstein, Richard	Merrill Lynch	1
Quantitative Strategy	Goldstein, Michael	Sanford C. Bernstein	2
Quantitative Strategy	Sorensen, Eric	Salomon Smith Barney	3

Appendix B

Online Brokers 2000:
A Reader Survey by TheStreet.com

There are more than 100 online brokers for investors to choose from, offering all combinations of low commissions, after-hours trading, IPOs, fancy quote functionality, and other gizmos. But which brokers are best? Better yet, which one is the best *for you?*

TheStreet.com is in a superb position to help investors answer those questions, because so many of our readers have firsthand experience with online brokers. Rather than evaluate the brokers on our own, we have asked our readers to tell us what they think of the brokers they've used for their trading.

Through several interactive reader surveys, we first asked readers what features and services are most important to them in a broker. Then we asked, How does your broker fare on those features?

Below you'll find the results of our Online Brokers 2000 survey, in which more than 10,000 readers submitted ballots. We present the performance ranking here on the seven brokers who received more than 650 votes.

You can find more information from this extensive survey, and our methodology, on www.thestreet.com in "Investing Basics." We also update news on the brokers through our reporting and subsequent surveys on our Web site. The results below should give you a good start if you're selecting a broker for the first time, or switching brokers.

The Best Brokers and What They're Best At

Criteria*	1 Datek datek.com	2 Fidelity fidelity.com	3 Schwab schwab.com	4 DLJdirect dljdirect.com	5 Ameritrade ameritrade.com	6 E*Trade etrade.com	7 TD Waterhouse waterhouse.com
Reliability: access even in times of heavy volume	3	2	4	1	5	6	7
Real-time quotes	1	5	2	3	6	4	7
Fast order confirmation	1	2	4	3	5	6	7
Easy account administration & portfolio tracking	2	4	1	3	6	5	7
Customer service	4	1	2	5	3	6	7
Best execution price	1	2	3	4	6	7	5
Easy to implement complex trades	1	4	2	3	6	5	7
Low commissions	1	4	7	6	2	5	3
Real-time market & company news	4	5	3	1	6	2	7

Criteria*	1 Datek datek.com	2 Fidelity fidelity.com	3 Schwab schwab.com	4 DLJdirect dljdirect.com	5 Ameritrade ameritrade.com	6 E*Trade etrade.com	7 TD Waterhouse waterhouse.com
Investment research	6	4	1	2	7	3	5
IPO Availability	7	3	4	1	6	2	5
Breadth of investment product offerings	7	1	2	4	6	3	5
Level II Nasdaq quotes	3	2	5	4	6	1	7
Email alerts	5	6	3	1	4	2	7
Easy options trading	7	5	3	1	4	2	6
After-hours trading	1	5	4	3	6	2	7
Banking services	5	2	1	6	7	4	3
Bond trading	7	2	3	1	6	4	5

* In order of importance to readers, according to our survey results

Note: The brokers are listed overall best to worst, from left to right. The numbers indicate their rank in specific categories.

The Trader's Tongue: A Glossary

James J. Cramer

When Jim Cramer says "naked," do you know what he means?

Let's face it, in investing, knowing the right lingo is like knowing the secret handshake. This is where Jim Cramer comes in. The long-time hedge fund manager and columnist for *TheStreet.com* not only knows the business, he doesn't like to beat around the bush. While other glossaries may delineate "security selection decision," Cramer just talks about picking stocks. Other definitions read like solemn prayers; his come across like machine-gun fire. Cramer will tell you what's good, what's bad, and what's definitely "ugly" (see "buy-in").

Here's the word, straight from *The Trader's Tongue*.

Analyst estimates: Published numbers put out by the research departments of different brokerages gauging how much companies are expected to earn in a quarter and in a year. For these companies' stocks to go higher, they must exceed these estimates.

Beta: How much up-down action you get out of a stock.

BGL: This is a game where people bag stock (B) and gun it (G) by going to a message board and hyping it or getting a reporter to predict some takeover that you know can't be proven. Then they liquidate it (L) into the unsuspecting public after CNBC picks up the bogus takeover deal. This BGL game gets played out every day on Wall Street; it makes me sick.

Bid: Traders bid for stock when they want to buy. We hit bids when we want to sell. Traders speak in terms of bids and takes. And the order is different for each. You want to buy 10,000 shares of Intel (INTC: Nasdaq) at 70? Bid 70 for 10,000 Intel. You want to sell 10,000 Intel?

Then it's take, as in "Take10,000 Intel at 70." Different order; no confusion about buying and selling.

Borrow: A technical term describing the process in which you find out if a brokerage house has any stock in its vault to loan you (the borrow) so you can sell the stock short. You have to deliver something to the buyer; it will be borrowed stock. You have to get a borrow before you short or you could be in violation of exchange rules forbidding the shorting of stocks that can't be borrowed.

Bottom: When a stock stops going down and begins to head up.

Break a trade: When you do this, your name is mud on Wall Street. We do everything verbally. If you buy stock, you buy it. You can't come back and say, "Sorry, I don't want to buy." This isn't Wal-Mart (WMT: NYSE). Never break a trade.

Brokerage: A business that employs brokers who buy and sell stocks and bonds.

Buyback: When a company buys its own shares, typically as a way to stabilize the market. Can't be done in the last half hour of trading.

Buy-in: When you can't find any stock to borrow for a short sale and have to buy in the open market, the brokerage used by the buyer might buy the stock in the open market and hose you after you've failed to deliver yours. Result: You pay the brokerage through the nose. Really painful.

Call: A call is an option, a right to buy at an agreed-upon price. People who buy calls are bullish; they profit from a rise in the stock price. People who sell calls are neutral or bearish. The call's value decreases if the stock stays flat or falls, and the call can expire worthless. Options are a leveraged way to play the game, because one option is equal to 100 shares.

Chasing a stock: Another sin. You should never chase a stock, buying it as it's spiking or plummeting. You should use a limit, and if it goes past your limit, forget it. You missed it. Bidding is better than chasing anytime.

Church of what's happening now: This phrase, originally coined by Flip Wilson, came to be applied to me by my friend and colleague Mark Haines. It has to do with liking what works and hating what doesn't. I think it fits me and I don't fight it.

Collateral damage: When one company blows up and takes down all of the similar companies in the industry.

Commission: The payment a broker receives for executing an order.

Commit capital: When a large mutual fund or other sell-side player wants out of a stock, sometimes he will ask the firm doing the trade to commit capital to take him out of it. Why would a broker commit capital? He hopes to get both sides of the trade—meaning commissions from the buyer and seller—and he wants to please the seller, so the seller will come back and give him some easier business.

Conference call: The discussion with management after a quarter is reported.

Cover: People use this term to describe closing out a short. Let's say you are short National Gift at 33 and it drops to 23. You have to buy it back to make the 10 bucks. That buyback is called *covering*.

Cross markets: In really fast markets when someone wants out quickly, markets can go crossed, in that a seller is willing to sell stock below the price that the buyer is willing to pay. Or vice versa. So if National Gift is 32 bid, 31.75 offer, that's a crossed market. Happens on the Nasdaq in times of real stress.

Cyclicals: Stocks of companies that need a strong economy to do well. These companies' fortunes are directly tied to the economy.

Dead Head: Street slang for Dayton-Hudson (DH:NYSE).

Dead money: Means the stock isn't going anywhere.

Deal pipeline: The queue for underwritings.

Delist: Game over when a company gets delisted from the NYSE, the Nasdaq, or the Amex. Worthless stock.

Discount bid: When an institution wants out so badly it is willing to accept a price below where the stock is currently trading. Bad sign for your stock if you see this.

Done: You should never say this. You should never say you are "done." You should say you have bought the stock. Or sold the stock. Done means nothing. Yet people use it all the time. Don't fall into this shorthand.

Downgrade: When an analyst pulls his buy recommendation, or changes any recommendation to a lesser one.

Dumb money: Slow money, usually mutual-fund or pension money.

Earnings report: A company's quarterly report card of how much money was made or lost.

E-commerce: Business conducted on the Web.

Express: Short for American Express (AXP:NYSE).

Fast money: The type of account that would scalp a point. Hedge funds are fast money.

Fedex: Short for Federal Express (FDX:NYSE).

Fizzy: Street slang for Pfizer (PFE:NYSE).

Flip: When you get a hot stock and you blow it out immediately. The brokerages try to discourage flipping, but in this crazy market where only small bits of stock get floated at the beginning, there are a ton of flippers on these pops.

Full up: The excuse an account gives when it's not possible to buy any more of a falling stock.

Gaff: When a trader screws you on an execution, the same as what fishermen do to fish.

Handle: This is the first digit of a two-digit number. If National Gift is trading at 23, the handle is a two. If it's trading at 33, the handle is a three.

Hot deal: This is an initial public offering that goes above the price it was issued at.

I-Beam: Street slang for IBM (IBM:NYSE).

Indications: Where a stock might open. Right before the start of the day, we get indications of interest about where a stock might open. You say the stock is "looking" and then you mention a range of prices. So people can figure out where they want to buy or sell.

Insiders: People inside a company that know of material, market-moving information. They cannot trade on it because it would violate securities laws.

JohnnyJohn: Street slang for Johnson & Johnson (JNJ:NYSE).

Knockout: Street slang for Coke (KO:NYSE).

Listed: The Big Board is listed; so is the Amex. Non-Nasdaq.

Long: To own. Journalists always get this wrong. They talk about being "long on." You are simply long or short. As opposed to owning or betting against.

Long-term strategies: Strategies that eschew trading and bet on the long-term appreciation of stocks.

Margin: On borrowed money. Buying on margin is buying with the brokerage's money.

Margin call: When you don't have enough cash in your account to cover purchases that you have made. You must wire money in to cure these.

Margin clerk: Someone who reviews all accounts every night to see if the collateral in an account is high enough so that, if the market were to plummet, the brokerage would get its money back. A margin clerk is basically a loan officer in the bank of the brokerage.

Markdown: When someone places a sloppy order at the bell to make a stock close lower than it really did. This is done to beleaguer the bulls and make a stock look bad.

Market order: Go ahead and buy it. Go ahead and sell it. Hurt me as much as you want. I gave you that right by using a market order instead of a limit order.

Markup: The opposite of markdown. This is when a sloppy order is entered at the bell to make a stock look like it was up more than it was. A favorite device of the bulls to make a stock look rosier than it actually is.

Mister Softee: Slang for Microsoft (MSFT:Nasdaq).

MOAT: Shorthand for Motorola (MOT:NYSE).

MOSH: Street slang for the Morgan Stanley High Tech Index.

Motors: The auto stocks.

Naked: When you are selling a derivative without owning the underlying security. Can be very dangerous. If you sell calls naked, you are selling calls on a stock that you don't own. If it gets a takeover bid, you could be history. You might sell out-of-the-money puts on something that you aren't short, and you will end up owning it if the stock gets really hammered.

New Tech: Typically, companies that have been created to take advantage of the Internet in some way, shape, or form.

Noaks: Shorthand for Nokia (NOK:NYSE).

Nose Tackle: Slang for Nortel (NT:NYSE).

Old Economy/New Economy: Stupid journalistic shorthand distinguishing between companies that have earnings vs. ones that don't. I prefer Net vs. non-Net.

Old Tech: Pre-Internet tech stocks.

Orders: Requests to buy or sell stocks. A buy order and a sell order can be done "at the market," where you get the current price, or by "limit," where you get the price you specify. The first is always executed immediately; the second may not be.

P/E: That is the price of the stock divided by its earning. You have to know this stuff because otherwise you might not understand why a stock is expensive or cheap. A high P/E means it is expensive; a low P/E means it is cheap.

Piece: A piece of merchandise, as in, there is a large block of stock for sale, or a piece. Bad sign. A piece usually means it is too big to handle where the bid side may be.

Pin action: From bowling, when one stock's movement sends up other stocks. If Texas Instruments (TXN:NYSE) goes up, Micron (MU: NYSE) and Intel should go up.

Pop: This is a quick move up, a pop. Always want to catch one of these.

Portfolio manager: Someone who selects equities for a portfolio.

Position: The technical term for a stock you own. For example, I have a "position" in Cisco.

Preannouncement: Could be great or bad. If a company screws up, they have to preannounce when they know they have screwed up. If they are exceeding estimations, they preannounce to the upside. A great event. A preannouncement to the upside when you are long is pure bliss. A preannouncement to the downside when you are short is pure bliss.

Premium bid: When someone attempts to buy stock above where the market currently is. Good sign.

Primary seller of equity: The company itself issuing shares. The proceeds go to the company.

Profit-taking: The natural process where people take stocks off the table. Meant to imply there is no change in the fundamentals of the company.

Program trading: Any large-scale orders done swiftly, usually by machine, to take advantage of disparities between where stocks and futures are. Buy programs move stocks up. Sell programs move stocks down.

Put: A way to bet against a stock that you think is going down. If you buy a put on National Gift when it is at $90, you are betting that it is going to go lower. You buy a $100 put for 10 bucks and you make one-for-one profits on the way down. That is an in-the-money put. An out-of-the-money put would be an $85 put. You probably won't make money until the stock really gets hammered. You don't have to concern yourself with a short squeeze when you buy a put, which is why, in part, people buy them. You can only lose your investment. Theoretically on a short, you could lose everything because stocks could go up forever.

Q: Shorthand for "quarter."

Raid: When a group of short-sellers get together to spread rumors about a stock in order to drive it down.

Ramp: This is a slang term for a market that is going into orbit. When the market "ramps," it is screaming upward.

Range: The pricing band for an IPO. Sixteen to 18 might be the range. Top of the range means there is good demand. Low end of the range means that demand is lukewarm.

REIT buy: When a firm re-recommends a stock after it has been hammered.

Research: Any report that advises you to buy or sell a security based on either fundamental or technical information. Wall Street research typically includes earnings estimates and projections of prospects for a publicly traded company.

Restricted stock: This is stock that has a legend on it. It is not free to trade. Most insider stock is restricted. It can come off only over time, so as not to deluge a stock's float.

Revenue: The sales a company had. Often a better indicator of the health of a company than profits, because it measures sheer growth.

Reverse split: Typically, a desperate company tries to disguise how low it has gone by doing a reverse stock split. Avoid these like the plague.

Risk arb: This is someone who sells one security and buys another to lock in a return, because the two are basically the same but aren't trading at the same price. Risk arbs should be able to buy one and sell the other and wait around until they meet. They can profit from that.

Rocks: Shorthand for Xerox (XRX:NYSE).

Scale: A method of buying a stock or selling a stock by waiting for small increments (tight scale) or big increments (wide scale) to execute orders. You could buy Intel every quarter point down—tight scale—or every two points, wide scale.

Scale-down buyer: A buyer who is using a scale to buy, as in buy 5,000 shares every half point down beginning at 90.

Scalp: Trying to make a buck or two on a quick trade.

Secondary barometer: Most trades tell you nothing because they are too small. When you want to find out if the bull or the bear is in command, you evaluate how secondaries do, because they are big slugs of stock put on the market at one level. If they hold the price where the secondary was placed or go higher, that is great. If they fail to hold or go down big, the market is probably weaker than you think.

Secondary seller of equity: When individuals offer equity as part of an underwriting. The proceeds don't go to the company.

Short squeeze: A phenomenon involving the inability of the market to accommodate all of the people who want to bet against a stock. In order to short a stock you have to be able to borrow the stock. Remember, the buyer has to get something. If there is no stock to loan out, you can't borrow it. Sometimes you get a "borrow" and then it is taken away. Nothing is guaranteed. And you have to scramble to cover your short. A squeeze may ensue where you have to pay up drastically to buy the stock back. Huge bummer.

Short-term strategies: Strategies that try to have as much money as possible in the market during the best times and as little money in the market during the worst times.

Silly Graphics: Slang for Silicon Graphics (SGI:NYSE).

Size buying: Typically, buying more than 100,000 shares at a time.

Slob: Shorthand for Schlumberger (SLB:NYSE).

Small unit: Military term meaning a typical skirmish. I use it as a metaphor when the bulls and the bears are skirmishing in a particular stock, as opposed to in the market as a whole.

Snapback rally: Another term for a "V-bottom whoosh" (see page 317). It means a market that rallies quickly, too quickly for the bears to bring in their shorts or for the longs to get longer. A good sign.

Soaps: The soft-goods stocks like Colgate (CL:NYSE) and Procter & Gamble (PG:NYSE).

Split: When you get a different number of shares for the same amount of money.

Sponsorship: When an analyst backs a company's stock with a buy recommendation.

Spread: The space between the bid and the offer. If National Gift trades at 24 bid, 25 offer, that's a dollar spread. Some stocks have tight spreads; others are very wide.

Squawk box: The sound system that each brokerage has to inform brokers of changes in recommendation and of merchandise to buy or sell.

Stock split: When management authorizes the division of its shares to facilitate easier buying in smaller amounts.

Supply/Demand: Stocks are bid up when there is not enough supply of stock and demand is great. But when supply overwhelms demand, you get a big selloff.

Sweep: To take all of the offerings currently available on a stock.

Take: We don't buy in this business. We take. As in take 10,000 Intel at 70. That means buy it.

Taking it off the table: Taking some of your winnings out of circulation and putting them in a safe place where the market can't hurt them. A commonsense strategy, in my book.

Tape: Slang for the action, as in a good tape or a bad tape.

Teenager: Disparaging term for a stock that used to be higher but has now traded down to the teens.

Tell: A clue, something that signals the next move in the market.

Ten-percenter: A giant order in a secondary or an IPO, meaning that the account wants 10% of the stock on the deal, the most one account can have.

Texan: Short for Texas Instruments (TXN:NYSE).

Trade by appointment: A very thin stock where it is hard to find buyers or sellers. These are dangerous stocks to try to buy a lot or sell a lot of.

Trade to a premium: When a new stock or a piece of stock trades above the offering price.

Trans: The transport averages.

Treasuries: U.S. government bonds; the most liquid market in the world.

Twix: Shorthand for Time Warner (TWX:NYSE).

Underwriters: The brokers who are selling the stock to the public.

Underwriting: The sale of stock by a brokerage firm.

Upgrade: When an analyst raises a recommendation, such as hold to buy.

Utes: The utility averages.

V-bottom whoosh: Technical term for when a stock market that is headed down takes an abrupt move up. The chart looks like a V. Very bullish. Means selling may have ended.

Index